SECOND EDITION

Scenic Routes & Byways™
VIRGINIA

JUDY COLBERT

gpp®

travel

Guilford, Connecticut

To buy books in quantity for corporate use or incentives, call **(800) 962-0973** or e-mail **premiums@GlobePequot.com.**

Photos by Judy Colbert unless otherwise noted

Project Editor: Staci Zacharski
Layout: Casey Shain
Maps: Tony Moore, updated by Alena Joy Pearce © by Morris Book Publishing, LLC

ISBN 978-0-7627-8653-4

Printed in the United States of America

CONTENTS

ABOUT THE AUTHOR

Judy Colbert's mother, Bernice Smith Mudrick, was from the Tidewater (or Hampton Roads) area of Virginia, so she has been wandering around the state, visiting relatives and exploring the interesting and beautiful aspects of the Old Dominion, her whole life. Her first book for Globe Pequot, nearly 3 decades ago, was *Virginia Off the Beaten Path*. Since then, she has written *The Spa Guide, Maryland and Delaware Off the Beaten Path, Insiders' Guide to Baltimore, It Happened in Maryland,* and *It Happened in Delaware*. She has written numerous books for other publishers, on topic ranging from *Super Bowl Trivia to Peaceful Places Washington DC* to a cookbook called *Chesapeake Bay Crabs*. Her current goal is to leave her land-based existence and spend a year or two cruising the seven seas and writing about her experiences and the people she meets.

ACKNOWLEDGMENTS

Although I wander around Virginia for articles and updating my *Virginia Off the Beaten Path* book, I rely on my online and real-life friends who find interesting things and let me know about them. The people who live and work in Virginia and would never think of going anyplace else provide the southern hospitality for which the state is known and make my life and research worthwhile and fulfilling. I also depend on the people who help promote the state and its attractions. From cartographers to historians and many other professionals, I'm in their debt. Special thanks go to Dwayne Altice, Mary Ann "Maggie" Anderson, Curt and Kim Arney, Erin Bagnell, Bridgitte Belanger-Warner, Karen Beck-Herzog, Brenda Black, Margie Boesch, Tom Bonadeo, Danya Bushey, Jennifer Buske-Sign, Shuan Butcher, Briana Campbell, Lois Chapman, Jean Clark, Sally Coates, Kelly Connor, Kevin Costello, Lynn Crump, Rebecca M. Cutchins, Sally Dickinson, Margie B. Douglass, Rich Ellis, Danielle Emerson, Pamela M. Flasch, Betsy Fields, LuAnn Fortenberry, Catherine Fox, Ranger Janice Frye, Mary Fugere, Jack Gary, Ranger Peter S. Givens, Ranger Sharon Griffin, Brenda Griggs, Leah Harms, Dave Harris, Karen W. Hedelt, Beth Homicz, Lisa Hull, Courtney Hunter, Denise Jackson, Erica Jeter, Randall "Randy" Jones, Kari Journigan, Jennifer Keck, Maureen Kelley, Ryan LaFata, Richard Lewis, Travis C. McDonald, Kathy Moore, Lisa Moorman, Gena S. Morris, Claire Mouledoux, Christopher Nicholad, Beckie Nix, Kelli Norman, Cara O'Donnell, Laura Overstreet, Gina L. Sandy Patterson, Catherine Payne, Julie Perry, Deborah H. Pitts, Marie Plank, Carolyn Pottowsky, Jackie Saunders, Catherine Slusser, Mayumi Smitka, Jim Stallard, Kelcey Thurman, Tonya H. Triplett, Sergei Troubetzkoy, Sheryl S. Wagner, Jen K. Ward, Beverly Watson, Tiffany White, Charlotte Whitted, Christopher L. Williams, Jennifer L. Williams, Natalie Wills, and Judy Winslow.

Other thanks go to Ted Becker, Liz Griffith, Mary Lou Malzone, Mary-Lynne Neil, and Bev Westcott.

Legend

Interstate Highway/ Featured Interstate Highway	——(95)—— / ——(95)——		
US Highway/ Featured US Highway	——(13)—— / ——(13)——		
State Highway/ Featured State Highway	——(55)—— / ——(55)——		
County Road/ Featured County Road	——[631]—— / ——[631]——		
Local Road/ Featured Local Road	———— / ————		
Railroad	┥┝┥┝┥┝		
Trail	- - - - - - - -		

Airport	✛	Lighthouse	🕯
Bridge	⌣⌢	Museum	🏛
Building or Structure	■	Picnic Area	🛦
Capital	✪	Point of Interest	▫
Campground	⋀	Scenic Area/Overlook	◪
Cemetery	⚰	Small State Park, Wilderness or Natural Area	▲
City	◉	Town	○
Cliff	🗻	Trailhead	⑩
Dam	—	Visitor, Interpretive Center	⑦
Gap/Pass	) (	Waterfall	〣
Historic Site	⛪		

Mountain, Peak, or Butte
▲ *Stony Man Mountain*
4,010 ft.

River, Creek, or Drainage

Marsh

Body of Water

State Line   VIRGINIA

National/State Park Area

National/State Forest Area

Wilderness/Wildlife/Natural Area

Miscellaneous Area

Locator Map

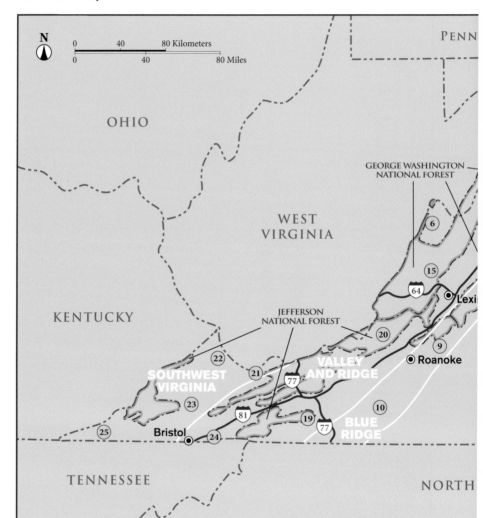

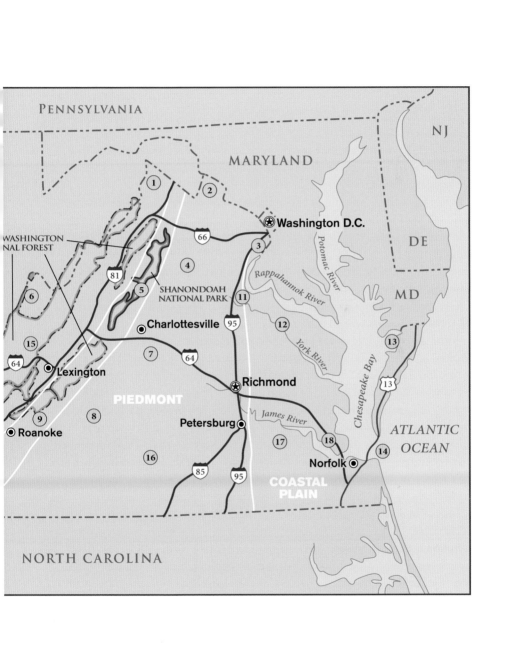

PENNSYLVANIA

MARYLAND

NJ

DE

MD

Washington D.C.

66

3

WASHINGTON
NAL FOREST

81

SHANONDOAH
NATIONAL PARK

Potomac River

Rappahannok River

1

2

4

5

11

York River

12

13

Charlottesville

95

13

6

15

64

7

64

Chesapeake Bay

Lexington

Richmond

PIEDMONT

9

8

Petersburg

James River

17

ATLANTIC
OCEAN

Roanoke

16

18

14

85

95

Norfolk

COASTAL
PLAIN

NORTH CAROLINA

INTRODUCTION

... It's that time when the pull of the blue highway is strongest, when the open road is a beckoning, a strangeness, a place where a man can lose himself.

William Least Heat Moon
Blue Highways

As a child, my travels were pretty much limited to visiting relatives in the Tidewater or Hampton Roads area of Virginia and annual trips to Miami Beach, Florida.

When we weren't heading to one of those places, mother and I would drive around the Metropolitan Washington area and "get lost." Long before GPS (they would probably take all the fun away for her), mother and I would just go for a drive and enjoy the countryside. She was totally confident that she'd find her way back, and who was I to dispute that? I thought of it as exploring or unexpected sightseeing, but never as being lost—misplaced, not lost.

Whether it's nurture or nature, I'm sure those drives sparked my wanderlust. I still treasure the days when I'm exploring.

Fortunately, Virginia is one of the most spectacular states to explore. Yes, there are 1,118 miles of interstate highway crisscrossing in the state. However, there are more than 8,000 miles of primary state highways and more than 48,000 miles of secondary roads. There are plenty of places to discover. Several roads have been designated as Scenic Byways. They go through the Shenandoah Valley with mountains cradling you within their gentle slopes or stretch out over flat country on the Eastern Shore (the other side of Chesapeake Bay). They are defined by history and natural growth. From Cumberland Gap in the southwest corner to Cape Charles on the southern tip of the Eastern Shore, you're sure to find something to fascinate you.

The plethora of route classifications can be confusing, but only if you let it. There are:

National Scenic Byways: This is a road recognized by the US Department of Transportation because it has archaeological, cultural, historic, natural, recreational, and/or scenic qualities. The US Congress established this program in 1991 to help promote tourism and protect these often less-travel roads. Some of these routes are designated All-American Roads if they have at least two of those qualities and the road is unique and important. Within Virginia, the Blue Ridge Parkway, the Colonial Parkway, and the George Washington Memorial Parkway are All-American Roads, and Skyline Drive is a National Scenic Byway.

Virginia welcome sign located along the state line
©KATHERINE WELLES/SHUTTERSTOCK.COM

Virginia Scenic Byways: According to the Virginia Department of Transportation (VDOT), there are "nearly 3,000 miles of special roads that offer something for everyone." These byways offer an uncommon view of the state and lead to places of natural beauty and historical and social significance.

The VDOT website, virginiadot.org, provides links to major construction sites, travel advisories, lane closures, traffic cameras, E-ZPass details, hurricane and tornado warnings, maps, truck restrictions, and a wealth of other information.

Virginia extends 200 miles north to south and about 500 miles east to west. Its varied topography and geography range from coastal estuaries and beaches in the east to mountains more than 5,000 feet high in the south and west. Scenic routes cover all portions of the state and were selected to display the most interesting scenic, historical, and unique features. Many routes extend into two or more sections. From east to west, geologists divide the state into the sections shown below, under which are listed the routes that pass through each.

Tidewater and Coastal Plain: Virginia's Coastal Plain includes the land areas adjacent to the Atlantic coastline, both shores of Chesapeake Bay, and the tidal reaches of the Potomac, James, Rappahannock, and other rivers. An area of

Shenandoah National Park, Green Tunnel Section
©ZACK FRANK/SHUTTERSTOCK.COM

low relief, it is underlain by unconsolidated, sandy sediments and encompasses the bays, estuaries, offshore islands, and saltwater marshes along the coast.

Virginia's Coastal Plain was the site of some of the first European settlements in North America, and it played a vital role in the birth and early years of the US. Today it includes the thriving cities of Williamsburg, Newport News, Norfolk, and Virginia Beach, and surrounding areas, including the beaches and bird-watching areas of the Eastern Shore and the Northern Neck. Routes 3, 11, 12, 13, 14, 17, and 18 lead to scenic, historic, and natural points of interest on Virginia's Coastal Plain.

Piedmont: The Tidewater ends at the Fall Line where the sediments of the Coastal Plain overlap the older crystalline rocks of the Piedmont. Because the rocks of the Piedmont are much harder than the soft, unconsolidated sediments of the Coastal Plain, they do not erode as easily, so rapids have formed in rivers as they cross this boundary. The Fall Zone marks the head of navigation on the rivers, where many of the major cities, such as Washington, DC, Fredericksburg, and Richmond, were built. The Fall Zone is less prominent south of Petersburg.

The Piedmont stretches westward from the Fall Zone to the foothills of the Blue Ridge, covering a broad area of the state. The rocks here are deeply eroded with thick soil and rich farmlands. The northern Piedmont has rolling hills, flattening out in the southern part of the state. This is the breadbasket of the state with acres and acres dedicated to growing apples, corn, cotton, grains, melons, peanuts, pecans, soybeans, sweet potatoes, tobacco, and wine grapes. Hanover tomatoes were bred to be ripe in time for Fourth of July picnics. Halifax cantaloupes are unique and the center of a major annual festival. Livestock, including bison, cattle, and poultry are also raised here, and great swaths are known as horse country. Routes 2, 3, 4, 7, 8, 11, and 17 pass through at least part of the Piedmont.

Blue Ridge: The Blue Ridge is Virginia's easternmost range of mountains, including several peaks exceeding 4,000 feet in elevation. The Blue Ridge extends in an almost unbroken span the length of the state in a northeast-southwest line from the Potomac River in northern Loudoun County to the North Carolina and Tennessee border. The rocks of the Blue Ridge are mainly Precambrian metamorphosed sediments and lava flows. It's a long story and it happened a long time ago, but there were no volcanoes in Virginia and there still aren't.

Some of the most outstanding scenery and scenic routes in Virginia lie along the Blue Ridge and its ridgeline, including Skyline Drive and the Blue Ridge Parkway, routes 5, 6, 9, and 10.

Valley and Ridge: The Valley and Ridge section consists of the broad valleys and long, even ridgelines west of the Blue Ridge. It is made up of folded, faulted, and eroded Paleozoic sedimentary rocks. The ridges are underlain by sandstone, which is resistant to erosion; less resistant limestone and shale make up the valleys. The folding has in places resulted in five or six parallel ridgelines and adjacent valleys.

Immediately to the west of the Blue Ridge in the northern part of the state is the wide Shenandoah Valley, which has a continuation farther south in the Great Valley. These limestone valleys are known for their numerous caves, many of which can be seen on guided tours. In the northern half of the state the Valley and Ridge region extends into West Virginia; farther south it is bordered on the west by the Appalachian Plateau. The George Washington and Jefferson National Forest covers much of the area, particularly the heavily wooded ridges.

For convenience, Mount Rogers is considered part of the Valley and Ridge section, although its enigmatic, Precambrian geology puzzles earth scientists; some think it belongs in a province of its own. Scenic routes in the Valley and Ridge are routes 1, 15, 19, 20, and 24. Note that the Shenandoah River travels south to north, so you'll head south if you're going upriver and north downriver.

Southwest Virginia: This area is mostly part of the Appalachian Plateau, a region of high cliffs and thick, horizontal beds of sandstone with numerous seams of coal. The boundary between the Valley and Ridge and southwest Virginia is hard to distinguish in places:

The difference is that while the rocks of the Valley and Ridge were folded, those of the Appalachian Plateau formed from thrust faults. The rocks remained relatively flat and slid over on top of each other like a spread-out deck of cards. Routes 21, 22, 23, and 25 pass through southwest Virginia.

Virginia's climate east of the Blue Ridge is moderate and variable. In non-mountainous areas you can expect warm to hot summers and mild to cold winters. The hottest region of the state is the southern Piedmont. In the Tidewater and Eastern Shore areas the climate is moderated by the waters of and breezes off of Chesapeake Bay and the Atlantic Ocean. Most parts of the state, particularly in the northern half, get a few snowstorms each winter, averaging about 16 inches. There may be no measurable snow for a year or two and then a blizzard the next.

The climate in the mountains of the western and southwestern areas of the state depends on the altitude. Summer temperatures in the high mountains can be several degrees lower than in nearby lowlands. At higher elevations winter can be severe with heavy snows that cause mountain roads to close to vehicular traffic. The most severe weather is in the high country around Mount Rogers, where an average of more than 70 inches of snow falls each winter.

In addition, the weather—both summer and winter—can vary with changes in elevation, from summer-like conditions in the valleys to wintry conditions a few thousand feet higher. That means you can snow ski and play golf on the same day at the Wintergreen Resort. Summer thunderstorms are common. Because many of the mountain routes go rapidly up and down, you should be prepared for cooler weather at higher elevations.

With its varied habitats, Virginia also has diverse bird, animal, and plant life. Some 400 species of birds are known in the state. Migrating shore and wading birds follow the marshes and estuaries of the Eastern Shore; hawks, falcons, and passerine birds ride the thermals along the windswept ridges of the Blue Ridge on their spring and fall journeys. Bald eagles, one of the largest populations in the East, inhabit the estuaries of the Potomac, Rappahannock, and other rivers, and are also found in some mountain areas.

The state also supports a rich mammal population. Two species of deer—the common Virginia white-tailed deer and Chincoteague's sika elk—plus raccoon, possum, skunk, a growing black bear population, and many smaller animals call Virginia home.

The forests have thick growths of hardwoods and softwoods. Wildflowers bloom from early spring to late fall. Spring is especially beautiful when the majority of the wildflowers bloom, and the slopes are covered with rhododendron, redbud, and mountain laurel blossoms.

The Virginia Department of Conservation and Recreation manages about 35 state parks and related sites throughout the state. Many parks are along or close to

Skyline Drive as the leaves start their annual fall fashion show.
PHOTO COURTESY OF NATIONAL PARK SERVICE

the routes and many are mentioned as points of interest. Some parks are free; others charge a modest day-use fee in season. Additional fees are levied for camping and lodging or for special use, such as the chairlift at Natural Tunnel State Park. For information on fees or to make reservations, call toll-free (800) 933-PARK.

The George Washington and Jefferson National Forest (now operated under a single administration) covers 2 million acres of public land in western Virginia. Many routes pass through or around the forest. The Forest Service maintains numerous recreation areas and campsites, of which only a few are mentioned here. For detailed maps or other information, call the Forest Supervisor at (540) 265-5100.

The National Park Service administers numerous sites in Virginia, both historic and scenic, including such diverse areas as George Washington Birthplace National Monument and Shenandoah National Park. Phone numbers for additional information on these sites are given in the Appendix.

Virginia is steeped in history, from Jamestown to the Civil War to the terrorist attack on the Pentagon. The Civil War permeates the state, with 70 percent of the battles fought here. Twenty-six major battles and more than 400 smaller engagements took place on Virginia soil. Two routes cover specific campaigns and battles of that war, and many other routes mention Civil War sites along the way.

The routes are described from a starting point to an end point, or from a starting point in a loop back to the beginning. However, if your time is limited, you can begin most routes at many places in the middle.

Information for each route starts with a "General description," which gives a one-paragraph summary of the route. "Special attractions" point to key features. "Location" ties the route to a nearby large town or general area within the state, and "Route numbers" tell you the highways covered on the drive. "Travel season" gives you the time of year when the route looks especially attractive, such as during spring blossoming or autumn leaf changing. "Camping" points you to any private and public campgrounds along or near the route. "Services" tell you where to get gas for the car and food and lodging for the motorists. Except for a few routes, these services are readily available at several places. Many points of interest are located off the main route; "Nearby attractions" will help you decide if you want to visit them. "For more information" offers a quick list of reference numbers, although the Appendix also lists phone numbers and addresses of visitor information centers and some local points of interest. It is arranged numerically by route for convenience.

Getting to scenic routes is made easy by Virginia's excellent interstate highways. I-81 and I-95 cover the state from north to south, while I-64, I-66, and I-77 provide access east to west. And some portions of the interstates themselves are scenic: Mountainous I-77 is part of Route 195.

. . . Where has nature spread so rich a mantle under the eye? Mountains, forests, rocks, rivers. With what majesty do we there ride above the storms!

Shenandoah Valley Loop

Winchester-Luray-Strasburg-New Market

General description: This 143-mile loop tours much of the northern Shenandoah Valley from the valley floor to the ridgeline of surrounding mountains. This tour provides you with varied, sweeping views alternately looking up at the mountains and down at the valleys. The route goes past small towns, both branches of the Shenandoah River, Civil War battle sites, and several caverns with guided tours.

Special attractions: The Shenandoah Valley and the Blue Ridge Mountains are the trip's star. Features include a stretch along the ridgeline of Massanutten Mountain, the opportunity to visit some of the Shenandoah Valley's world-famous caverns, a route through a covered bridge, and several Civil War battlefields.

Location: The trip begins and ends at Winchester in the northwest corner of the state off exit 313 of I-81, about 10 miles from the West Virginia line.

Route numbers: US 522, 340, 211, and 11; VA 600, 55, 678, 675, and 720.

Travel season: The trip can be made at any time. Heavy snows in winter may temporarily close some mountain roads. Some facilities may be closed in winter.

Camping: Camping and trailer facilities are available at the Elizabeth Furnace Recreation Area in the George Washington and Jefferson National Forest, at several areas in Shenandoah National Park, and at Jellystone Park in Luray.

Services: Gasoline, motels, hotels, and restaurants are available in all towns along the route.

Nearby attractions: Shenandoah National Park and Skyline Drive (see Route 5), various caverns, and Shenandoah Valley Music Festival.

For more information: Winchester Frederick County Convention & Visitors Bureau, (540) 542-1326 or (877) 871-1326, visitwinchesterva.com; Shenandoah County Tourism, (540) 459-6227, shenandoahtravel.org; Virginia's Heritage Migration Route or the Wilderness Road, virginia.org/wildernessroad; Strasburg Virginia Chamber of Commerce, (540) 465-3187, viststrasburg.com; Museum of the Shenandoah Valley, (888) 556-5799 or (540) 662-1473, themsv.org; Old Court House Civil War Museum, (540) 542-1145, civilwarmuseum.org; Stonewall Jackson's Headquarters Museum, (540) 662-6550, winchesterhistory.org; Kernstown Battlefield, (540) 869-2896, kernstownbattle.org; Shenandoah Valley Discovery Museum, (540) 722-2020, discoverymuseum.net; Rock Harbor Golf Course (540) 722-7111, rockharborgolf.com; Rocking S Ranch, (540) 678-8501, therockingsranch.com; Blandy Farm/State Arboretum of Virginia, (540) 837-1758, virginia.edu/blandy; Luray Caverns, (540) 743-6551, luraycaverns.com; Endless Caverns, (540) 896-2283, endlesscaverns.com; Shenandoah Caverns, (540) 477-3115 or (888) 422-8376, shenandoahcaverns.com; Belle Grove Plantation, (540) 869-2028, bellgrove.org; Cedar Creek & Belle Grove National Historic Park, (540) 868-0176, nps.gov/cebe.

Shenandoah Valley Loop

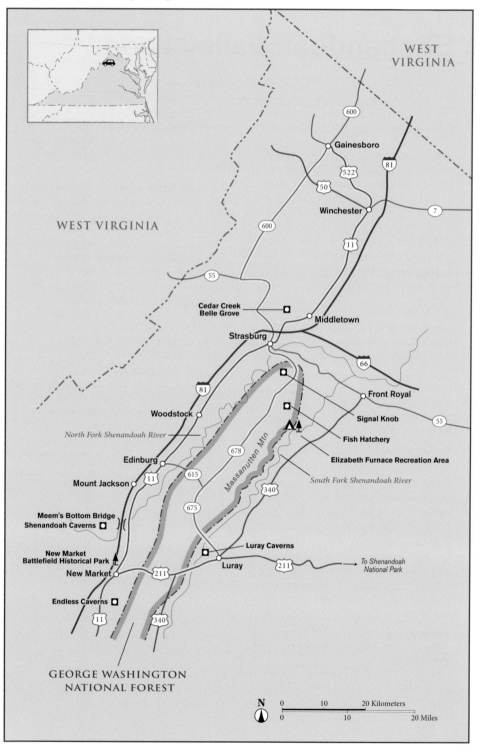

WEST
VIRGINIA

WEST VIRGINIA

600

Gainesboro

522

81

50

Winchester

7

600

11

55

Cedar Creek
Belle Grove

Middletown

Strasburg

66

81

Front Royal

Woodstock

Signal Knob

55

North Fork Shenandoah River

Fish Hatchery

Edinburg

678

Massanutten Mtn

Elizabeth Furnace Recreation Area

615

Mount Jackson

11

340

South Fork Shenandoah River

675

Meem's Bottom Bridge
Shenandoah Caverns

Luray Caverns

New Market
Battlefield Historical Park

Luray

211

To Shenandoah
National Park

New Market

211

Endless Caverns

11

340

GEORGE WASHINGTON
NATIONAL FOREST

N

0   10   20 Kilometers

0   10   20 Miles

The Route

The Shenandoah Valley of Virginia stretches for about 200 miles in a northeast-southwest line from the West Virginia panhandle to Roanoke. Europeans started settling in the valley in the early 1700s, and they adopted the Indian name "Shenandoah," which means "daughter of the stars." It soon became a major farming area and corridor for westward expansion.

The valley lies between the Blue Ridge Mountains to the east and the Alleghenies to the west. Its rich, limestone soils continue to support Virginia's extensive apple orchards, cornfields, soybeans, other crops, and poultry farms. The long ridge of Massanutten Mountain dominates the northern Shenandoah Valley The South Fork of the Shenandoah River drains the southeastern section; the North Fork of the Shenandoah River drains the northwestern. The two forks unite to become the Shenandoah River at Front Royal, which flows to Harpers Ferry, West Virginia, to join the Potomac River.

Below the valley floor several thousand caverns have formed in the limestone and dolomite carbonate rocks; the biggest and most interesting caverns provide guided, lighted tours.

Because the valley was such an important farming area and was used as a thoroughfare for both Union and Confederate troops during the Civil War, several major battles and numerous skirmishes and encounters took place here. Today the valley is traversed by high-speed I-81, used by several million vehicles each year, and roughly parallels its predecessor, US 11. This surface route winds its way through the various towns and offers a great respite from the mind-numbing traffic speeding along the interstate. It's part of Virginia's Heritage Migration Route or the Wilderness Road; 43 million people can trace their heritage to families that migrated from Europe to this area of Virginia.

The route begins in the historic town of Winchester and follows back roads to Strasburg, "the Antique Capital of the Blue Ridge," with 50,000 square feet of antiques. You then cross the North Fork of the Shenandoah River and enter the George Washington National Forest. After traversing a short canyon you cross the twin ridges of Massanutten Mountain. As you descend the mountain, you have superb views of the South Fork of the Shenandoah and the fertile Shenandoah Valley.

The route then joins US 211, passes by Luray Caverns, and crosses Massanutten Mountain again to New Market. You then head north on old US 11 with magnificent views of the Blue Ridge, past some of the Civil War's bloodiest battlefields, and return to Winchester where the route ends. The total distance is about 143 miles, and the trip can be made in one day. Schedule more time if you're going to visit a cavern, a battlefield, a historic site, or browse through the antiques.

Meem's Bottom Bridge is the only covered bridge on Virginia public lands that you can drive a car through.

The town of Winchester has been rich in history since colonial days. The oldest building in town, known as Abram's Delight, has been restored to its original 1754 splendor and is open to the public, including an herb garden and formal boxwood garden. You can also visit George Washington's Office Museum, used by the young officer as both a surveying office and later as headquarters during the French and Indian Wars.

More than 100 years later, the town, strategically located at the head of the Shenandoah Valley, was a pivotal spot during the Civil War. The valley provided a north/south transportation corridor, and its rich farmlands of food crops and—farther south—tobacco, were coveted by both sides. Winchester's importance is shown by the fact that the town changed hands some 72 times during the 4-year conflict, more than any other town in the country.

Winchester to Strasburg

Your logical first stop is the **Winchester–Frederick County Visitors Center** with a staff of travel counselors who will help you plan your tours. Also at the center, you can view the exhibits at the area's **Civil War Orientation Center** and take away local and state maps, brochures, and souvenirs, Then, stroll along the 2-block pedestrian mall in Old Town with restaurants, specialty shops, and boutiques. **Old Town Winchester** was one of the state's first designated Main Street Communities, and the pedestrian mall was one of the first in the state.

To better understand the valley's arts, history, and culture, visit the **Museum of the Shenandoah Valley.** The 4 galleries, 6 acres of gardens, a house built in 1794, a cafe and a museum store provide a fascinating interpretation of our ancestors' lifestyle.

Area Civil War attractions include the **Old Court House Civil War Museum,** used as a prison and a hospital during the war and located in the antebellum Frederick County Courthouse; **Stonewall Jackson's Headquarters Museum,** used by the Confederate general while he planned his famous Valley Campaign in 1861–62; **Stonewall Cemetery,** the resting place for more than 2,500 Confederate soldiers; **Winchester National Cemetery,** the final resting place for Union soldiers; **Kernstown Battlefield,** 315 acres of green space; and the **Third Battle of Winchester Path,** a 5-mile walking/mountain bike trail on battlefield land.

Other attractions are a **Korean War Memorial** and a **POW/MIA Memorial** in the Jim Barnett Park, a statue of polar explorer **Rear Admiral Richard E. Byrd, Abram's Delight Museum, Shenandoah Arts Council Gallery, Dinosaur Land, Shenandoah Valley Discovery Museum,** and numerous fruit orchards and farmers' markets throughout Frederick County. Popular outdoor activities include **Rock Harbor Golf Course, Rocking S Ranch,** and **Blandy Farm/State Arboretum of Virginia.**

To begin the actual route, head northwest out of Winchester on US 522. Once out of town, this 4-lane highway with its gentle curves and grades winds through several road cuts where the folded limestones, dolomites, shales, and mudstones that make up the valley floor are exposed.

At **Gainesboro,** about 10 miles from Winchester, the route turns left onto 2-lane VA 600 which winds through town and heads into the open country. This narrow road passes farms growing corn and hay and numerous herds of both dairy and beef cattle.

The level valley floor ends in hardwood ridges that parallel both sides of the road; most farms are maintained as open fields up to the steeper part of the ridge. These ridges, like most of the higher points in the Shenandoah Valley, are made up of sandstone rocks folded into an anticline, or arch. Because the sandstone does not erode as easily as the limestones, shales, and mudstones that underlie most of the valley, the sandstone forms resistant ridges.

Four miles from Gainesboro, VA 600 crosses 4-lane US 50. Continue on VA 600 past the stop sign and several other stop signs farther along. Virginia 600 ends at VA 55 in about 13 miles. Turn left on VA 55, a broad 2-lane road. The ridgeline you see ahead on the horizon stretching to the right is **Massanutten Mountain.** The prominent high point at the left-hand end is **Signal Knob,** a Civil War observation and message station.

Cross I-81 and enter the town of Strasburg. The town calls itself "the Antique Capital of the Blue Ridge," with almost 100 antiques dealers in the **Strasburg Emporium** on VA 55. (Yes, purists, that probably should be "antiques" capital. Just appreciate that you'll find a lot of antiques and collectibles here.) Although they are busiest in the warmer months, most dealers are open year-round. On Main Street are the **Strasburg Museum** and the elegant **Hotel Strasburg,** furnished to restore its 1890 Victorian splendor.

Strasburg to Luray

Follow VA 55 through town. For a few blocks the road parallels US 11 which you will use on the return end of the driving loop. VA 55 soon leaves town and crosses the North Fork of the Shenandoah River. You are now at the base of **Signal Knob** whose steep slopes have been visible for many miles. The road curves gently around the mountain's wooded base.

At the other side of the mountain, about 5 miles past Strasburg, turn right on VA 678. VA 55 continues straight ahead to Front Royal, starting point for Skyline Drive (Route 5). Continue on VA 678, which enters George Washington National Forest.

The forest name may confuse you. Originally there were two national forests in Virginia: **George Washington National Forest,** primarily in the northwestern part of the state and neighboring West Virginia, and Jefferson National Forest in southwest Virginia and nearby parts of West Virginia. They have since been consolidated into one mouthful of an entity: George Washington and Jefferson National Forest. However, the northern section is still known as the George Washington section, and the southern section continues to be known as . . . right, you get the idea. Most maps and most people still refer to the original names.

At any rate, you enter thick woods in the national forest, and the road begins to climb. A road to the left leads to a fish hatchery. Many open views through the hardwood trees show conical peaks and cliffs to the left. VA678 follows the small wooded canyon of Passage Creek with several unmarked parking areas and turnoffs for swimming, fishing, and picnicking. The creek flows over steeply dipping beds of sandstone, forming small rapids in places.

Winchester's native son Rear Admiral Richard E. Byrd
PHOTO COURTESY WINCHESTER–FREDERICK COUNTY CONVENTION & VISITORS BUREAU

About 3.5 miles from VA 55, you pass the parking area and trailhead on the right for a 10-mile circuit hike to **Signal Knob.** Just past the trailhead, a road leads left to the **Elizabeth Furnace Recreation Area,** a hiking, camping, and picnic area; a trail here leads to the ridgeline of **Massanutten Mountain.**

After several miles the road leaves the creek bed and the grade steepens. You level off and emerge from the woods in a small valley with ridgelines to the left and right. This is the eroded axis, or center, of the anticline; the sandstone has been worn away here, like a truncated McDonald's archway. Most of the land here is privately owned although surrounded by the national forest. Lush farms alternate with woods.

About 10 miles from VA 55, go left on VA 675. The road narrows and climbs steeply with many bends up a wooded ridge. At the crest of the ridge, park at the side of the road and cross the road for an outstanding view of the fields and farmlands of the Shenandoah Valley east of Massanutten Mountain. The view includes the South Fork of the Shenandoah River, the town of Luray, and on clear days, the distant peaks of the Blue Ridge and Shenandoah National Park.

Past the viewpoint, VA 675 quickly descends to the valley floor. Turn left at the stop sign at the T-intersection at the edge of the South Fork of the Shenandoah River. You will see a bridge that crosses the river. Turn right over the bridge, still following VA 675.

Follow VA 675 into **Luray,** crossing over US 211 and following VA 675 through the outskirts of town to the stop sign at US 340. Turn left (north) on US 340. (Turn right to visit the town of Luray.) You will see US 211 a quarter of a mile ahead. Turn left on US 211 (west, toward New Market). (In the other direction, to the east, US 211 twists and climbs the Blue Ridge to Shenandoah National Park and Skyline Drive, intersecting Route 5 in the middle; it then descends to the Piedmont at Sperryville in the middle of Route 4.)

Luray to New Market

US 211 is a 4-lane divided highway that will seem like a speedway after the narrow mountain roads. You are in a wide valley. The taller Blue Ridge Mountains are behind you to the east; **Massanutten Mountain** is straight ahead. On clear days mountains will stretch to the horizon in all directions.

In 2 miles you pass the entrance to **Luray Caverns,** the most famous, most popular, and most advertised cavern in Virginia. Discovered in 1878, the cavern was soon open to the public. It became immensely popular, attracting visitors from around the world, and the tourist money they brought was a major factor that helped the area recover from the ravages of the Civil War. The cavern features large rooms and an underground organ, the "Stalacpipe," which strikes stalactites

A garden at Abram's Delight Museum, the oldest home in Winchester

(which hang down from the ceiling) and stalagmites (which grow up from the floor) to generate musical tones. In addition to cavern tours, the cavern properties include an old-time car and caravan museum, garden maze, and singing tower with a carillon of 47 bells.

The carbonate rocks (limestone and dolomite) in which Luray Caverns and other caverns are formed were deposited from organic material at the bottom of shallow tropical seas during early Paleozoic times, some 300 to 500 million years ago. These seas were similar to the Bahama Bank that surrounds today's Bahama Islands.

The limestone and dolomite contain small amounts of the sulfide mineral pyrite. The caverns were dissolved out by slowly percolating groundwater which contained small amounts of sulfuric acid from oxidation of the pyrite. The solution followed cracks and fissures in the rock, dissolving the limestone and dolomite, forming many caverns with large rooms and spacious passages. The same groundwater also deposited calcite on the walls, ceilings, and floors of the caverns, leaving festoons of stalactites, stalagmites, flowstone, and other picturesque formations.

All caverns mentioned on this route offer safe, comfortable, well-lighted guided tours on paved and improved trails. Because these are commercial enterprises, fees are charged.

As you approach Massanutten Mountain and enter **George Washington National Forest,** you can clearly see the break in the ridge at New Market Gap, which you will soon cross. At the top of the ridge is a Forest Service center with exhibits. Several trailheads lead off from the center.

The road descends to **New Market** to a stop sign at US 11. The main route turns right (north) on US 11.

To the left (south) on US 11/211 are side trips to **New Market Battlefield Historical Park** and **Endless Caverns.** In 1864, Confederate General John Breckinridge, outnumbered two to one, defeated Union troops in one of the most dramatic battles of the Civil War. Some 257 cadets from Virginia Military Institute (VMI) participated, and 10 cadets were killed. The battlefield park details this story. The facilities, operated privately by VMI, include battlefield tours and perhaps the finest Civil War museum in the state.

To visit the battlefield and museum, go left (south) on US 11/211 for 2 blocks and then turn right on US 211. Cross I-81 and take the first right to the park. The entrance is well marked. To return to the route, turn left on 211 as you leave the park and turn left (north) on US 11.

To visit Endless Caverns, drive south on US 11 for about 3 miles. Turn left at the well-marked turnoff. A beautiful cavern, Endless Caverns was developed into a tourist attraction in the 1880s to compete with Luray Caverns. After visiting the cavern, turn right on US 11 to New Market to rejoin the tour.

New Market to Middletown to Winchester

About 4 miles north of New Market, as you're approaching Mount Jackson, turn left at the "Covered Bridge" sign on VA 720. The bridge lies about half a mile from the highway down a tree-shaded road. The **Meem's Bottom Bridge,** built in 1892, spans the North Fork of the Shenandoah River and is the only covered bridge in the state open to vehicular traffic. It is about 200 feet long. There are a few parking spaces just before the bridge. When you return to US 11, turn left to continue the route.

In about 5 miles you pass the entrance to **Shenandoah Caverns,** another popular tourist stop. This cavern features an elevator ride to the cavern floor. Or, you can continue to Mount Jackson, where you can stop by the **Mount Jackson Confederate Cemetery,** the **Route 11 Potato Chip Factory,** and a few wineries.

The winding route continues by **Edinburg** and **Woodstock.** Low hills and occasional views of the river add variety. Mount Jackson is the gateway to the **Shenandoah Valley Music Festival,** held each summer at Orkney Springs, about 15 miles west of Mount Jackson. The festival features a varied program from classical to western to light pops.

Patsy Cline Historic House in downtown Winchester
PHOTO COURTESY WINCHESTER–FREDERICK COUNTY CONVENTION & VISITORS BUREAU

At Woodstock the road skirts the well-kept grounds of the Massanutten Military Academy.

You reach **Strasburg** again about 30 miles from New Market. Follow US 11 through town, crossing VA 55.

A few miles north of Strasburg, before reaching Middletown, you see to your left the entrance to **Belle Grove Plantation.** Designed in part by Thomas Jefferson, this restored, historic mansion was the honeymoon site for James and Dolley Madison and the 1797 manor house is on the list of the National Trust for Historic Preservation.

The area was also the scene of the **Battle of Cedar Creek,** the last major Civil War engagement of the Shenandoah Valley. More than 6,000 soldiers died here when Union General Philip Sheridan narrowly defeated Confederate General Jubal Early. The actual battlefield extended from Strasburg almost to Middletown. Numerous roadside markers point out places and describe events of the Civil War.

On the right side of US 11 in Middletown, traveling north, is the **Cedar Creek & Belle Grove National Historic Park** visitor contact station which is open year-round. Park rangers conduct numerous seasonal educational programs throughout the area.

The route continues on US 11 to end where you began in Winchester.

Leesburg Loop

Hunt Country & the Snickersville Pike

General description: This 98-mile (if you take the side trips) loop route passes through the hilly hunt country west and north of Leesburg in the northern tip of the state. This is a varied area of scenic and historical interest with many large estates, horse farms, open fields, small towns and villages, and historic Leesburg itself.

Special attractions: Of special interest is White's Ferry across the Potomac, and the historic village of Waterford. Snickersville Turnpike's up-and-down hills provide a scenic and memorable driving experience and Dodona Manor (George C. Marshall's home), and the 19th-century mansion and grounds at Oatlands will give you a glimpse of how the privileged lived at the turn of the 19th century.

Location: The route, beginning and ending in Leesburg in north-central Virginia is easily reached in about an hour from Washington, DC, via the Dulles Toll Road extension or VA 7.

Route numbers: US 15, US Business 15, and US 50; VA 655, 7, 9, 662, 665, 672, 673, 690, 9, 719, and 734.

Travel season: The route can be followed at any time. Most attractions are busiest—and have the most activities—during the warmer months; they may have reduced hours or limited operations from late Oct through May.

The crafts festival in Waterford the first week in Oct attracts large crowds.

Camping: Not available.

Services: Gasoline, motels, hotels, and restaurants are abundant in Leesburg; gasoline and restaurants can be found in all towns along the route.

Nearby attractions: Leesburg is less than an hour from Washington, DC, and all the attractions in the nation's capital. Route 3, George Washington Memorial Parkway, provides views across the Potomac of many of the Washington sights when you're traveling north.

For more information: Town of Leesburg Economic Development and Tourism, (703) 737-7019, leesburgva.gov; Dodona Manor, (703) 777-1880, georgecmarshall.org; Visit Loudoun, (703) 771-4964 or (800) 752-6118, visitloudoun.org; Morven Park and the Museum of Hounds & Hunting, (703) 777-2414, morvenpark.org; Loudoun Museum, (703) 777-7427, loudounmuseum.org; White's Ferry, (301) 349-5200, visit loudoun.org; Waterford Foundation, (540) 882-3018, waterfordfoundation.org; Willowcroft Farm Vineyards, (703) 777-8161, willowcroftwine.com; Aldie Mill Historic Park, (703) 327-0777, nvrpa.org/park; and Oatlands Plantation, (703) 777-3174, oat lands.org.

The Route

Horses, hounds, and hunting have been the traditional trademarks of the rolling Piedmont area around Leesburg since colonial days. Just a short distance from Washington, DC, its bucolic nature has been a magnet for many who want to dwell in the country while their business requires them to be near the hustle and bustle of the nation's capital.

Leesburg Loop

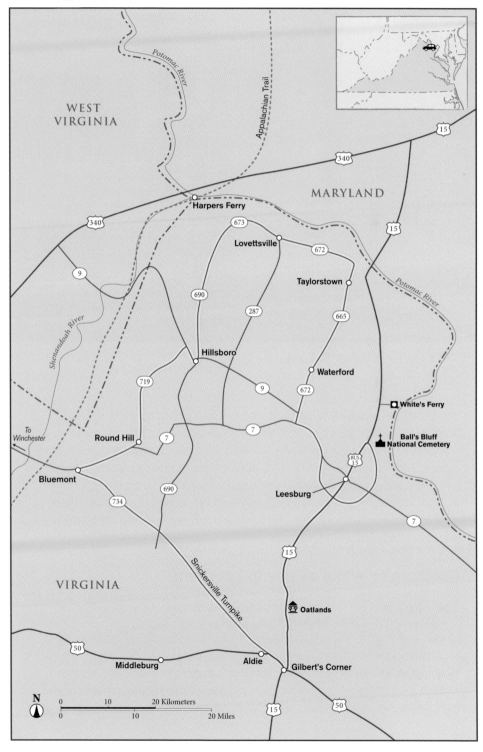

Dodona Manor, home of General George C. Marshall
PHOTO COURTESY TOWN OF LEESBURG, VIRGINIA

On this 98-mile loop route you'll pass many large mansions with manicured lawns, long wooden fences, and horse barns and trailers. The hills, vales, curves, and woods that attract foxhunters (and sometimes attract foxes) pass through sleepy villages, often through open country with distant views of gentle peaks and ridges.

You'll view (and can ride on) the last operating ferry on the Potomac, drive through the historic village of Waterford—restored to look as it did 150 years ago—ride up and down the hilly Snickersville Turnpike, and tour the restored plantation and gardens of Oatlands.

Leesburg to White's Ferry to Leesburg

The route begins and ends in historic **Leesburg.** Originally known as George Town, the settlement broke ties with England in 1758 and took the name Leesburg in honor of Virginia's prestigious family. Today its narrow downtown streets are filled with tony shops and restaurants, with the delight of an occasional colonial-era building.

While in the area you may want to visit **Ball's Bluff Regional Park,** which describes the retreat of Union soldiers across the Potomac in a small battle fought here in 1861. North of town is the columned mansion at **Morven Park,** home to several 19th-century Virginia governors. On the grounds are extensive boxwood gardens and, if you want to learn more about foxhunting history, the **Museum of Hounds and Hunting.** To learn more about the city's history, visit the **Loudoun Museum** (it does have limited hours).

Dodona Manor is a local attraction that's historic and relatively new on the tourism scene. It was formerly the home of General George C. Marshall and his wife Katherine Marshall, purchased in 1941. He was the mind behind the Marshall Plan that saved much of Europe after World War II and the man who invited other great minds to discuss the important matters of the day. General Marshall lived here until his death in 1959. When the home and property were scheduled for sale in the early 1990s, a George C. Marshall Home Preservation Fund (now the George C. Marshall International Center) was established to purchase the home, renovate it, and open it as a museum. Much of the funding came from those countries that had been the beneficiary of the Marshall Plan. The center conducts educational and leadership programs and offers exhibits, lectures, and community outreach events.

When you visit, note the furnishings—including a painting by Sir Winston Churchill—for most of them were owned by the Marshalls. The house is open on Sat 10 a.m. to 5 p.m., Sun 1 to 5 p.m., and from June to July, it's open on Mon 1 to 5 p.m.

The actual route begins with a short side trip to **White's Ferry.** Head north from Leesburg on either US 15 or Business 15. The two roads rejoin just north of town. Follow US 15 north for about a mile to the "Ferry" sign and turn right onto VA 655.

VA655 leads directly to the Potomac River's shores. It then turns sharply to the left along the riverbank on a tree-shaded road for about 0.5 mile to White's Ferry, the only car ferry across the Potomac. There are a few parking spaces near the ferry landing.

A ferry has run from this spot since 1786. The current boat, named for the Confederate general Jubal Early, was installed in 1988 and can carry 24 cars; commuter traffic in the morning and evening often fills the vessel to capacity. If you have time, you can ride the ferry over and back as a pedestrian for a nominal sum.

The ferryboat is run by a diesel engine that pulls the boat along a cable stretched across the river. The town of White's Ferry is actually in Maryland, about 1,000 feet away across the Potomac River.

When you leave to continue the route, follow VA 655 back to US 15 and turn left, retracing your route to Leesburg. You can take either Business 15 (shorter and more congested) through Leesburg or US 15 (longer and, theoretically, faster) around town to VA 7. Whatever route you take, turn right (west) onto VA 7.

Leesburg to Waterford

Follow VA 7 west a few miles to VA 9. Go less than 0.5 mile on VA 9 and turn right (toward Waterford) onto VA 662. This curvy Virginia Byway passes numerous cattle and horse farms and open fields.

When you arrive in **Waterford,** you may think you have stepped back 100 years in time as you drive past several blocks of lovingly restored, 2- and 3-story colonial and federal houses. Settled by Quakers in 1733, the village became a thriving crafts and farming community. During the Civil War, Confederate harassment led many townspeople to support Union troops, despite the traditional Quaker belief in nonviolence.

The village did okay until the 1940s when it had something of a jump-start because the Waterford Foundation began sponsoring an **annual crafts fair.** The fair's success resulted in extensive renovations and restorations including of the **Corner Store** that sells foundation books, gifts, crafts, and other "small town" items. It's open on Fri and Sat 10 a.m. to 2 p.m. Today the fair, held the first weekend in Oc, attracts some 150 craftspeople. This has given rise to a series of concerts in the new Waterford Old School auditorium, replacing the building that burned in early 2007. In addition, there are public tours of a dozen or more restored homes along its tree-shaded streets. The entire village is listed as a National Historic Landmark.

Waterford to Hillsboro

From Waterford, follow VA 665, Royalton Road, north. The countryside here is wilder and less settled, with more woods and unused fields. You pass the old general store in **Taylorstown** and cross **Catoctin Creek,** a state scenic creek.

At the stop sign north of Taylorstown, turn left onto VA 672, Lovettsville Road. The narrow road twists and turns its way toward Lovettsville. Bear right on VA 673. At the stop sign in Lovettsville, cross VA 287 and continue straight ahead on VA 673. About 2 miles out of town, turn right onto VA 690, also known as Mountain Road.

The **Appalachian Trail** follows the top of the ridge on the low hills to the right, which also marks the Virginia–West Virginia boundary. When West Virginia seceded from Virginia and joined the Union in 1863, the boundary in this area was set as the watershed divide between the Potomac (on this side of the ridge) and the Shenandoah (on the other side of the ridge). This sounds simple, except it took satellite surveys in 1997 before the two states agreed on an exact line. This was a relief to many residents, who until then were not sure what state they were living in (and should pay taxes to).

South King Street in Leesburg
PHOTO COURTESY TOWN OF LEESBURG, VIRGINIA

At the stop sign in Hillsboro, turn right on VA 9. A former mill town, **Hillsboro** has several blocks of beautiful, 100-year-old stone houses. The town is the birthplace of Susan Koerner Wright, mother of airplane inventors Wilbur and Orville. Follow VA 9 through town.

Hillsboro to Bluemont

On the other side of Hillsboro, turn left onto VA 719, Woodgrove Road. Follow this wooded country lane for about 7 miles to Round Hill. Turn right in Round Hill onto VA Business 7, and turn right again in about 0.5 mile when the route joins the main VA 7, a 4-lane highway.

VA 7 climbs a long hill with several vistas to your left. After 4 miles, turn left onto VA 734 towards Bluemont. You are entering the **Snickersville Turnpike,** a Virginia Byway. This narrow, 2-lane road makes several hairpin turns and heads downhill like a runaway roller coaster. You soon pass by the stately stone houses and Bluemont Country Store in the little town of **Bluemont** and cross a 1-lane bridge.

After several miles of mostly downhill travel, the landscape levels out, while the sharp curves continue. Horse farms and executive-type mansions are intermixed with farmland; the predominant crops in season are hay, corn, and soybeans. To the left you pass the entrance to **Willowcroft Farm Vineyards.** Like most of the wineries (as of this writing) in the state, Willowcroft Farm provides tours and tasting rooms. Check its website for days and hours of operation.

Bluemont to Middleburg

VA 734 and the Snickersville Turnpike end at US 50. The main route turns left (east) on US 50.

For a side trip to **Middleburg,** a popular weekend destination from the DC suburbs, turn right on US 50 and drive about 5 miles to this historic town known for its upscale shops, inns, and restaurants. The nineteenth-century buildings in the center of this charming town are the Middleburg Historic District that's listed on the National Register of Historic Places. As you may have surmised, from driving around, this is horse country with lots of foxhunting and steeplechasing activities. It's been going on since just after the turn of the twentieth century. Fans of the Kennedy dynasty may remember when President John F. Kennedy had a country home nearby. When you are ready to leave Middleburg, turn around and drive east on US 50 to continue with the main route.

Middleburg to Oatlands to Leesburg

Back on US 50 you soon pass through **Aldie,** known for its antiques shops and old mill. The **Aldie Mill** has been restored, including its original millstone hoist. Just past the mill the route crosses a historic, narrow, 2-lane stone bridge built during colonial days.

At Gilbert's Corner roundabout, a mile past Aldie, turn left onto US 15 and head back toward Leesburg. Most of the route follows a discontinuous ridge with downhill views to the right of open fields, farms, and wooded estates.

Just past Goose Creek you come to the long, tree-shaded entranceway to **Oat-lands,** an expansive early federal period mansion and gardens. Turn right up the drive to visit, or continue on US 15 for 6 miles to Leesburg.

Oatlands is part of an 11,500-acre tract purchased by the Carter family from Lord Fairfax. In 1804 George Carter built his country house on the estate. The house served as a boardinghouse during the Civil War; like so many others in Virginia, the estate fell into disrepair after the conflict. It was reclaimed and restored by William Corcoran Eustis, grandson of the founder of the Corcoran Art Gallery in Washington, DC.

In addition to the 3-story mansion with its stately columns and spacious wings, Oatlands contains extensive terraced gardens with shady boxwood tunnels,

With plenty of trees available, a split rail fence was an attractive and practical means of marking a boundary.

wisteria walkways, and herb plantings. The mansion contains a mix of American and European furnishings, including some dessert plates that belonged to George Washington. Other interesting features are the octagonal drawing room—very stylish in the early 1800s—and elaborate plasterwork in several rooms.

When you leave Oatlands, turn right on US 15. In a few miles the condos and developments south of Leesburg appear, and in 6 miles you reach Leesburg, the route's beginning and end.

3

George Washington Memorial Parkway

Capital Views

General description: This 25-mile route following the western shoreline of the Potomac River is unlike the other routes in this book. Although it's a national parkway under the same jurisdiction as Skyline Drive and the Blue Ridge Parkway, it's different. It is a spectacular route, offering vistas and snapshots into daily life and history as no other piece of roadway does. Sometimes the parkway is within eyesight of the river and sometimes it veers away a little. Given good traffic conditions, you can drive it in about 45 minutes. Or, you can stop at any of a half-dozen parks along the way and spend an entire day taking in the sights and sounds along the Potomac.

Special attractions: George Washington's home at Mount Vernon; open stretches of the lower Potomac; Old Town Alexandria; intimate moments with Mother Nature; close-ups of takeoffs and landings at Reagan National Airport; views of the Washington, DC, skyline, including the Washington Monument, the Lincoln Memorial, and the US Capitol; and the gorge of the upper Potomac. The 7,374 acres of the parkway are home to at least 81 species of plants and animals that are considered rare, threatened, or endangered.

Location: The route, which is across the Potomac River from Washington, DC, in northern Virginia, starts at Mount Vernon, about 15 miles south of Washington. You can also join the ride mid-route from Washington by crossing the Potomac on one of the many bridges out of Washington (see details in the Route section) and following signs to the parkway. It ends at the Capital Beltway, about 10 miles north of Washington.

Route numbers: Starting at Mount Vernon, the route is VA 235 until Alexandria where it becomes Washington Street/VA 400 and retains the VA 400 designation to the northern end at the Capital Beltway (I-495).

Travel season: Avoid rush hour. The day and time of day are more important than the time of year with early morning weekend days the least crowded. The parkway is a major weekday morning and evening commuter route for the more than 7 million people traveling the system in 2012, making it the fourth most visited park in the National Park System. The best views of the Washington skyline are in winter when leaves are off the trees. Spring and fall are best for flowering plants and trees. Except for occasional winter snowstorms, the ride can be made anytime. An after-dark ride provides an almost star-studded view of the Washington skyline decorated in streetlights and memorial illumination (until midnight).

Services: Motels, hotels, restaurants, gasoline, and shopping malls are available in abundance in Alexandria, and hotels and restaurants are even more abundant in Washington, DC.

Nearby attractions: All of the monuments and buildings of the nation's capital are nearby, including the US Capitol, the National Mall, the Lincoln and Jefferson Memorials, the Washington Monument (temporarily closed), the Korean War Veterans Memorial, the Vietnam Veterans Memorial, and the Martin Luther King Jr. National Memorial. The various components of the Smithsonian Institution (including the zoo) are also in Washington, DC, just across the Potomac. The parkway runs more-or-less parallel to the Mount Vernon Trail used by walkers, joggers, and bikers.

George Washington Memorial Parkway

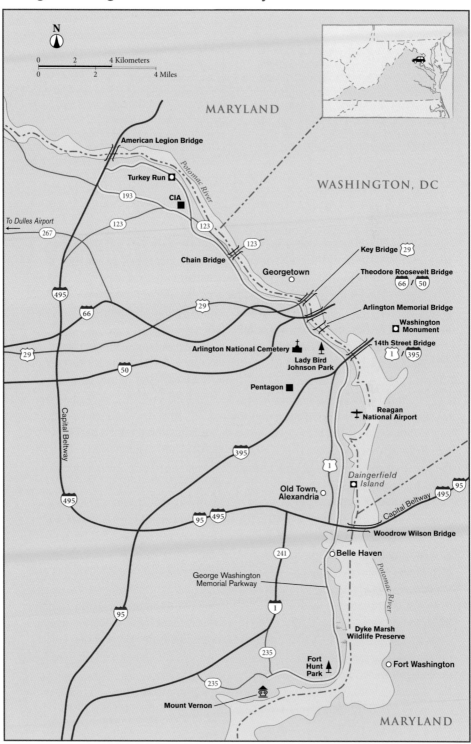

N

0   2   4 Kilometers
0   2   4 Miles

MARYLAND

WASHINGTON, DC

American Legion Bridge

Potomac River

Turkey Run

193

CIA

To Dulles Airport

267

123

123

123

Chain Bridge

Georgetown

Key Bridge 29

Theodore Roosevelt Bridge
66 / 50

Arlington Memorial Bridge

Washington
Monument

14th Street Bridge
1 / 395

495

66

29

50

Arlington National Cemetery

Lady Bird
Johnson Park

Pentagon

Reagan
National Airport

Capital Beltway

29

395

1

Daingerfield
Island

Old Town,
Alexandria

495

95   495

Capital Beltway

495 95

Woodrow Wilson Bridge

241

Belle Haven

Potomac River

George Washington
Memorial Parkway

95

1

Dyke Marsh
Wildlife Preserve

235

Fort
Hunt
Park

Fort Washington

235

Mount Vernon

MARYLAND

For more information: Alexandria Convention & Visitors Association, (800) 388-9119 or (703) 652-5360, visitalexandriava.com; Arlington Convention and Visitors Service, (703) 228-0875, stayarlington.com; Mount Vernon, (703) 780-2000, mountvernon.org; Fort Hunt Park, (703) 289-2500, nps.gov/gwmp; Dyke Marsh Wildlife Preserve, (703) 289-2500, nps.gov/gwmp; Jones Point Park, (703) 289-2500, nps.gov/gwmp; Netherlands Carillon, (703) 289-2500; nps.gov/gwmp; Women in Military Service for America Memorial, (703) 533-1155, womensmemorial.org; US Marine Corps War Memorial, (703) 289-2500, nps.gov/gwmp; Turkey Run Park, (703) 289-2500, nps.gov/ns/gwmp; Lady Bird Johnson Park, (703) 289-2500, nps.gov/gwmp.

The Route

The George Washington Memorial Parkway, or GW Parkway, was opened on May 29, 1930. The cloverleaf interchange at the 14th Street Bridge was built in 1932 and is one of the oldest cloverleaf interchanges in the country.

The parkway is narrow, windy, and the strictly enforced speed limit can be 25 miles per hour up to 50. Much of the road is lined with forests housing deer, wild turkeys, box turtles, and numerous other reptile species.

You should know the height of your vehicle because some of the bridges passing over the GW Parkway have limited clearance. As an example, the CSX Railroad Bridge has a clearance of 12'3" in the left lane, 13'9" in the right lane, and 14'7" in the middle lane going north, and 13'8", 12'10", and 14'7" in the left, center, and right lanes, respectively, going south.

Commercial trucks, even personal ones, are not allowed on the parkway.

Although the parkway is open all day, the parks and facilities that are part of the park system have limited hours, generally 6 a.m. to 10 p.m. or, in some cases, dawn to dusk.

The route, as described here, starts at Mount Vernon. It can be picked up at several points along the way as well. This can be convenient for visitors to Washington, DC, who can cross one of the several bridges to Virginia.

Starting from the south, the bridges that can be navigated by car from the Maryland/Washington side of the Potomac to Virginia and the GW Parkway are: Woodrow Wilson (I-95/495/Capital Beltway), Rochambeau Memorial Bridge (I-395 HOV, 14th Street Bridge), George Mason Memorial Bridge (I-395 South), Arlington Memorial Bridge, Theodore Roosevelt Bridge (I-66/US 50), Francis Scott Key Bridge (US 29), Chain Bridge (Clara Barton Parkway), and the American Legion Memorial Bridge (I-495/Beltway and also sometimes still referred to as the Cabin John Bridge).

The southbound part of the parkway is a pleasant drive. However, most of the overlooks and turnoffs are only accessible from the northbound lanes.

Mount Vernon gateway and driveway
©JOEL SHAWN/SHUTTERSTOCK.COM

Reversing directions is easy at the Mount Vernon end. The parkway terminates in a broad circle, or you can pull into the Mount Vernon parking area to head the other way.

Scenic it may be, but this route becomes a bumper-to-bumper commuter route every weekday between 6 and 9:30 a.m. and 3:30 and 7 p.m. (and sometimes on weekends, too). Although it was designed as a recreational drive, it has become a favored commuter route. Traffic can move fast when it isn't gridlocked with an accident.

Mount Vernon to South of Alexandria

The route begins at **Mount Vernon,** George Washington's primary home and estate from 1754 until his death in 1799. Washington considered himself to be a farmer, although the duties of war and a young country kept him away from his beloved home for much of this time. After his death, Mount Vernon eventually passed out of family control and fell into neglect. In 1858, some women, organized as the Mount Vernon Ladies' Association, bought the run-down buildings and grounds for $200,000, an enormous sum in those days. Through their fund-raising efforts and with the help of Washington's detailed notes and writings, the estate

Military battery remains are one feature of Fort Hunt Park, with picnic areas, flora and fauna, and other activity options.

has been restored to reflect his life as a gentleman farmer and landowner. Guided tours show the mansion, Washington's tomb, and numerous outbuildings, and give a detailed view of early colonial life, including the lives and work of the many slaves who operated and maintained the estate. If you have all day for this route, spend a few hours seeing how our first president lived or take an hour and have a picnic or walk or jog along the **Mount Vernon Trail** (or bike if you've brought your wheels).

Four miles north of Mount Vernon is **Fort Hunt Park** which, over the years, has been used as a farm (Washington's), a Spanish-American War coastal fort, a Civilian Conservation Corps camp, and the site of secret World War II military intelligence activities known as "PO Box 1142." Now, the park has six picnic areas (for 100–600 people per site) set among the trees, plants, wildlife, and the remains from the war batteries. Pull up a chair or bring your extended family for games on the fields and softball diamonds. Climb on the old batteries or just enjoy the playgrounds. Restroom facilities, water fountains, and trash cans are provided.

Heading north again, you pass **Dyke Marsh Wildlife Preserve** and the **Belle Haven Marina,** a popular spot for weekend boaters who sail the sparkling Potomac waters. You can rent a canoe or kayak at the **Mariner Sailing School** at Belle Haven and then visit the Dyke Marsh Wildlife Preserve. Or just stop at the preserve, a place that's adored by birders (and people who want to feel away from the city). Take the 0.75-mile-long **Haul Road Trail** (paved with pea gravel or boardwalk) through the estuary wetland of the 485-acre Dyke Marsh Wildlife Preserve to an elevated platform that overlooks the marsh and the Potomac

River. This is one of the largest tidal freshwater marshes within the National Park System. The brackish nature of the river (part fresh, part salt) attracts many wading birds, both freshwater flyers and shorebirds—about 300 species—including ospreys, bald eagles, great blue herons, red-winged blackbirds, wood ducks, and belted kingfishers. You can also spot beavers, muskrats, red foxes, cottontails, and shrews. And if you're a flora lover, the marsh has more than 375 species. The National Park Service schedules hikes, bird walks, bike lessons, and tours as a lighthouse keeper at Dyke Marsh and the surrounding area. The Friends of Dyke Marsh conduct a bird walk every Sun at 8 a.m., departing from the trail entrance.

Alexandria

After you pass under the Capital Beltway (here called I-95/I-495), you have about 2 miles of surface streets to navigate as you drive through Alexandria. Your first optional stop is **Jones Point Park** which is, literally, in the shadow of the 12-lane bascule Woodrow Wilson Memorial Bridge. Take a right on Green Street, go 2 blocks and turn right on South Royal Street. Drive to the cul-de-sac and turn left into the park. This 65-acre park, with an 1856 lighthouse, has playgrounds (one for children 5 and under), basketball courts, and other recreational and ranger-led educational options. Picnic tables, a canoe/kayak launch, restrooms, water fountains, and a dog drinking bowl are provided. Pets must be on a leash. Fishing from two piers for catfish, rockfish, and American eels is allowed with a license. Most people recommend you catch and release rather than eat what you bring in here.

Improvements have been made to the park that included renovation of the lighthouse, pedestrian and bike trails, playgrounds, historic interpretations, and, perhaps most important, the removal of invasive plant species and replacement with native plants.

As inviting as it may look, swimming and wading in the Potomac are prohibited.

Alexandria was founded in 1749 and became a major colonial port. Visit **Old Town Alexandria** with its restored colonial and federal homes, or tour such historic buildings as **Gadsby's Tavern, Carlyle House,** and the **boyhood home of Robert E. Lee.**

The arts are a major part of life, and you can see examples of the visual arts at the **Torpedo Factory Art Center.** Munitions were manufactured here during the two world wars, but the facility is now the home of the urban **Alexandria Archeology Museum** and studios for working artists, potters, sculptors, and other craftspeople who invite you to view their work. Shops and walks along the river have replaced the colonial trading ships, although river tours of Alexandria and the Washington skyline are available in modern vessels.

The Woodrow Wilson Memorial Bridge understructure is easily visible from Jones Point Park where you can jog, picnic, fish, and watch local neighbors tend their part of a community garden.

To continue on the parkway, stay on Washington Street. The parkway resumes as a 4-lane, divided road just north of Alexandria.

The route curves away from the river as you pass Reagan National Airport on the right. As you drive by, you will see the modernistic new control tower and the numerous "Jeffersonian domes" of the terminal that opened in 1997. The airport, inaugurated in June 1941, was known as National Airport or Washington National Airport, but renamed the Ronald Reagan National Airport by Congress in 1998.

Just past the airport, you can stop at **Gravelly Point** to watch planes take off and land. It's a great place for a picnic if you've brought lunch (no food kiosks here). There are outhouses and water. This spit of land is separated from the main airport runway by a few hundred feet of water. Jets roar by just overhead as numerous airplane watchers crane their necks skyward. Depending on the wind and runway use, you may see (and hear), close up, takeoffs or landings. Part of the 18-mile **Mount Vernon Trail** goes through the Gravelly Point area, and volunteers periodically patrol the trail. Look for one if you have a question about the area or need some minor first aid (Band-Aid category). This is about 15 miles north of Mount Vernon. You do need a helmet if you are biking the trail.

As soon you cross I-395 and pass several auto and railroad bridges, you'll see the easily recognizable **Washington, DC skyline** with the Jefferson Memorial (another Jeffersonian dome) and the columns of the Lincoln Memorial. Above all stands the Washington Monument tucked in between are the National Mall and the US Capitol. To the left, in Virginia, is the huge **Pentagon Building,** headquarters for the Department of Defense.

Arlington to the Beltway

Arlington National Cemetery is on your left; just follow the direction signs before the Memorial Bridge to visit the cemetery. President Lincoln established the cemetery in 1864 to bury the slain Civil War soldiers from a nearby Arlington tent hospital. Today representatives of those killed in all US wars are buried here.

Well-known sites inside Arlington National Cemetery include the eternal light at the **grave of President John F. Kennedy, the Tomb of the Unknowns,** and the mast of the **USS *Maine*** that sank off Havana, Cuba, in 1898 igniting the Spanish-American War. Unless you are part of a funeral or use a wheelchair, you are not allowed to drive through the cemetery. Park and walk or take the shuttle.

Nearby are the **Netherlands Carillon,** the **Women in Military Service for America Memorial,** and the **US Marine Corps War Memorial,** a bronze statue of the famous World War II photograph showing marines raising the flag at Iwo Jima.

Continuing on the route, you pass under the Theodore Roosevelt Memorial Bridge with views of the green woods of **Theodore Roosevelt Island** (formerly Mason's Island) in the Potomac. A parking lot past the bridge gives access to a footbridge to the 88.5-acre island, which contains 1.6 miles of a looped wooded trail and boardwalk and a statue of President Roosevelt. This little bit of tranquility in the middle of the river is a sharp contrast to the noise and activity on either side of it.

The Potomac narrows and the flat, open vistas are replaced by tree-covered slopes as you drive under the graceful arches of the Key Bridge, a memorial to Francis Scott Key, author of the Star-Spangled Banner. **Georgetown,** once one of the busiest ports in the nation, is across the river, with its historic houses and upscale shopping. Small rapids in the river mark the head of navigation, known as the Fall Line, and the end of the tidal Potomac.

The towers and spires you see are part of **Georgetown University.** Founded in 1789 as the first Catholic university in the country, the school is known today for its prestigious international affairs programs.

The route passes under Chain Bridge and continues through woods. For a view of the rapids in this part of the river, turn into the picnic grounds at the

Arlington National Cemetery
©DMVPHOTOS/SHUTTERSTOCK.COM

Turkey Run Park. Note that venomous copperhead snakes make their home in Turkey Run Park. Should you see any snake in the park or on the trail, do not disturb it.

When you pass the entrance to the Central Intelligence Agency, think for a moment that this part of the parkway was completed, in large part, so employees there would have an access road.

As you approach I-495, the Capital Beltway, signs announce the end of the GW Parkway. To head north to Maryland (toward Baltimore), bear right and follow the signs; to head south (toward Richmond), bear left.

To reverse direction and return to the parkway heading south, go south on the Beltway (toward Richmond) for 0.8 mile and exit at VA 193, Georgetown Pike, cross the Beltway, staying in the left lane and enter the Beltway going north (toward Maryland) until the very next exit which is the GW Parkway. Or, if you don't want to drive on the Beltway again, take VA 193 to VA 123, turning left onto Dolley Madison Boulevard and following it to the end to reenter the parkway.

If you think this is confusing, imagine a few decades ago when some brilliant minds decided the parkways on both sides of the Potomac should be called the George Washington Memorial Parkway. Fortunately, saner heads prevailed, and as of late 1989, the Maryland road was renamed Clara Barton Parkway.

The Beltway to Alexandria

As you're driving back down the GW Parkway, you can stop at the **Lady Bird Johnson Park,** just 0.5 miles before the I-95/I-395 bridges. This park is testimony to her work in beautifying the country. In the spring, it looks like a huge piñata has been ripped open with thousands of daffodils and hundreds of tulips scattered on the ground instead of pieces of candy. The turning leaves of the deciduous hardwood trees close the curtain of another fall.

Besides picnicking, photography, birding (wading birds, raptors, and warblers), and just enjoying nature, you can visit the **Navy and Marine Memorial** and the **Lyndon Baines Johnson Memorial Grove** on the Potomac. Johnson came here often, and the serpentine paths, white pines, a granite monolith (carved by sculptor Harold Vogel), and an open meadow are a tribute to his accomplishments in the fields of social justice and conservation. Landscape architect Meade Palmer designed the grove as a living memorial to our 36th president

The **Mount Vernon Trail** goes through this park and you can paddle the flat water through the **Boundary Channel** by the Pentagon, allowing you to see how the Potomac shapes the park.

4

Piedmont–Blue Ridge Vistas

Warrenton to Charlottesville

General description: Beginning at Warrenton, this 94-mile route takes you past the rolling hills of Piedmont horse country to imposing views of the Blue Ridge Mountains and Shenandoah National Park. The route then winds through the foothills of the Blue Ridge with constant views of the ridgeline through several picturesque small towns. The route ends at the outskirts of Charlottesville.

Special attractions: Rolling hills of Piedmont area, extended scenic vistas of the Blue Ridge Mountains, including Old Rag and the F. T. Valley, Montpelier, and the Barboursville Ruins.

Location: North-central Virginia. Warrenton is about 50 miles west of Washington, DC, via I-66 and US 29.

Route numbers: US 211, 522, and 29; VA 231 and 20.

Travel season: All year long, although roads may be temporarily closed during occasional heavy winter snows. Winter also brings the clearest days for exceptional views without intervening vegetation. Spring is the best time for flowering trees and shrubs. Hot, hazy summer days can obscure the views. Fall leaf colors can be outstanding, so this attracts large numbers of visitors.

Camping: Available in several campgrounds in Shenandoah National Park. These often are filled on summer weekends. Check with the park for dates and availability.

Services: Gasoline, motels, and restaurants are available in Warrenton and Charlottesville. Numerous gas stations and restaurants can be found in the small towns along the route.

Nearby attractions: Monticello, Charlottesville, Montpelier, Shenandoah National Park, Skyline Drive (Route 5), and Blue Ridge Parkway North (Route 9).

For more information: Fauquier County Chamber, (540) 347-4414, fauquierchamber.org; Charlottesville Albemarle Convention & Visitors Bureau, (434) 970-3635, visitcharlottesville.org; Nelson County Economic Development and Tourism, (434) 263-7015, nelsoncounty.com; The Inn at Little Washington, (540) 675-3800, theinnatlittlewashington.com; Rappahannock County Office of Tourism, (540) 675-5330, visitrappahannockva.com; Barboursville Vineyards, (540) 832-3824, barboursvillewine.com.

The Route

On this 94-mile route you cross rolling Piedmont country with distant views of the Blue Ridge Mountains. The countryside alternates between hardwood forest and open fields of cattle and hay. Gradually you approach the mountains and then drive along the base of the Blue Ridge for 30 miles on a state scenic road with many spectacular views. Optional side trips allow you to visit a town surveyed by George Washington, a mansion and plantation that belonged to James Madison, and the remains of a mansion designed by Thomas Jefferson.

Piedmont—Blue Ridge Vistas

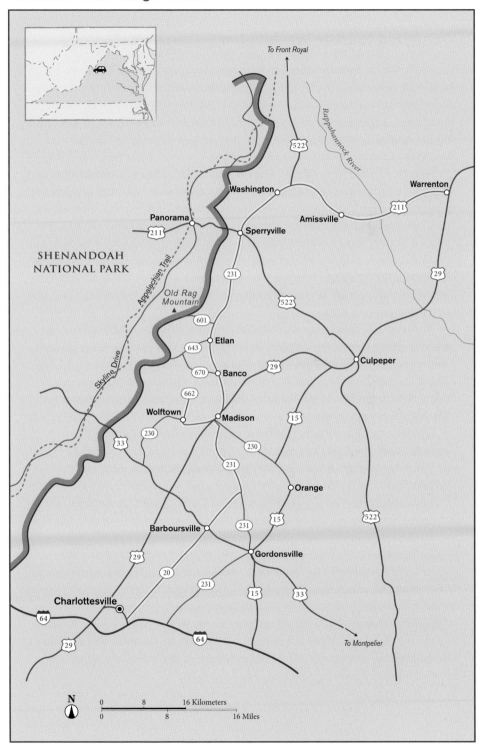

Warrenton to Little Washington

The route begins in **Warrenton,** county seat of Fauquier County. The town started out as a trading post in the 1700s, and until late in that century it was considered to be the western frontier of English civilization in the Virginia colony. Several old buildings are open to the public, including the **Old Court House** and **Old Jail Museum,** which once sported a three-person gallows. During the Civil War, Warrenton was headquarters for the Gray Ghosts, a vigilante group led by Confederate Colonel John Mosby. The colonel, whose group was also known as Mosby's Raiders, is buried in a nearby cemetery along with 600 other Confederate soldiers.

The route heads west on 4-lane US 211 through the open, gentle hills of the Fauquier County horse country. Virginia likes to name its highways after favorite sons and calls US 211 the Lee Highway. On non-hazy days the Blue Ridge Mountains appear on the distant horizon. You pass numerous large mansions and well-kept fields, with grazing horses and cattle. You may even see several practice rings with jumps and bars.

The road descends to cross the **Rappahannock River,** a designated state scenic river. About 10 miles from Warrenton on the left, just past the small town of Amissville, are the **Gray Ghost Vineyard** grapevines, the first of several wineries along this drive. Most wineries, including the Gray Ghost, welcome visitors and provide tasting rooms and guided tours. Highway signs direct you to numerous offerings off the main route.

Several long hills provide panoramic mountain views, which present an unbroken, undulating line of peaks stretching left and right as far as you can see. The mountains get the name "Blue Ridge" from their typical hazy blue appearance.

Continue straight on US 211 where it joins US 522 South. To the right, US 522 goes to Front Royal, the northern entrance of Shenandoah National Park and the starting point for Skyline Drive (Route 5).

The road, now US 211/522, makes a series of lazy S-turns that bring you closer to and parallel with the mountains. In a few minutes you pass US Business 211 on the right, which leads to the town of Washington, county seat of Rappahannock County. There are more than 25 towns named "Washington" in the US (plus Washington state and the federal city, of course) and Washington, Virginia, lays claim to it being the first Washington of all. It is sometimes known as **"Little Washington"** to distinguish it from the somewhat larger federal seat of government 70 miles to the east.

Virginia Piedmont countryside

An early morning swim under a weeping willow tree before the mist burned off.

The town was laid out and surveyed by George Washington in 1747 when the future president was 17 years old. This project brought Washington's first paid remuneration; he received 2 pounds, 3 shillings. The town is also the home of the country's only five-star restaurant, the **Inn at Little Washington,** renowned for chef Patrick O'Connell's signature dishes. (Reservations are required.) Also in town are several small craft shops and an art gallery. You can follow Business 211 through the town and back out to the main highway without retracing your route.

Little Washington to Sperryville

Back on US 211/522, turn right. The mountains and **Shenandoah National Park** are on your right, with rounded peaks 2,000 to 3,000 feet above you. In places, the wooded foothills of mixed hardwood extend down almost to the highway; in other places, broad valleys, known locally as hollows, provide open vistas to the distant peaks.

At **Sperryville,** just after the 4-lane highway ends, turn left and follow US 522 where it branches off from US 211. US 211 continues straight ahead before it climbs up the mountain to intersect with Route 5, Skyline Drive, at Panorama.

Cross the river and turn left again in the middle of **Sperryville** on US 522. The quaint look of the town is enhanced by many buildings preserved to look much as they did in the 1920s. It is also a craft and art center with numerous shops.

Sperryville to Madison

Follow US 522 about a mile to the intersection with VA 231. Turn right on VA 231, a Virginia Scenic Byway. For several miles this winding road follows the **F. T. Valley,** snuggled between the **Blue Ridge Mountains** on the right and the hills of the Piedmont on the left. The valley gets its name from Francis Thornton, an early landowner, who notched his initials on trees to mark the way; travelers learned to follow the F. T. Trail.

The mountains are beautiful year-round, with each season having special merits. In summer, verdant slopes stretch from the foothills to the highest summits. As the shortening days of autumn approach, the countryside is bathed in a thousand shades of orange, yellow, brown, and red as the leaves turn. Winter days are often the clearest. The lower hills look gray and black, contrasting with the higher peaks that are often coated with snow. Occasional snowstorms at lower elevations turn the landscape into a stark contrast of black and white. As the weather turns warmer, the hillsides turn yellow and then green as spring creeps up the mountainsides day by day.

About 3 miles from Sperryville is a good view of **Old Rag Mountain,** a popular destination for hikers in **Shenandoah National Park.** "Old Rag" is short for Old Raggedy, so named because of several prominent, steplike ledges that give the mountain its distinctive, serrated appearance. The mountain is composed of some of the oldest rocks in the chain, from about 570 million years ago, when tectonic plates were shifting and molten rock—not from a nearby volcanic eruption—rose through rifts in the ground and spread over thousands of square miles in Virginia, Maryland, and southern Pennsylvania. It's referred to as the Catoctin Formation. These seeping, spreading, and cooling phases create the stair pattern you'll see in some mountain formations. The original basalt contains chlorite and epidote that are not usually found in basalt which have changed under the heat and pressure of the centuries and turned the rock shades of grey and dark green. Hence, it's called greenstone.

Several side roads off VA 231 lead to hiking trails in the park. However, stay on VA 231 for the main route. Eight miles from Sperryville, VA 601 turns right to lead to the **Old Rag trailhead.** This trail has become so popular that the National Park Service now limits the number of hikers on busy summer weekends. At Etlan, 10 miles from Sperryville, a right turn on VA 643 takes you to the **White Oak Canyon Trail,** known for its steep canyons and numerous waterfalls.

View of Old Rag

Continue on VA 231, crossing the Robinson River and after passing through the town of Madison, county seat of Madison County, VA 231 turns right to join 4-lane US 29. Service stations and restaurants are available along this stretch.

Madison to Barboursville

VA 231 turns left in 3 miles, leaving US 29. Turn left here for a ride away from the mountains into wooded and rolling Piedmont country. There are numerous herds of beef and dairy cattle. About 10 miles from US 29, turn right onto VA 20.

To see James Madison's **Montpelier,** turn left onto VA 20 toward Orange and follow the signs. Montpelier, a 2,700-acre plantation and mansion, was the retirement home of James and Dolley Madison after he completed his second presidential term in 1817 until his death in 1836. The mansion was renovated extensively by later occupants, and has now been restored to its state during Madison's occupancy. There are extensive gardens and plantings.

VA 20 continues to the right through woods and open country. The Blue Ridge is visible occasionally in the distance to the right. A low, tree-covered ridge parallels the road for several miles. Continue on VA 20 and cross US 33, about 15 miles from US 29.

Just past the intersection with US 33, turn left off VA 20 and follow the signs for a side trip to the **Barboursville Ruins** and the **Barboursville Vineyards.** Here are the remains of a mansion Thomas Jefferson designed for James Barbour, governor of Virginia from 1812 to 1814. The building burned in 1884, leaving only the massive brick foundation and walls for today's visitors. The ruins are on the grounds of the Barboursville Vineyards, which is open daily for tastings, tours, and picnics (bring your own).

Barboursville to Charlottesville

Return to VA 20 and turn left. The route continues through rolling country with several sharp turns past fields of grazing sheep, cattle, and horses. The route ends where VA 20 crosses US 250 south of Charlottesville, about 14 miles from Barboursville. Turn right on US 250 to go downtown.

Charlottesville has many attractions, including the beautiful grounds of the **University of Virginia** and **Ash Lawn-Highland,** James Monroe's Virginia home. Nearby is **Monticello,** Thomas Jefferson's magnificent mansion and gardens, and within a few miles are wineries, cideries, and a distillery. The starting point for the Blue Ridge Parkway North (Route 9) is about 20 miles west of Charlottesville on I-64. The starting point for the Jefferson Heritage Trail (Route 75) is at Monticello, outside of Charlottesville.

5

Skyline Drive

Shenandoah National Park

General description: Skyline Drive in Shenandoah National Park winds for 105 miles along the crests of the Blue Ridge Mountains. On one side of this crest—to the west—is the Shenandoah Valley; to the east is the rolling Piedmont area. Numerous scenic turnouts provide views in all directions. The route can be made in 1 day, or you can take a more leisurely trip, recommended to let you stop and enjoy more of the features.

Special attractions: Spectacular vistas of mountains, valleys, ridges, and thick hardwood and pine forests. Wildlife (deer, black bear, wild turkey, coyote, etc.), birds (about 200 species, mostly living in the canopy so they're heard rather than seen), wildflowers (trillium, azaleas, cardinal flower, black-eyed Susans, and goldenrod), century-old trees, exhibits, visitor centers, waterfalls, hikes, and trails all add to your understanding and enjoyment. You can see many of the blossoms along the roadside. Sixty-six scenic overlooks let you peek into the park, dedicated in 1936. You are allowed to bring your pet, on a leash no longer than 6 feet, on most trails. However, they are not allowed on ranger programs. To protect the park forests from invasive pests, do not bring firewood into the park.

Location: Northwestern Virginia outside of Front Royal, about 75 miles west of Washington, DC, via I-66.

Route numbers: Skyline Drive. There is no route number since the road is completely within the boundaries of Shenandoah National Park. Skyline Drive is accessible via four entrance stations: Front Royal (via I-66 and US 340), Thornton Gap (US 211), Swift Run Gap (US 33), and Rockfish Gap (I-64 and US 250).

Travel season: All year. Summer weekends can be crowded; the heaviest visitation is in mid-Oct during peak leaf season. Inclement weather can temporarily close Skyline Drive, which is also closed at night during deer-hunting season (mid-Nov through early Jan). You may still enter the park on foot when the road has been closed. Although RVs, camping trailers, and horse trailers are allowed, you should be ready to shift into low gear. Also, the vertical clearance for Marys Rock Tunnel (south of Thornton Gap entrance at US 211) is only 12'8".

Camping: Campgrounds at Mathews Arm, Big Meadows, Lewis Mountain, and Loft Mountain provide a total of about 650 campsites. Advance reservations are accepted for Mathews Arm, Big Meadows and Loft. Campgrounds are usually open Apr through Oct, and are often full on summer and fall weekends. Other overnight stops along the drive are Skyland Resort (mile 41.7), Lewis Mountain Cabins (mile 57.5), campgrounds, and picnic grounds. The Potomac Appalachian Trail Club (PATC) has some cabins which are in remote areas and require a hike. Except for some of the picnic grounds that are open all year, the other Shenandoah facilities close for the winter, some as early as late Oct and others in Nov and Dec. Opening dates range from late Mar through mid-Apr.

Services: Gasoline, lodgings, motels, and restaurants are available in Front Royal, Waynesboro, Harrisonburg, and Charlottesville. From mid-spring to late fall, overnight accommodations in the park are at Skyland Resort, Big Meadows Lodge, and the Lewis Mountain cabins. Within the park, gasoline is available at Big Meadows only (mile 52), in the center of the park.

Nearby attractions: Museums, historic sites, vineyards, and farms in the Shenandoah Valley, Winchester, Front Royal, Luray,

Skyline Drive

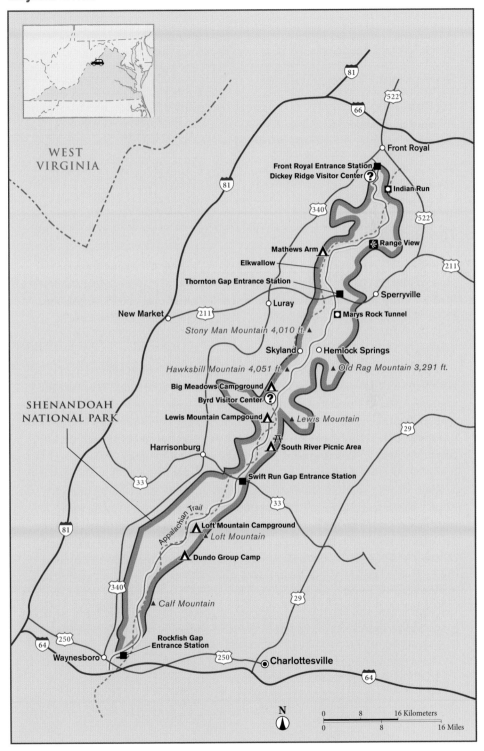

WEST
VIRGINIA

81

522

66

81

340

⛝ Front Royal

Front Royal Entrance Station ■
Dickey Ridge Visitor Center ?

□ Indian Run

522

Mathews Arm ▲
Elkwallow

Thornton Gap Entrance Station ■   ⛝ Sperryville

522

211

211

⛝ Luray

New Market ⛝   211

□ Marys Rock Tunnel

Stony Man Mountain 4,010 ft. ▲

Skyland ⛝   ⛝ Hemlock Springs

Hawksbill Mountain 4,051 ft. ▲   ▲ *Old Rag Mountain 3,291 ft.*

Big Meadows Campground ▲
Byrd Visitor Center ?

Lewis Mountain Campgound ▲   ▲ *Lewis Mountain*

29

SHENANDOAH
NATIONAL PARK

Harrisonburg ⛝   🌲 South River Picnic Area

Swift Run Gap Entrance Station ■

33

33

81

Appalachian Trail

340

Loft Mountain Campground ▲
Loft Mountain

Dundo Group Camp ▲

29

▲ *Calf Mountain*

250

64

Rockfish Gap
Entrance Station ■

Waynesboro ⛝

250   ⊙ **Charlottesville**

64

N
▲

| 0 | 8 | 16 Kilometers |
| 0 | 8 | 16 Miles |

Harrisonburg, Waynesboro, Staunton, Skyline Caverns, Luray Caverns, the Shenandoah Valley, Virginia Quilt Museum, Charlottesville, and the Blue Ridge Parkway which extends south from Skyline Drive (see Routes 9 and 10).

For more information: Shenandoah National Park, (540) 999-3500 (particularly for current weather and roadway conditions), nps.gov/shen or visitskylinedrive .org; Shenandoah Valley Travel Association, (540) 740-3132, visitshenandoah.org; Front Royal Department of Tourism, (540) 635-5788, frontroyalva.com; City of Waynesboro, (540) 942-6644, visitwaynesboro.net; Charlottesville Albemarle Convention & Visitors Bureau, (434) 970-3635, visitcharlottesville .org; Blue Ridge Parkway, (828) 670-1924, blueridgeparkway.org Virginia Quilt Museum, (540) 433-3818, vaquiltmuseum .org; Shenandoah National Park concessions, (877) 847-1919, goshenandoah.com.

The Route

Skyline Drive and Shenandoah National Park in northwest Virginia are nearly synonymous. Shenandoah National Park is a long and narrow park that straddles the Blue Ridge Mountains, the easternmost and highest range of the Appalachian Mountains. It includes steep mountains, quiet valleys, streams and waterfalls, and green forests. The 197,000-acre park includes 79,000 acres of designated wilderness.

Skyline Drive is a 105-mile-long, mountaintop road within Shenandoah National Park that winds along the rolling peaks of the Blue Ridge. It provides sweeping vistas of the surrounding mountains and valleys and is the only public road through the park. There are four entrances (and exits), at Front Royal (where this route starts), Thornton Gap at US 211, Swift Run Gap at US 33, and Rockfish Gap at I-64 and US 250 (the northern entrance to the Blue Ridge Parkway and Route 9). Milepost markers are placed on the west side of the road (your right as you're driving south) to help you find your way. They start with 0.0 at Front Royal. Shenandoah National Park was authorized by Congress in 1926, with many of the park's facilities constructed by Civilian Conservation Corps workers. The final section of Skyline Drive was opened in 1939. Previously inhabited and clear-cut in some places, the area slowly reverted to its natural state so that now, nearly 75 years later, 100 species of trees cover about 95 percent of the park. The updrafts and thermals created by the ridges turn the area into an aerial highway as well each spring and fall; it is one of the major flyways for migrating birds. Some spotters have seen flocks of thousands of broad-winged hawks during the fall migration.

The winding Skyline Drive caressing the mountain folds
PHOTO COURTESY OF NATIONAL PARK SERVICE

A portion of the Appalachian Trail (AT) runs for 101 miles along almost the full length of the park. This famous footpath stretches about 2,200 miles from Maine to Georgia. The section in the park parallels and crosses Skyline Drive numerous times. It varies in difficulty from easy to strenuous. More than 500 miles of trails of all types spiderweb the park, the most popular ones leading to mountaintops or waterfalls. Many radiating from Skyline Drive are mentioned below. For a more thorough guide to 59 of the most interesting hikes, see *Hiking Shenandoah National Park 4th* by Bert and Jane Gildart (Falcon Publishing, 2012).

Remember that this is a national park; all plant and animal life is protected. That means it's illegal to feed the wildlife. Do not offer food to deer or other animals. Collecting of any sort is prohibited. The maximum speed limit is 35 miles per hour, but the rate is often slower as drivers take time to appreciate the scenery. This is an attitude-adjustment time, and yes, this is what meandering means. An entrance fee is charged. As of this writing, it's $15 per private (noncommercial) vehicle for 7 consecutive days March through November. That drops to $10 the rest of the year. Motorcycles are $10 each. Other fees apply for individuals in other conveyances and on commercial tours. Or, you can buy an annual pass for $30 that provides unlimited access to Skyline Drive and the park for a year from the month of purchase.

Front Royal to Panorama

The route begins at the north end of **Front Royal** about 75 miles from Washington DC, via I-66. The town gets its name because its large oak trees—known as royal oaks—were cut for masts for sailing ships. A mile north of the park entrance is **Skyline Caverns,** known for its delicate, needlelike anthodite crystals.

At the entrance station pay your fee and pick up a park brochure. The road heads uphill through a thick forest. Road cuts reveal numerous outcrops of Catoctin basalt or greenstone, an extensive series of lava flows that covered the region in late Precambrian time. The geology of the park is complex. The road curves steadily uphill to the first scenic overlook at mile marker 2.8, a view of the **Shenandoah Valley.** The prominent ridge is the northern end of **Massanutten Mountain,** which bisects the Shenandoah Valley and extends south for about 40 miles. **Signal Knob,** the prominent high point, was occupied by both sides during the Civil War (at different times) as a lookout post. Route 1 follows the ridgeline of Massanutten Mountain. The South Fork of the Shenandoah River lies between the park and Massanutten Mountain; the North Fork of the Shenandoah River flows on the far side of the mountain. The two forks meet just north of Front Royal.

At the **Dickey Ridge** information center, mile marker 4.5, are exhibits and more views of the Shenandoah Valley. Detailed hiking and other maps are available.

A deer in the grass along Skyline Drive
PHOTO COURTESY OF NATIONAL PARK SERVICE

The building originally served as a tavern in the 1930s. A popular hang-gliding launch area is nearby. The center's operating hours is subject to budget. It should be open weekdays in the winter and daily starting in early May for the season.

The first view to the east at **Indian Run,** mile marker 10.1, reveals the low mountains of the Piedmont area. Like ripples spreading in a pond, the hills decrease in elevation away from the park, and eventually die out to a gently rolling plain.

The Appalachian Mountains and the Blue Ridge formed about 320 million years ago when the great continental plates of what are now Africa and Europe slowly crashed into ancestral North America. This continental collision first started to fold the existing rocks and then the forces over time were so powerful that the rocks to the east—today's Blue Ridge—broke, or faulted, in what is known as a thrust fault, and slid over the younger rocks to the west—today's Shenandoah Valley. The rocks of the Shenandoah Valley were also thrust faulted over still younger rocks west of them. These huge thrust faults extend for more than 100 miles along the Blue Ridge.

The **Range View** overlook at mile marker 17.1 is aptly named. In one direction lies the irregular, craggy crest of the Blue Ridge; in the other, across the Shenandoah Valley, are the parallel ridge lines of the Valley and Ridge province.

At **Panorama,** mile marker 31.3, you'll find the **Thornton Gap Entrance Station** where the drive crosses US 211, which goes west to Luray, New Market, and I-81; to the east it hits Sperryville, Culpeper, and Warrenton.

Routes 1 and 4 are nearby: Route 1 to the west traverses the Shenandoah Valley; Route 4 to the east has excellent views of the Blue Ridge from the Piedmont. From Panorama, you can follow the **Appalachian Trail** uphill to the cliffs at **Marys Rock** for excellent views of **Thornton Gap.**

Panorama to Big Meadows

Just beyond Panorama, Skyline Drive passes through 600-foot-long **Marys Rock Tunnel,** the only tunnel on the drive, which was cut through billion-year-old metamorphic rocks.

Stony Man Mountain, with its steplike profile, looms straight ahead at the overlook at mile marker 38.6. The peak is 4,010 feet high, the second highest in the park. To the right in the Shenandoah Valley lies the town of Luray. The gap on the horizon is New Market Pass in Massanutten Mountain.

A half-mile beyond this is the trailhead for the **Little Stony Man Cliffs,** which follows along the base of one of the lava flows. Longer, circular hikes can also start here.

The turnoff for **Skyland** at mile marker 41.7 is the highest point on the drive, at 3,680 feet. Just inside the turnoff is the trailhead for the **Stony Man Nature Trail.** This 1.5-mile, round-trip hike probably gives you the best view for the effort of any hike in the park. A brochure guides you along 20 interpretive signs, culminating at the rocky summit of Stony Man Mountain, which you saw earlier from the road. Nearby are several nesting sites for the endangered peregrine falcon—known for its high-speed dives—which the National Park Service has been successfully reintroducing.

Skyland Resort itself, with its lodge, dining room, gift shop, stables, and riding horses, is a popular destination for some travelers. Rangers conduct guided walks and evening programs. The resort was established in the 1890s by naturalist George Pollock, whose continuing efforts helped to establish the park.

Back on Skyline Drive, at mile marker 42.4, is the trailhead for **White Oak Canyon,** known for its waterfalls. The first waterfall requires a 4.6-mile down-and-up hike; to visit all six is even more strenuous.

The least strenuous hike in the park is just past White Oak Canyon: the wheelchair-accessible **Limberlost Trail.** The trail passes through groves of red spruce and hemlocks, some of the largest and oldest trees in the park.

The best view of **Hawksbill Mountain,** at 4,051 feet the highest in the park, is from the **Crescent Rock Overlook** at mile marker 44.4. Trailheads at miles 45.5

The dining room, taproom, and gift shop at the Skyland Resort
PHOTO COURTESY OF NATIONAL PARK SERVICE

and 46.5 lead to the summit and an unsurpassed 360-degree view of mountains in all directions.

The waterfall closest to Skyline Drive is the 70-foot cascades of **Dark Hollow Falls.** It is about a 1.5-mile round-trip from the trailhead at mile marker 50.4.

Just beyond the Dark Hollow trailhead is **Big Meadows,** the largest treeless area in the park. In the 1920s some of the future park had been cut for timber and looked like this. This flat plain is known for its wildflowers, strawberries, and blueberries, which attract grouse, mice, rabbits, deer, and other birds and animals. More than 430 rare plant populations—including 66 rare plant species—have been identified within the park, with the largest number of them in the Big Meadows area.

Turn into the Big Meadows facilities at either mile marker 51.0 or 51.2. The **Byrd Visitor Center,** named for former Virginia Senator Harry F. Byrd, contains numerous exhibits and information on activities, including guided nature hikes along several nearby trails. The Byrd Visitor Center was closed as of December 1 through early April (weekends only) and then early May for the season during 2012–13. Operational hours will be determined by budget availability.

A trail of historical interest takes you to **Rapidan Camp** where President Herbert Hoover came to relax and to escape the pressures of Washington. Several original structures can be seen at the site, including the president's cabin. Other facilities at Big Meadows are a restaurant and store, gas station, the Big Meadows Lodge (MP 51), and a campground.

Children may enjoy the self-guided **Story of the Forest Nature Trail** accessible by paved path from the Byrd Visitor Center or at mile marker 51.10. This 2-mile round-trip walk has 22 interpretive signs describing forest sights and ecology.

Big Meadows to Rockfish Gap

The **Bearfence Mountain Trail** at mile 56.4 is a strenuous, 0.8-mile round-trip scramble, much of it over jumbled rocks to an excellent 360-degree view.

A picnic area and another campground are at **Lewis Mountain** at mile marker 57.2. A few cabins are available for overnight stays.

The South River picnic area, mile marker 62.5, marks the trailhead to **South River Falls.** This is a strenuous, 2.6-mile, round-trip hike to an 83-foot-high waterfall.

The drive crosses US 33 and the **Swift Run Gap Entrance Station** at mile marker 65.5. To the west, US 33 goes to the West Virginia border; to the east it goes to Stanardsville and US 29.

The developed area at **Loft Mountain** at mile marker 79.5 features a campground, restaurant, and gift shop. The **Loft Mountain Trail** is a moderate, 2.7-mile loop with views of **Flat Top Mountain** and, to the east, the Piedmont.

The valley at **Big Run,** to the left of the overlook at mile marker 81.8, is almost entirely enclosed by mountains. Heavy rains from the large watershed occasionally fill the narrow outlet with resultant floods. At mile marker 83.4 is the entrance to the **Dundo picnic grounds**, a former Civilian Conservation Corps (CCC) center. It's ideal for group picnicking if you're making this route a "y'all come" event.

Calf Mountain at mile marker 98.5 provides an expansive view. You can see the full width of the Shenandoah Valley, undivided here by Massanutten Mountain. The drive and park narrow beyond here to little more than a road bordered by a fence.

The road descends to the entrance station and then to **Rockfish Gap** to end at mile marker 105.5 and I-64 and US 250. Go east (left) to go to Charlottesville, or go west (right) to Waynesboro and I-81. The Blue Ridge Parkway (Routes 9 and 10) begins just across I-64; the Humpback Visitor Center is 5 miles south.

6

Highland County Barn Quilt Trail

Looking for Gorgeous Graffiti

General description: This 52-mile route explores Highland County, frequently called "Virginia's Switzerland" (or "Virginia's Little Switzerland") because of the mountains. The route adds a scavenger hunt quality to the natural beauty of the mountains and valleys. You'll be looking for barn quilts. For you quilters, this is not the barn quilt pattern. Rather, it's a collection or exhibition of quilt patterns that are painted on wood and mounted, usually, on the side of a barn. Sometimes, however, you'll find them on homes and other outbuildings.

Special attractions: Mountains, valleys, woodlands, sugar maple camps, Civil War historic spots, barn quilts.

Location: Shenandoah Valley, western highlands.

Route numbers: US 250 and 220; VA 654, 622, 624, 640 600, and 678

Travel season: All year long, although winter weather conditions might suggest another time of the year.

Camping: Not available.

Services: Gas and restaurants are available at McDowell, Blue Grass, Monterey, and other little stops along the road. The historic Highland Inn is in Monterey. Several bed-and-breakfast and farm stay options are available throughout the county.

Nearby attractions: Highland County Museum, Maple Sugar Camp exhibit.

For more information: Highland County Visitor's Center, (540) 468-2550, highland county.org; Highland County Museum, (540) 396-4478, highlandcountyhistory .com; Sugar Maple Camp, (540) 458-2550, highlandcounty.org/sugartours; Shenandoah Valley Battlefields Foundation, shenandoah atwar.org; McDowell Battlefield, civilwar.org/ battlefields; Ginseng Mountain Farm, Store & Lodging, (540) 474-3663 or (540) 474-5137, ginsengmountain.com; The Highland Inn, (540) 468-2143, highland-inn.com.

The Route

The Highlands is an area with one of the highest mean elevations of any county east of the Mississippi River, hence the name. Germans settled the northern part of the county and the Scots/Irish settled the southern part. Designated Highland County in 1847, the county was formed by taking land from Bath County, Virginia, and Pendleton County, West Virginia (still part of the state of Virginia at the time). The south branch of the Potomac River and the James River start in these Allegheny Mountains. The mountains framing your route are Jack (4,373-foot elevation), Bearcamp Knob (4,170 feet), and Bullpasture (3,240 feet), and the change in altitude spans more than 2,000 feet with the Bullpasture River dropping

Highland Barn Quilt Trail

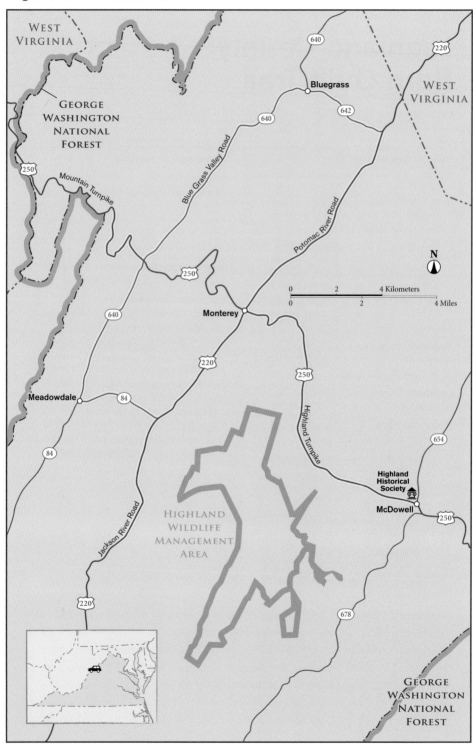

Autumn among the high mountains and valleys of Highland County
PHOTO COURTESY OF SHARON HEAVENER

to 1,800 feet from the top of Sounding Knob on Jack Mountain. The landscape is filled with sheep (which tend to outnumber humans, particularly in the Blue Grass Valley) and cattle grazing the days away and farm acreage with a variety of crops. Wool remains an important agricultural resource. Mature oak and hickory hardwoods and red spruce are home to scarlet tanagers; rose-breasted grosbeaks; and Kentucky, hooded, black-throated blue, and black-throated green warblers. Birders can also see pileated woodpeckers, ruffed grouse, red-shouldered hawks, and wild turkeys. Migratory birds pass this way in the spring and fall. Black bears and red and gray foxes live in the woods but tend to hide very well.

You'll start this 52-mile route in McDowell, about 30 miles west of Staunton. The area, whose population was divided about secession, was drawn into the Civil War as a personal matter on May 8, 1862. A battle raged around McDowell with the Confederates under the direction of General Thomas J. "Stonewall" Jackson fighting the Union forces as part of his Shenandoah Valley Campaign. Because there has been so little settlement in this area, the site is considered one of the most pristine of all Civil War battlefields.

Several years ago, Margie Boesch, a flight attendant and active quilter, and her husband Mike, a teacher turned farmer, retired to Highland County where

Clay's Choice, named for the owner, is what this barn quilt on Mountain Turnpike goes by.
PHOTO COURTESY OF MIRRORSLAP PHOTOGRAPHY

she started exploring the growing art form of barn quilts. She painted three for their farm (Sunset Star, Maple Leaf, and Turkey Tracks) and realized she preferred brushing on colors to piecing them. He does the heavy-duty work of moving the signboard around, delivering and cutting wood to keep her studio warm, and installing the quilts when necessary. She showed some photos of her painted quilts and Jacob Hevener's nieces ordered one for him—Jacob's Ladder—as a Christmas gift. The quilt's name is in reference to the Old Testament story of Jacob's dream of angels ascending and descending on a ladder to heaven.

The idea of a barn quilt trail caught on and has been growing ever since. A half-dozen are 8 by 8 feet while the others are in the 4-by-4-foot neighborhood. A brochure is available that shows 27 barn quilts and gives some directions. Several others quilts have been mounted although they aren't in the brochure, so you can enjoy a scavenger hunt within the drive.

Almost all have a personal significance to the owner. Birds in the Air, Clay's Choice, Jacob's Ladder, and Robert's Choice include the owner's name. One quilt, not in the current brochure, is Pomegranate Basket (on US 220), named for the owner's mother whose name means "seller of pomegranates" in Italian. Sunset

Star, Virginia Reel, and Puss in the Corner are named for quilts the owners have pieced and quilted themselves. Additionally, Puss in the Corner is owned by a woman named Kitty. Flying Geese is named for the Flying Geese Studio, while Mare's Nest is appropriate for the horse farm riding ring. Maple Leaf is on Margie's Highland Barn Quilts Studio which was once a sugar house.

Between McDowell & Monterey

While you're on US 250 (Staunton-Parkersburg Turnpike, which links the upper Shenandoah Valley to the Ohio River), cross the Crab Run Bridge and turn right on VA 654 (Doe Hill Road) by Stonewall Grocery. Turn left onto Mansion House Road. The Sugar Tree Country Store will be on your right and then the **Highland County Museum.** For wheelchair access, pull into the driveway behind the museum. As with many fine old buildings along the Shenandoah, this Greek Revival–style home was built for a wealthy family and then served as a hospital during the Civil War and then a hotel, serving as an important stagecoach stop along the turnpike. This was the first large brick home in McDowell and faced the turnpike. The bricks were made on the property, and because it was so large, it was called "the Mansion." The Highland Historical Society became owners of the Mansion in 2001.

The museum's permanent exhibits show the county's history from the first pioneering families settling in the area (descendants still live around here) to the effect of the Civil War with displays and a 20-minute film covering Jackson's battle. Two changing exhibit rooms have previously explored clothing, quilts, toys, country stores, feedsacks, and the Maple Queen contest. The museum is open Thurs through Sun, Mar 1 through Nov 1, and at other times by appointment. Admission is free although donations are accepted.

In the center of **McDowell** is the **Sugar Tree Country Store & Sugar House** where they use modern equipment to produce maple syrup and have antique sugaring tools on display. Look for jams and other country store items.

Another favorite stop in McDowell is **Mountain Oasis,** where they bake their own bread.

During the **March Maple Festival**—the second and third weekends of March—there are tours and opportunities to buy a variety of home-cooked goodies. Other sugar maple producers in the county are **Laurel Fork Sap Suckers** on Clay Hise Lane, 10 miles west of Monterey; **Puffenbarger's Sugar Orchard,** on VA 637 (Maple Sugar Road), is southwest of Blue Grass; **Rexrode's Sugar Orchard** is 7 miles west of Monterey, over Monterey Mountain, on US 250; **Southernmost Maple Products** is 15 miles south of Monterey on VA 607 (Big Valley Road) at Bolar, where you can find a country store with plenty of maple

Virginia Reel, also on Mountain Turnpike, was chosen because the owner had made a fabric quilt in the Virginia Reel pattern.

PHOTO COURTESY OF MIRRORSLAP PHOTOGRAPHY

goodies and other products; and **Duff's Sugar House,** 3 miles southwest of Monterey on US 220 South and then 3 miles west on VA 84, is a sugar house that uses old-fashioned equipment, and during the festival, which draws about 50,000 people, you're encouraged to participate in the sugaring.

Three barn quilts are located in the immediate McDowell area. The first is Mosaic Star, at 9023 Highland Turnpike (north side of VA 250, 0.2 miles east of VA 654). The quilt was drafted by Lucille Maloy and painted by Lyle and Georgianne Hull.

On Bullpasture River Road (west side of VA 678, 2.2 miles south of VA 250) is a barn with a variety of quilt patterns including Triple Sunflower, Four Leaf Clover, Star of the East, Blue Birds Flying, and Bear's Paw. Take time to enjoy the land that appears to be quilted, too, with crops growing along the irregular path of streams and forest climbing the higher terrains.

The Country Farm quilt is at 658 River Bend Ln. off Bullpasture Road (east side of VA 678), 2.7 miles south of US 250.

Now, head west on US 250 until you reach **Monterey,** the county seat, where you will turn north on Route 220 at the blinking light on Main Street. Almost 6 miles from the light is Robert's Choice, at 699 Potomac River Rd. The blue, green, and yellow Sister's Choice is nearby at 1115 Potomac River Rd., dedicated to sisters who are best friends.

Continue north on US 220 to **Forks of Water.** Daisy is at 154 Forks of Water Rd. (south side of VA 625). Turn left or west on Blue Grass Valley Road (VA 642) to see Cactus Star on the north face of **Rexrode's Country Store.** Mare's Nest is at 807 Blue Grass Valley Rd. (south side of VA 642), 1.7 miles from the intersection with VA 640. It's on **Peppermin Farm**'s riding ring building.

As you're approaching the town of **Blue Grass,** you'll see Moon & Star Over Mountains on your right at 2479 Blue Grass Valley Rd. just east of the intersection with VA 640.

Turn left on Blue Grass Valley Road (VA 640) and take it until you intersect again with US 250 (you've made a large U-turn). Turn right for four more quilts. Jacob's Ladder is at 5573 Mountain Turnpike (north side of US 250), 0.1 mile west of the intersection where you just turned. That's the one that was made for Jacob Hevener on a barn at **Dividing Waters Farm.** This was settled by the Hevener family in 1790 and Jacob was the last of seven generations to work the 875-acre property. A familiar figure at the Hightown General Store, he would tell tales of Highland, including the reason the farm has its name—at Hightown, the river waters flow north into the Potomac River and south into the Jackson River. Jacob died in 2011, and the farm is for sale as of this writing.

Drive a scant 0.2 mile to see Clay's Choice, at 5948 Mountain Turnpike. The third, Virginia Reel, is just 0.1 of a mile west at 6054 Mountain Turnpike. A fourth along this stretch is just 0.5 of a mile more.

Now, make a U-turn when you can to return to VA 640 and turn right (south) toward **Meadowdale.** Sunset Star is on the east side of Meadowdale Road (VA 640). The next one you'll come to Maple Leaf, which is on the west side of the road. Turkey Tracks follows, this time on the east side of Meadowdale Road. Turn left (east) on VA 84 and take it until you join up again with US 220 at **Vanderpool.** The last barn on this trail is Log Cabin at 2554 Jackson River Rd. (west side of US 220), 2.5 miles south of Monterey.

There are about a dozen other barn quilts that you can visit if you pick up (or download) the brochure from the museum or on the website.

Pleasant scenery is abundant, particularly views of the **Blue Grass Valley,** whether or not you're looking for quilts. Once back in Monterey, stop by the historic **Highland Inn,** built in 1904 under the name Hotel Monterey. Listed on the National Register of Historic Places and a Virginia Historic Landmark, this 3-story Queen Anne building has 18 guest rooms and suites and is ADA compliant.

If the thought of all that maple syrup has whet your appetite, stop by **High's Restaurant** where, during the Maple Festival, they serve pancakes all day with

Flying Geese barn quilt
PHOTO COURTESY OF MIRRORSLAP PHOTOGRAPHY

Highland-made maple syrup. They also offer fried chicken, pulled-pork barbecue, local trout, and house-made pies and cakes. They're open 7 days a week. You can also eat at the **Mountain Hideaway** and the **Highland Inn,** where you're pretty sure to find local trout.

Should you be interested in touring the area for another reason or via another mode of transportation, Highland County also offers information about a collection of Highland artists and artisans; trails for hiking, cycling, and horseback riding, and a wildflower trail.

7

Jefferson Heritage Trail

From Monticello to Lynchburg

General description: This 90-mile route starts in the foothills of the Blue Ridge Mountains outside of Charlottesville, just south of I-64, and follows US 29 for the most part. Add a couple of miles for the round-trip if you stop at the Snowflex Centre in Lynchburg. South of Charlottesville, you may see Carters Mountain (1,600 feet) and Horseshoe Mountain (2,533 feet). The route connects Jefferson's home at Monticello and his rural retreat, Poplar Forest. You can bypass this more congested local area of US 29 Business by picking up the 4-lane divided US 29 at Amherst and exiting at US 501 (Lynchburg Expressway) to continue to Poplar Forest.

Special attractions: Mountains, valleys, vineyards, and farmland.

Location: Central Virginia.

Route numbers: US 29S, US 29Bus; VA 53W, VA 20S, VA 616, VA 634, VA 6, VA 718, VA 56, VA 653, VA 56W, US 460W, VA 678; CR 708, CR 631, CR 692.

Travel season: All year long, although summer and fall are the more popular seasons.

Services: All services are available along the trail.

Nearby attractions: Monticello, Poplar Forest, Walton's Mountain Museum, Oakland Nelson County Museum of Rural History, Inglewood Lavender Farm, Monocan Indian Nation Ancestral Museum, Amherst County Museum, Wintergreen Resort, Point of Honor, plus numerous wineries, a brewery, many orchards, and a distillery.

For more information: Jefferson Heritage Trail, jeffersonheritagetrail.com; Thomas Jefferson's Poplar Forest, (434) 525-1806, poplarforest.org; Charlottesville Albemarle Convention & Visitors Bureau, (434) 970-3635, visitcharlottesville.org; Nelson County Economic Development and Tourism, (434) 263-7015, nelsoncounty.com; Bedford City and County Department of Tourism, (540) 587-5682, visitbedford.com; Amherst County Tourism, (434) 946-9400, county ofamherst.com; Snowflex Centre, (434) 582-2308 or (866) 504-7541, liberty.edu/ snowflex; Lynchburg Regional Convention and Visitors Bureau, (434) 845-5966 or (800) 732-5821, discoverlynchburg.org.

The Route

Thomas Jefferson's ride between Monticello and Poplar Forest would have been arduous, particularly in inclement weather. It would have taken 2 days by horseback or 3 days by carriage. He would spend the night at an inn or with friends who opened their homes to him. This route mimics Jefferson's travels by offering several places to stop and spend some friendly time, talking about the day's events, sharing a meal, sipping some wine or another beverage, and generally making the trek more pleasant.

As you leave the mountains and enter the gently rolling hills of the Piedmont plateau area, you pass forestlands, vineyards, and small communities until you

Jefferson Heritage Trail

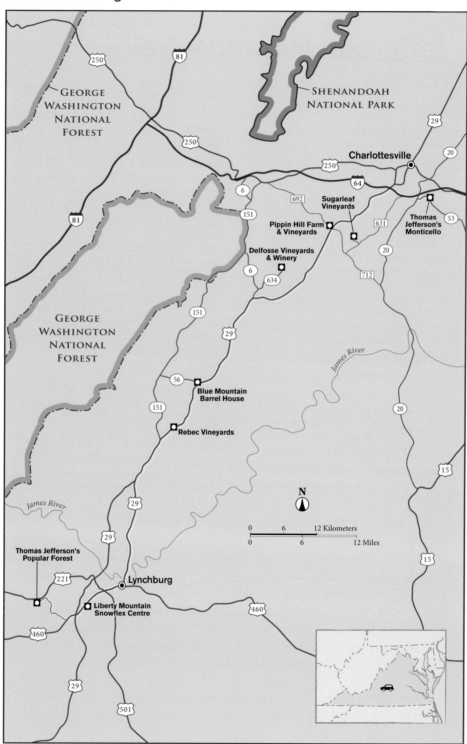

GEORGE
WASHINGTON
NATIONAL
FOREST

SHENANDOAH
NATIONAL PARK

Charlottesville

Sugarleaf
Vineyards

Pippin Hill Farm
& Vineyards

Thomas
Jefferson's
Monticello

Delfosse Vineyards
& Winery

GEORGE
WASHINGTON
NATIONAL
FOREST

James River

Blue Mountain
Barrel House

Rebec Vineyards

James River

N

0   6   12 Kilometers
0   6   12 Miles

Thomas Jefferson's
Popular Forest

Lynchburg

Liberty Mountain
Snowflex Centre

Vineyard view near Charlottesville
©HEATH OLDHAM/SHUTTERSTOCK.COM

start reaching the outskirts of Lynchburg, considerably more suburban and congested. Nelson County is mostly rural, with apple orchards and farms, wineries, a brewery, and a distillery.

As oenophiles and local historians know, Jefferson started cultivating grapes from France, Italy, and Spain as early as 1774. The fertile soil, warm temperatures, and protecting eastern slopes of the Blue Ridge Mountains make this an excellent place to grow the grapes and fruits used to produce interesting wines. Whatever winemaking was happening in Virginia sustained a nasty blow with a blight in the 19th century that became part of a lethal punch when Prohibition was enacted in 1919.

The industry returned to Virginia in 1976 and took about a decade to convince people that maybe it is here to stay. Trial and error and intense research at the Virginia Polytechnic Institute helped refine the right and wrong ways to excellent production. The tourism industry saw a good thing and has worked hard to promote various wine trails throughout the state.

Virginia is now the fifth-largest wine-producing state in the country, after California, Washington, New York, and Oregon. For the most part, Virginia winegrowers grow what the land loves and not necessarily what's popular in surveys.

On this route, you can stop at Virginia's first winery and some of the newer ones. When you stop for a tasting, you'll find some locales charge a fee, some charge a fee that's refunded if you buy a certain amount of wine, and some don't charge at all. If you'd rather drive a loop, consider the Bedford Wine Trail (Route 8) that stops by five wineries.

Starting at Monticello in Charlottesville and traveling 90 miles to Poplar Forest outside of Lynchburg you follow US 29 and much of the same route Jefferson would have traveled. You can stop by wineries, a brewery, museums, bed-and-breakfasts, and other attractions. You can see the Blue Ridge Mountains to your right (as you're traveling south) and the occasional mountain to your left. You also cross the scenic Tye and James Rivers.

Monticello & Wineries

As the Thomas Jefferson Foundation says, "**Monticello** is the autobiographical masterpiece of Thomas Jefferson—designed and redesigned and built and rebuilt for more than 40 years—and its gardens were a botanic showpiece, a source of food, and an experimental laboratory of ornamental and useful plants from around the world." Enjoy a guided tour about his home, gardens, or even the plantation's slave history.

When you leave Monticello, head west and then take a right on Monticello Loop. Follow the loop until you turn right onto VA 53W (Thomas Jefferson Parkway). Stay on the parkway for almost 2 miles and turn left onto VA 20S (Scottsville Road) and continue for 7.3 miles. Turn right onto Red Hill Road, go about 3 miles, and then turn left onto Old Lynchburg Road followed by a right turn 1 mile later on Walnut Branch Lane. You've arrived at **Wisdom Oak Winery** (you're allowed and maybe encouraged to say WOW), a winery started as a hobby by Jerry Bias in 2000. The first vines were planted by hand in 2002 when the vineyard/winery was called Sugarleaf Vineyards, and now all 2,075 plants take advantage of the cool breezes coming down the mountain slopes and have matured nicely. The tasting room, overlooking the vineyard, is where you can sample their petit manseng, petit verdot, cabernet franc, and viognier. There is a tasting fee. Check the drive-in movie schedule for free films; you might see *Sideways* or *A Good Year* (do you sense a theme here?).

The winery is open Wed through Sun and Mon holidays Mar through Dec and weekends in Jan and Feb and by appointment.

The next stop after WOW is 7.6 miles away. Start by heading west on Walnut Branch Lane for a mile, turning right onto CR 631 (Old Lynchburg Road) which becomes Plank Road. After 6.6 miles, you'll be at **Pippin Hill Farm & Vineyards,** where owners Lynn Easton and Dean Andrews joined with George Abetti, the

The library at Monticello that Jefferson designed so that only the ends of the bookcases are visible from the center of the room and plenty of light cascades in through the windows between the bookshelves.

founder of GeoBarns, to create their idea and ideal of a Virginia farm winery. Starting with the concept of a thoroughbred horse barn that uses post and beam construction, diagonal framing, and cupolas, they created a space that combines refined elegance with a casual touch. The tasting room has a hand-carved bar and a stone terrace that overlooks the vineyard. The couple promotes farm-to-table dining sourced from local farmers and their own garden and then pairs the cuisine with their wines. Among their leading wines are chardonnay, petit manseng, viognier, a white wine blend, and cabernet franc. The farm table and wine bar are open Tues through Sun 11 a.m. to 5 p.m.

From Pippin Hill, head southeast on CR 692 (Plank Road) to US 29S (Monacan Trail Road). Then follow US 29S for 9.5 miles. Turn right onto Hickory Creek Road and go a mile before a slight left onto VA 6161 (continuation of Hickory Creek Road) and then another slight right onto VA 634 (Old Roberts Mountain Road). After 1 mile, you'll be at **DelFosse Vineyards and Winery.**

You're invited the stop by DelFosse for a wine tasting, a quiet picnic by their lake, to hike or bike the trails they're creating (eventually 5 miles) surrounding the winery, or to tour the terraced vineyards (one of the only terraced vineyards in the state). Claude, Genevieve, Oriane, Olivier, and Laurent DelFosse started the winery in 2000 on more than 330 acres with a natural spring and historically preserved buildings. Growing on those terraces are chardonnay, viognier, sauvignon blanc, petit manseng, pinot gris, cabernet sauvignon, cabernet franc, merlot, malbec, petit verdot, and chambourin. While the viognier and petit manseng are aged in stainless steel tanks, the rest spend their aging days in French oak barrels.

The winery is open Wed through Sun 11 a.m. to 5 p.m. and by appointment.

When you leave DelFosse, head southeast on VA 634 (Kermits Way) and then continue onto VA 616 (Hickory Creek Road) until you're back on US 29S/VA 6W (Thomas Nelson Highway). Drive for 9.6 miles and turn right onto VA 718 (Mountain Cove Road) until you reach **Mountain Cove Winery.**

This is an unusual winery in several respects. It was founded in 1973, making it the state's oldest winery. And, the tastings and tours are free. Although the views on your route have been nice so far, Mountain Cove offers vistas of apple orchards on the mountainside as its background. Stop for a picnic and a visit to the gift shop for wine and related items.

Al and Emily Weed moved here in 1973, planted the first 6 of 12 acres the following spring, and produced their first wine in 1976. He also became involved in the burgeoning industry by serving as president for the Virginia Wineries Association and coexecutive director of Public Policy Virginia, participating in legislative proceedings at the state level. They hired local artisan who used local stones and tinsmiths to create the roof. Wood came from nearby neighbors and was cut at a local sawmill. Events include Shakespearean performances and other gatherings.

The Weeds produce wines that meet vegan standards, from grapes and other fruits, and they are considering producing kosher fruit wines—perhaps the country's only kosher fruit wine—if there is enough demand.

Mountain Cove is open Wed through Sun noon to 5 p.m. Closed Jan and Feb.

Turn northeast on VA 718 (Mountain Cove Road) toward US 29S (Thomas Nelson Highway) and then turn onto US 29S and follow this for about 6 miles. Turn right onto Stage Road and then make another right onto Cooperative Way to the **Blue Mountain Barrel House,** where you can sample a flight of their beer selections, take a tour of the brewing process, and sit back with a glass of ale or lager. The Smack family seems to have combined and selected a variety of production techniques that you won't see at every brewery, not even those that are called boutique. Six of their beers are aged in once-used charred American white oak bourbon barrels. All of the beers have live, fermenting beer added to them just before they're bottled that makes for a nicer appearance than those that have forced carbonation. Among the beers they brew are an imperial stout aged in oak bourbon barrels, a chocolate orange bourbon porter, a pale ale, and a Bavarian-style wheat beer. Unlike at their older sister brewery in Afton where there's a full restaurant, here they focus on just the beer. Feel free to bring a picnic and spend a little time relaxing.

The tasting room is open Fri through Sun 11 a.m. to 8 p.m. for sampling. It's also open just for beer sales on Wed and Thurs.

Whether or not you've had your hops at the brewery, the next stop at **Rebec Vineyards** is just a little more than a hop, skip, and a jump away. Turn southeast on Cooperative Way and go for 0.5 mile, then take the second right onto US 29S (Thomas Nelson Highway) which will take you to N. Amherst Highway in 5.5 miles.

Rebec has been the home of the annual **October Virginia Wine and Garlic Festival** almost since soon after opening in 1987. Richard Hanson started the winery and planted the first 8 acres in 1980. He and his son-in-law Mark Magruder designed and built the winery with weather chestnut siding and exposed beams that they reclaimed from a 200-year-old tobacco barn. Among the 15 wines they sell are dry white wines, sweet wines, dry reds, and what they call their "one-of-a-kind Autumn Glow and Sweet Sofia," which are created by winery owner Svet Kaney. This 70-acre estate in Amherst County lets you enjoy your wine with views of the Blue Ridge Mountains and you're encouraged to bring a blanket and picnic under the trees. Oh, and the *rebec* is a medieval stringed instrument and the use of it as the winery's name symbolized their belief in old-world craftsmanship.

You can tour and taste daily 10 a.m. to 5 p.m. from spring through fall.

Other wineries populate the area only a few miles off US 29. Check with the Virginia Wine organization for details.

Snowflex Centre to Lynchburg

Leaving Rebec, head southeast on US 29S (N. Amherst Highway) for 7.6 miles and exit on US 29 Business South. Go 16 miles and take the ramp onto Candlers Mountain Road and follow this for 1.6 miles if you're going to Snowflex Centre, then turn left onto Monogram Road, exit 11, and then turn left onto Graves Mill Road and go 1.7 miles.

Whether you adore cold weather or think skiing, snowboarding, and tubing would be fun if you could do it in summer clothing, the people at the **Snowflex Centre** (the first of its kind in the country) will make you happy. This is a one-of-a-kind year-round attraction with a synthetic ski slope surface that simulates snow and offers beginner, intermediate, and advanced slopes. Everyone starts on the beginner slope to prove their proficiency. Instructors are available for beginners. You should wear long-sleeve shirts, long pants, and gloves (or short sleeves, pants, and elbow and knee pads).

Misting devices (bring a change of clothing) give it the feel of the real stuff with extra padding underneath so the more experienced skiers and boarders can

Jefferson's Poplar Forest is at the southern end of the Jefferson Heritage Trail.

practice all sorts of maneuvers and stunts. This place is open day and night, offers rentals, and has a tow system to bring you back to the top of the easy or difficult slope. Yes, beginners are more than welcome and children under 16 must be accompanied by a parent. The 2-story lodge is ADA compliant.

To go to **Poplar Forest** after leaving Snowflex, turn onto Candlers Mountain Road and go 0.5 miles before taking a left onto University Boulevard. Take a left again to merge onto US 460W. Take CR 678 (Airport Road) exit toward Green-view Drive and stay on CR 678 for another 0.15 miles. Turn left onto Timberlake Road, right onto Enterprise Drive, right onto Homestead Drive, and then continue on Bateman Bridge Road after 0.9 mile.

Stopping by Poplar Forest lets us peek into a 14-year period of his private life of the so-very-public Thomas Jefferson after he turned 65. The home was sold after he died, altered, and then allowed to fall into disrepair. With scrupulous detail to research and attention, the home (including an attached office wing) and landscape are being restored in a mission that may—intentionally—never be complete. Preservationists are working with the incomplete and inconsistent notes made and plans drawn by Jefferson.

Fortunately, some things remain, and a couple of the most spectacular rem-nants are five original tulip poplar trees and a black walnut in the north yard that may have been on the property before the main house was constructed. Three more tulip poplars are about 200 yards northeast of the building and together they are the last trees from Jefferson's landscape.

The walls aren't finished, because part of our understanding is to see a wall's interior construction methods from the early 19th century and artifacts from the people—including slaves—who lived and worked on the plantation. You can explore exhibits at the restoration workshop and view a 15-minute film about the work and archaeological excavations. You're almost certain to see something new each time you visit.

This National Historic Landmark is open daily Mar 15 through Dec 30 (closed Easter, Thanksgiving, Christmas Eve and Day) and winter weekends. Although the home wasn't originally designed for wheelchair access, a lift is now available to the upper level when you request assistance at the museum shop. Events, including musical performances, lectures, and historical theater, are presented frequently. Forty-minute guided house tours and self-guided grounds exhibits are included in the admission fee.

Once you've toured Poplar Forest, you can return to **Lynchburg** by retracing your steps. The city has numerous reasons to lure you in for a visit including museums that seem to cover all ages and most interests and the particularly fascinating **Old City Cemetery.** As mentioned in Route 11 (Eastern Shore), the state started a LOVE art program in 2011, building on the state's tourism motto of "Virginia is For Lovers." The Lynchburg artwork was created by local artist Paul Clements and installed in May 2013 at the head of **Blackwater Creek Trail,** along the riverfront in downtown Lynchburg.

8

Bedford Wine Trail

Sip, Sip, Hooray!

General description: This 75-mile loop trail starts and ends in Bedford and visits five family-owned and operated wineries where you can sip, swirl, and spit. There are also two non-winery stops including the National D-Day Memorial, built with private funds in Bedford because the town gave up more lives per capita in the Normandy landings on June 6, 1944 during World War II than any other American community. Consider making Mountain Fruit and Produce your first stop or maybe saving the best, or sweetest, for last.

Special attractions: Wineries, farms, a Blue Ridge mountain backdrop.

Location: Central Virginia.

Route numbers: US 221, US 460, and US 460W; VA 668, VA 703, VA 811, VA 709, VA 24, VA 627, VA 628, VA 626, VA 608, VA 654, VA 655, V 616, VA 653, VA 756, VA 747, VA 122, and VA 680.

Travel season: All year long, except the wineries may have restricted hours during the winter. More events are scheduled during the growing season. Check the operating hours, so you're not out at the crack of dawn and waiting several hours before your winery opens.

Services: All services are available in Bedford.

Nearby attractions: National D-Day Memorial, Appalachian Trail, Bedford Museum and Genealogical Library, Historic Centertown Bedford, Blue Ridge Parkway, Smith Mountain Lake, Peaks of Otter.

For more information: Bedford City & County Department of Tourism, (540) 587-5682 or (877) 447-3257, visitbedford .com; Bedford Wine Trail, (877) 447-3257, bedfordwinetrail.org; LeoGrande Winery, (540) 586-4066, leograndewinery.com; Savoy-Lee Winery, (540) 297-9275, savoy-lee.com; Hickory Hill Vineyards & Winery, (540) 296-1393, smlwine.com; White Rock Vineyards & Winery, (540) 890-3359, whiterockwines.com; Peaks of Otter Winery, (540) 586-3707, peaksofotterwinery.com; National D-Day Memorial, (540) 586-DDAY or (800) 351-DDAY, dday.org; Appalachian Trail, (304) 535-6278, nps.gov/appa; Bedford Museum and Genealogical Library, (540) 586-4520, bedfordvamuseum.org; Smith Mountain Lake, (540) 721-1203, visitsmithmountainlake.com; Peaks of Otter, (800) 542-5927 or (877) HI-PEAKS, peaksofotter.com.

The Route

The wine-producing industry that Thomas Jefferson started (as described in Route 7 Jefferson Heritage Trail) has thrived in Virginia; it is now the fifth largest wine-producing state in the country. This loop allows you to sample wines from five wineries.

The mountains' blue haze presents a stellar backdrop to the vibrant green grape leaves. The vineyards hug the mountain slopes and nearly line some banks of Smith Mountain Lake. While most tours and even some tastings are free, if

Bedford Wine Trail

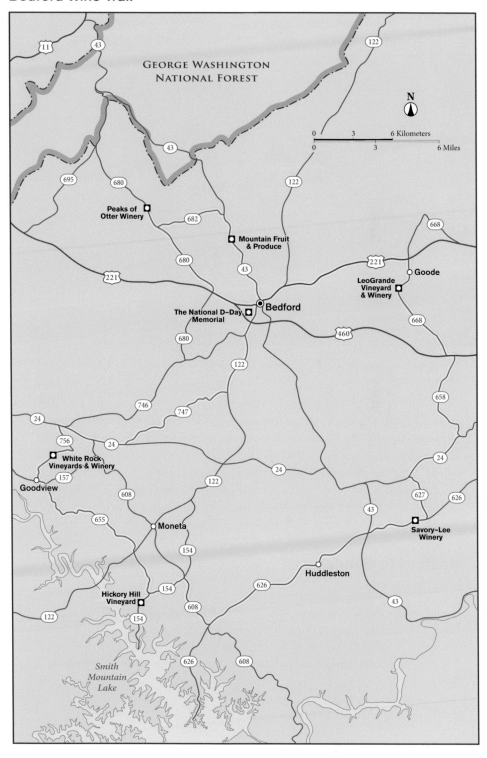

A model of the National D-Day Memorial is displayed at the Bedford City and County Department of Tourism.

there is a fee, it usually includes a free glass as a souvenir of your visit (along with any wine you may buy). Look for picnic areas, farm experiences, and musical and other events. Pick up a Bedford Wine Trail brochure and have it stamped at each winery, then bring it to the Bedford Welcome Center for a gift.

The route takes you on gently curving and undulating roadways, past acres and acres of farmlands, open pastures, forests, schools, community churches, cemeteries, neighborhood stores, and, of course, vineyards.

Bedford to Goode

You start your tour of the gorgeous scenery that includes the twin Peaks of Otter mountaintops in the Blue Ridge Mountains in **Bedford.** Take US 221N (Forest Road) for 6.7 miles and turn right onto VA 668 (Goode Station Road) and then get onto VA 668 (now Goode Road) for 1.3 miles, after which make a right onto VA 703 (Wingfield Drive) and continue until you reach **LeoGrande Winery in Goode.**

This family dream started in the 1990s and has been growing ever since. The tasting room was an old farmhouse that's been painstakingly remodeled. Norman

LeoGrande and his family started with 3 acres of grapes which they sold to local wineries until they bought some more land and decided they could produce the wine themselves. You're invited to taste their wines, including many Italian varieties, all made on the premises. The 400-acre farm also supports Black Angus cattle, horses, goats, chickens, dogs, and a potbellied pig. Sit on the veranda, have a picnic, and enjoy the vista that includes the **Peaks of Otter.** If you've made the loop the other way or this is the only winery you'll visit, time your journey to watch the sunset over the mountains. There is a gift shop.

Goode to Huddleston

When leaving LeoGrande Winery, head north on VA 703 (Wingfield Drive) for 0.5 miles, then turn left onto US 460E (East Lynchburg Salem Turnpike) for 4 miles. Turn right onto VA 668 (Blackwater Road) for 3 miles and then turn left to follow VA 668 for 1.4 miles. Turn right onto VA 709 (New London Road) for 0.6 mile and turn right onto VA 24W (Wyatts Way) for 3.4 miles. Turn left onto VA 627 (Preston Mill Road) for 2.5 miles, followed by a right turn onto VA 626 (Johnson Mountain Road) for 0.6 mile. After all that winding, you've arrived at the **Savoy–Lee Winery in Huddleston.**

Dave Wood started his winemaking hobby while he was serving in the Marine Corps. The winery was licensed in 2004 and released its first wines—chardonnay and cabernet sauvignon—the next year. Recently he has allowed area farmers to work his vineyards and grow the grapes while he concentrates on the wine production. Geoff Garcia joined Savoy–Lee in 2012 to help with events and the tasting room experience. Geoff apparently is the Kevin Bacon of the Virginia wine world. It's said he either knows everyone or is only one degree of separation from the rest. The winery now sells chardonnay, riesling, seyval blanc, various roses (blend of cabernet sauvignon and cabernet franc), cabernet franc, cabernet sauvignon, and a red wine blend. Volunteers are invited and encouraged to join the fun while pouring wine at festivals.

The winery is open Fri through Mon noon to 5 p.m., all year.

Huddleston to Moneta

Leaving the winery, head west on VA 626 (Johnson Mountain Road) for 12.2 miles and then turn right onto VA 608 (White House Road) and continue on for almost 3 miles. Turn left on to VA 654 (Radford Church Road), then make another left after 2 miles—to stay on VA 654 (now Hickory Cove Lane) for 1 mile to reach the **Hickory Hill Winery** in **Moneta** with a tasting room and gift shop in a converted 1923 farmhouse.

Roger and Judy Farrow invite you to bring a picnic and enjoy a meal in their scenic picnic area. They started dreaming about a winery in the mid-1980s and now share that dream with the rest of the family, particularly during harvest and festival time. Roger's mother Alberta also helps with the grape picking. It's her paintings that are hanging in the tasting room.

Picture an idyllic summer Saturday evening and place it at the winery where you can listen to music, enjoy conversation with new friends and old, and realize that your children will remember the good times they had here chasing lightning bugs at the Sunset Saturdays. Bring lawn chairs and a food of basket and sample some of their wines. For $10 you'll also get a souvenir glass and tasting.

Hickory Hill is always looking for volunteers, particularly when it's time to harvest. You have free admission to Sunset Saturdays when you're a volunteer. They have more than 100 volunteers and always welcome more.

The winery is open for tours and tastings Thurs through Sun 11 a.m. to 5 p.m. Apr to Oct, on Sat and Mon holidays the rest of the year, and by appointment. They are closed Thanksgiving Day and late December through early January.

Moneta to Goodview

Head northeast on VA 654 (Hickory Cover Lane) for a mile, then turn left onto VA 655 (Hendricks Store Road) for 6 miles. Bear left onto VA 616 (Horseshoe Bend Road) for 0.2 mile. Dogleg left onto VA 757 (Goodview Town Road) before getting back on VA 616 (Sandy Level Road), and then make a left on VA 756 (Bruno Drive). Follow this for 0.6 miles to find the **White Rock Winery** in **Goodview.**

Fred and Drema Sylvester started this vineyard and farm winery as their dream in the late 1990s. They toured vineyards, took some classes and seminars, and then planted their first vines in 2000. They added more each year through 2003, had their first vintage bottling in 2004, and opened their tasting room in 2005. They now offer five vinifera varieties—chardonnay, cabernet sauvignon, cabernet franc, merlot, and pinot gris—with two hybrids—charonell and traminette. As they're located in the town of Goodview, you can expect a spectacular view from the glass-walled tasting room and veranda. Special events include a portrait day when they invite one and all to have a free professional photograph taken in their beautiful natural setting in return for a canned food donation. They are open seasonally for tours and tastings Thurs through Mon noon to 5 p.m.

Virginia wineries offer tours, tastings, and visual harmony.

Mountain Fruit and Produce makes Bedford Peach ice cream and carries local produce.

Goodview to Bedford

This is the home stretch as you head back to Bedford with stops at the Peaks of Otter Winery and the National D-Day Memorial.

Leaving White Rock, head northeast on VA 756 (Bruno Drive) for 1.2 miles to VA 616 (Sandy Level Road). Drive for 1.5 miles and turn left to stay on VA 616 to an almost immediate right turn onto VA 24E (Stewartsville Road) and continue 3.5 miles. Make a left turn onto VA 747 (Joppa Mill Road) and drive for 6.2 miles to a left turn that puts you on VA 122N (Moneta Road). Drive for 3.9 miles to Overload Circle and the entrance to the **National D-Day Memorial.**

The privately funded memorial is set on 88 acres of land in **Bedford** because 19 soldiers from here, a town with about 3,200 people in 1944, died on D-Day and three others died later in the Normandy campaign meaning it had the highest number of deaths per capita of any city or town in the country. A total of 4,413 Allied soldiers died and all are remembered on plaques. This impressive memorial is a tribute to the Allied forces that were part of the Normandy invasion on June 6, 1944. The park has three parts. The first, in the shape of the Supreme Head-quarters Allied Expeditionary Force combat patch, is Reynold's Garden which represents the planning and preparation for the invasion. Gray Plaza, symbolizes the landing and fighting stages with an "invasion" pool with soldiers struggling to reach the shore amid beach obstacles and water jets embodying the water splashing around them from incoming live ordnance. Estes Plaza is capped with a triumph **Overlord Arch** (44 feet 6 inches tall) and the 12 flags of the nations that participated in the Allied Expeditionary Force.

While a stark winter day plays heavy contrast to this outdoor memorial, a summertime visit will see plants in bloom and fountains gushing (they are drained during the winter).

The memorial and gift shop are open daily 10 a.m. to 5 p.m., although it may be closed in inclement weather.

When you leave the memorial, go east on Overlord Circle toward Tiger Trail and then right onto Burks Hill Road and then right again to US 460W/US 460 Bypass West toward Roanoke for 2.5 miles. Turn right onto VA 680 (Patterson Mill Road) and go 4.6 miles, then staying on VA 580, take Sheep Creek Road for 1 mile and you're at **Peaks of Otter Winery.**

The Peaks of Otter Winery was the county's first winery and the state's first fruit winery. The Johnsons make 25 varieties of wine from fruits and vegetables they grow, a tradition that started in the 1700s. They've mixed chile peppers with vegetables for Kiss the Devil wine and with apple wine to make Chili Dawg, a top-selling flavor. Other favorites are apple truffles, blueberry muffin, wildflower honey, light pear, and light sweet peach. They also make jellies, jams, and butters. They're open on weekends Jan through Mar and daily the rest of the year.

Head southeast out of the Peaks of Otter Winery on VA 680 (Sheep Creek Road) for 1 mile and then, staying on VA 680, turn left onto Patterson Mill Road for a few seconds, then make the first left onto VA 682 (Kelso Mill Road) for 3.5 miles. Turn right onto VA 682/VA 43S (Peaks Road), and carry on for 1.4 miles so you can stop at the **Mountain Fruit and Produce** market. Pretend you're shopping for fresh fruits and veggies while the main reason you're here is to try the Bedford Peach ice cream. It should be there all year. In making the creamy goodness, they do more than add little chunks of peaches to the mixture. They puree the peaches as part of the mixture. Every bite is a spoonful of peach exploding on your taste buds. Maybe, if you bought some of the light sweet peach wine produced by Peaks of Otter, you could double your pleasure by pouring a little of it over the ice cream.

When you leave the market, head southeast on VA 43S (Peaks Road) for 3.5 miles and then turn right into North Bridge Street. Turn left onto East Main Street and you have finished your Bedford Wine Tour. If you're spending a summer night here, consider visiting the **Mayberry Drive-In Theatre & Diner** (Silver Diner) so you can have breakfast anytime or a meal before the movie. It's open on weekend nights.

9

Blue Ridge Parkway North

Rockfish Gap to Roanoke

General description: The northern section of the Blue Ridge Parkway in Virginia is a paved, 2-lane, mountain route along the ridgetops of the Southern Appalachians from near Charlottesville, Staunton, and Waynesboro in the north to Roanoke at the southern end. The 121-mile route winds up and down along the mountain crests from a low elevation of about 650 feet to almost 4,000 feet, with numerous scenic viewpoints and overlooks. This section is surrounded by the trees, shrubs, and flowers of the George Washington and Jefferson National Forest.

Special attractions: The forest and scenic mountain views are rightfully the main attractions of the route. Although many people treat the parkway as the experience, Ranger Peter S. Givens, interpretive specialist, says, "It's a window to those little communities alongside it where people should browse around the restaurants and craft shops. That's part of why the parkway is here."

Location: West-central Virginia.

Route numbers: There are no route numbers. The Blue Ridge Parkway is measured with cement mile markers or mileposts (MP), and distances and attractions are noted in tenths of a mile.

Travel season: Travel is heaviest on weekends during the summer months and in mid-Oct when autumn leaf colors of oak, hickory, tulip, buckeye, and ash trees are at their most brilliant with fir and spruce providing a constant coniferous background. As they occupy different elevations, the leaves don't turn at the same time offering a cascade of colors. However, the blooming rhododendrons, tulip trees, serviceberries, and dogwoods make spring a wonderful time to visit, too. The parkway is open all year, but portions may be closed temporarily

during winter storms or during times of icing, fog, snow, or other adverse weather conditions. Campgrounds are open during the warmer months. At this time, the only year-round lodging and facilities are at the Peaks of Otter, MP 86.0. Recent budget cuts may change that, so check before you start driving.

Camping: Campgrounds on this section of the parkway are at Peaks of Otter and Roanoke Mountain. The US Forest Service maintains a campground at Sherando Lake in George Washington National Forest, near MP 16.

Services: Gasoline is not available on the parkway, but stops can be made to fuel up on US 250 (MP 0), US 60 (MP 45.6), VA 130 (MP 61.6), US 501 (MP 63.9), US 460 (MP 106), VA 24 (MP 112.2), and US 22 (MP 121.4). Gas stations are not necessarily open 24 hours a day. Restaurants, motels, and hotels are available in Roanoke, Waynesboro, Lexington, Lynchburg, and Bedford. Gasoline, a restaurant, and year-round lodging are available at Peaks of Otter, MP 86.0.

Nearby attractions: Among the more interesting diversions off the route are Charlottesville, Lexington (Route 15), Natural Bridge, Buchanan (Route 20), Smith Mountain Lake, National D-Day Memorial, Wintergreen Resort, Booker T. Washington National Monument, and Roanoke. If inclement weather affects your view, venture off the parkway a few miles to explore some of these attractions. As sequestration budget cuts were just being implemented as of this writing, it's not known what operations will be closed or cut back. The NPS website has a list of what's being affected by the cuts.

Route 5: (Skyline Drive through Shenandoah National Park) terminates at the

Blue Ridge Parkway North

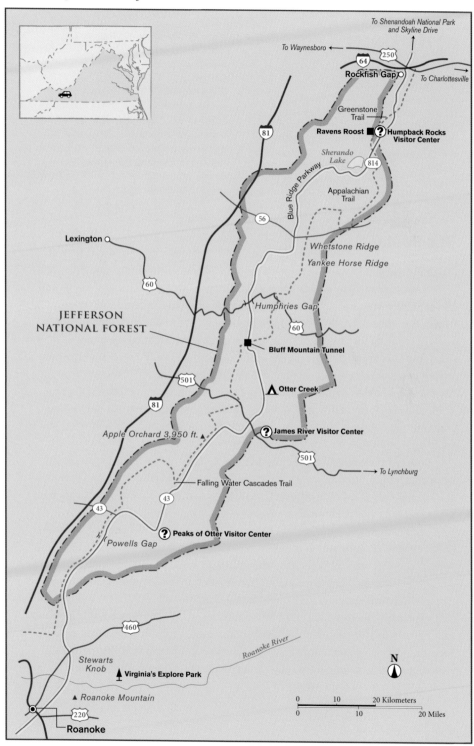

To Shenandoah National Park
and Skyline Drive

To Waynesboro ←

250

64

Rockfish Gap

To Charlottesville

81

Greenstone
Trail

Ravens Roost

Humbback Rocks
Visitor Center

*Sherando
Lake*

814

Blue Ridge Parkway

Appalachian
Trail

56

Lexington

Whetstone Ridge

Yankee Horse Ridge

60

Humphries Gap

JEFFERSON
NATIONAL FOREST

60

Bluff Mountain Tunnel

501

Otter Creek

81

James River Visitor Center

Apple Orchard 3,950 ft.

501

To Lynchburg

Falling Water Cascades Trail

43

43

Peaks of Otter Visitor Center

Powells Gap

460

Roanoke River

Stewarts
Knob

Virginia's Explore Park

N

▲ Roanoke Mountain

| 0 | 10 | 20 Kilometers |
| 0 | 10 | 20 Miles |

220

Roanoke

northern end of this route, and Route 10 (Blue Ridge Parkway South) is a continuation of the route.

For more information: Blue Ridge Parkway, (540) 767-2492, nps.gov/blri; Charlottesville & Albemarle County, (434) 970-3635, visitcharlottesville.org; Virginia's Blue Ridge, (540) 342-6025, visitvablueridge.com; Staunton Convention and Visitor Bureau, (540) 332-3865, visitstaunton.com; City of Waynesboro, (540) 942-6644, visitwaynesboro.net; Lexington & the Rockbridge Area Tourism Development, (540) 463-3777 or (877) 453-9822, lexingtonvirginia.com; Lynchburg Regional Convention & Visitors Bureau, (434) 845-5966 or (800) 732-5821, discoverlynchburg.org; Bedford area, (540) 587-5682 or (877) 447-3257, visitbedford.com; Roanoke Visitor Information, (540) 342-6025, visitroanokeva.com; Center in the Square, (540) 342-5700, centerinthesquare.org; Taubman Museum of Art, (540) 342-6760, taubmanmuseum.org.

The Route

The Blue Ridge Parkway is a ridgetop road that stretches 469 miles along the crest of the Appalachian Mountains linking Shenandoah National Park in Virginia and Great Smoky Mountains National Park and the Cherokee Indian Reservation in North Carolina. Because of the terrain and winding roads, you are warned not to use GPS routing for directions. Pick up a map from an information center or online.

There are about 200 overlooks, each of which will have a warning sign indicating it is coming up and whether it's on the right or the left. The overlook should come within a quarter mile of the sign. An apology is extended if a sign is missing; parkway staff are at work to replace those that go missing. Once you pull into the overlook, you'll see a sign with the name of the overlook, what you're looking at, elevation, and any other interesting facts.

Some of the overlooks only provide forest vistas rather than the details the designers had in mind in the 1930s and '40s. Sometimes trees encroach between the regular cutbacks made on public land, but other trees may be on private land where nothing can be done about them.

Senator Harry F. Byrd (D-VA) suggested the creation of the parkway to President Franklin D. Roosevelt in the early 1930s. Construction started in 1935 and wasn't complete until 52 years later when the last 7-mile section, around Grandfather Mountain (near the Linn Cove Viaduct) in North Carolina, was completed in 1987. The parkway was designed to harmonize with the natural beauty of the mountains and to preserve the historical and cultural features of the area, long a home to mountain farmers and hunters. The popularity of the route probably far exceeds anything Senator Byrd envisioned: More than 15 million people visited some portion of the parkway in 2012, making it the most visited site in the National Park System.

View from the Blue Ridge Parkway
©TIM MAINIERO/SHUTTERSTOCK.COM

The winding, 2-lane paved road has a speed limit of 45 miles per hour, but you'll often want to go slower to enjoy the scenery. Or others in front of you may be going more slowly, so relax and enjoy the views.

The Blue Ridge Parkway is maintained by the National Park Service. All plants and animals are protected. There is no fee, and you can enter and leave the parkway at numerous intersections. Commercial vehicles are not permitted on the parkway.

The Virginia portion of the parkway is about 217 miles long. This route covers the northern 121 miles of the parkway, from Rockfish Gap to US 220 outside Roanoke. Except for the few miles before Roanoke, this section is surrounded by heavily wooded George Washington and Jefferson National Forest with few intersections.

Rockfish Gap to Humphries Gap

The parkway and the route begin at **Rockfish Gap.** The entrance is at the intersection of exit 99 of I-64 and US 250, about 3 miles east of Waynesboro and 20 miles west of Charlottesville. It is directly across the highway from the southern terminus of Skyline Drive in Shenandoah National Park (Route 5). The **Appalachian Trail,** the ridgetop hiking trail from Maine to Georgia, parallels the parkway with numerous access points from Rockfish Gap to MP 103. If you are a birder and planning a fall visit, check out the Rockfish Gap Hawkwatch when hawks and other birds of prey are counted as they come through the gap. The results are submitted to the Hawk Migration Society of America.

Head south on the parkway on the steeply climbing road while the views of the Shenandoah Valley to the right and the Piedmont to the left slowly unfold as you ascend to the crest of the Blue Ridge. The **Humpback Rocks** area, from about MP 5 to MP 9.3, has a self-guided trail past several reconstructed Appalachian farm structures and pioneer log buildings, and several other short trails. A 0.75-mile trail to the **Rocks** starts at MP 6.1. The **Greenstone Trail** (MP 8.8) leads 0.2 mile through an oak and hickory forest to outcrops of Catoctin greenstone, an extensive late Precambrian lava flow exposed by many of the road cuts.

At **Ravens Roost,** MP 10.7, you'll see broad views of Torry Mountain and the Shenandoah Valley to your west.

Sherando Lake, a recreation area in **George Washington National Forest,** is accessible at MP 16 via VA 814. The lake, 4.5 miles from the parkway, features swimming, picnicking, and camping.

You may feel you're in spiritual surroundings with all this beauty, and at MP 17.6 is a view of the **Priest,** tallest of the Religious Mountains, that also include the Cardinal, Friar, Little Priest, and—no trees on the summit—Bald Friar.

View from Ravens Roost
©ALFRED WEKELO/SHUTTERSTOCK.COM

Near MP 27 is VA 56 to **Crabtree Falls,** 6 miles east of the parkway. This is the highest vertical-drop cascading waterfall east of the Mississippi River. It has five major cascades and numerous smaller ones falling a total distance of 1,200 feet. A trail leads to five overlooks, the first just a few hundred feet from the parking lot. The others are scattered along the 3-mile paved trail.

Whetstone Ridge, at MP 29 is where mountaineers sharpened their knives and axes on the "whetstone," a fine-grained sandstone deposited as invading seas covered the greenstone lava in early Cambrian time about 560 million years ago.

Until the early 1900s, lumbering was second only to farming as the region's most important industry, and many of the mountain slopes were clear-cut. The most prized wood was that of the American chestnut; unfortunately, the chestnut trees that were not cut down were all killed by the chestnut blight of the 1930s. The logs were hauled out by mule and horse. At **Yankee Horse Ridge,** MP 34.4, you'll find a reconstructed spur of an old logging railroad that ran along the ridge. A 10-minute trail leads to a logging exhibit and small waterfall.

The route descends to **Humphries Gap,** MP 45.6, where it crosses US 60. Lexington, the starting point for Route 15, is about 11 miles to the west. There's plenty of military history here inside the **George C. Marshall Museum, Lee Chapel and Museum, Museum of Military Memorabilia, Stonewall Jackson House,** and **Virginia Military Institute Museum.**

Past Humphries Gap to Peaks of Otter

Turn on your lights as you drive through the 630-foot-long **Bluff Mountain Tunnel,** just past MP 53 and the only Virginia tunnel on the parkway.

Otter Creek's 10-mile travels to the James River can be spotted between MP 58 and 63.6; **Otter Lake,** at MP 63.1, offers fishing and a trail.

At MP 63.8 you reach the **James River overlook** and the lowest elevation on the parkway, 649 feet above sea level. Until the advent of the railroad in the late 1800s, the James River was an important transportation link through the mountains. A footbridge spans the river, a favorite spot for anglers, with views both upstream and down through the river gorges. Across the river you can examine several restored locks of the James River and Kanawha Canal. The intention was to connect to the Ohio River, except when railroads replaced canals and towpaths as the main means of transportation, and the project was abandoned.

To the east, along US 501, is **Lynchburg** where, besides history, cemeteries, wineries, and other attractions, you can ski and snowboard all year at **Snowflex.** This is an artificial surface bearing beginner and moderate slopes. Yes, they have lessons. There's also a view of the mountains, particularly of the Peaks of Otter.

Back on the drive when you cross the James River and US 501 you leave the George Washington National Forest and enter the Jefferson National Forest. The route reaches its highest elevation in Virginia, 3,950 feet, at the **Apple Orchard** turnout, MP 76.5. (The highest point on the parkway, 6,047 feet, is at MP 431 in North Carolina.)

Bedford is just 10 miles east of the Peaks of Otter Visitor Center on VA 43. It's well-visited by those going to pay their respects at the **National D-Day Memorial** (in recognition of the town suffering the highest per capita D-Day losses in the nation). You'll feel very refreshed after trying some of the incredibly delicious (particularly in ice cream) Bedford peaches (see Route 8, Bedford Wine Trail).

The parking area at MP 83.1 is the trailhead for the **Fallingwater Cascades Trail,** a segment of the National Recreation Trail. This is a moderate loop hike of 1.6 miles through thick stands of rhododendron to a lacy cascade fringed by hemlocks. It involves a change in elevation, both up and down, of about 260 feet.

Just beyond, at MP 86.0, is the **Peaks of Otter Recreation Area.** Dominating the scene is conical 3,875-foot-high **Sharp Top Mountain,** and its taller and less conspicuous neighbor, 4,001-foot-high **Flat Top Mountain**. The two peaks are composed of a dark granite more than a billion years old.

Apple Orchard Fall near Peaks of Otter
©JON BEARD/SHUTTERSTOCK.COM

The Peaks of Otter has been a resort area since colonial days. In the early 1800s, Polly Woods operated her ordinary (inn) for travelers. Visitors today can dine in the restored ordinary and stay overnight in the Peaks of Otter Lodge (open all year) or camp in the campground. As of 2013, the Delaware North company is operating the lodge and other concessions.

Other facilities include a store, gas station, gift shop, and visitor center. Hikers have a variety of trails to choose from, including the strenuous **Sharp Top Trail.** The 360-degree view from the top takes in the Piedmont, Blue Ridge Mountains, Shenandoah Valley, and the distant Allegheny Mountains. There are frequent naturalist-conducted hikes and evening programs.

Peaks of Otter to Roanoke

The route continues around the big curve through **Powell's Gap.** Six species of oak are common to the forest, and at MP 90.0 you can examine all of them: red, black, white, scarlet, chestnut, and bear. If leaves are on the trees, an exhibit will help you find and identify each type.

A mile past there, VA 43 leads right 5 miles to I-81 and Buchanan, the start of Route 20.

As you continue south, the ridgeline starts to narrow, and you begin the long descent to the valley floor. At MP 99.6 is a view of the **Roanoke Valley** and gradually you emerge from the forest to views of open fields.

Houses become more frequent after you cross US 460 at MP 105.8. The last peak of note is **Stewarts Knob,** almost at the bottom of the long grade, viewed from the turnout at MP 110.6.

The route becomes somewhat urbanized as it skirts the southern edge of **Roanoke,** the largest settlement on the parkway. You pass over the Roanoke River on a high bridge; on the other side is the **Roanoke River Parking Overlook.** A path leads to a view 100 feet above the river gorge. The railroad along the river is the Norfolk & Western, which hauls coal from western Virginia and West Virginia. The railroad has its headquarters in downtown Roanoke.

At MP 115.8 the Roanoke River Parkway leads left in 1.5 miles to **Virginia's Explore Park,** formerly a frontier museum that emphasized the state's role in western expansion. It's now an information center with some historical exhibits.

East of Roanoke is **Smith Mountain Lake,** a popular resort area. Near the lake is the **Booker T. Washington National Monument,** marking the birthplace of this African-American educator.

At MP 120.3 is the entrance to the 4-mile loop road over **Roanoke Mountain,** with good views of the city and a short trail. The loop route is steep and winding and is not open to trailers. It is closed at dusk and during inclement weather. Just past the loop route is the entrance to the **Roanoke Mountain Campground.**

Roanoke is known for its museums, especially after the reopening of the **Center in the Square** held in May of 2013 after a 2-year, $30 million renovation. The **Harrison Museum of African American Culture, the History Museum of Western Virginia, Mill Mountain Theatre, O. Winston Link Museum, Opera Roanoke, Roanoke Ballet Theatre, the Roanoke Symphony Orchestra,** and the **Science Museum of Western Virginia** are all located here. Among the new features are fish tanks—including one that's interactive—a butterfly garden on the fifth floor (yes, you can walk among the butterflies or let them fly around you), and a seventh-floor view of the city that's unparalleled. Nearby is the **Taubman Museum of Art.** The building, designed by Randall Stout Architects, reflects both the nearby mountains and Stout's training under Frank Gehry.

For more nature, stop by the **Mill Mountain Zoo,** and for another panoramic view of the area, visit the top of **Mill Mountain** where the 100-foot-high **Roanoke Star** is located. Yes, that's the star you see shining down on the city.

The route ends at US 220, at MP 121.4, about 4 miles from downtown Roanoke. The Blue Ridge Parkway continues south, and the section from Roanoke to North Carolina is described in Route 10.

The new butterfly garden on the top floor of the renovated Center in the Square, Roanoke

10

Blue Ridge Parkway South

Roanoke to North Carolina

General description: This 97-mile section of the Blue Ridge Parkway is a paved 2-lane road along the edge of the Blue Ridge plateau with alternating views of mountains, the Piedmont, forests, and nearby farms. Many restorations and exhibits of 18th-century mountain life add to the interest. There are several hikes to points of interest along the route.

Special attractions: The scenic views of woods, farms, and distant vistas are outstanding. The most popular stop is the restored Mabry Mill and waterwheel and other buildings. At Smart View there is a restored mountain cabin and farm by a small lake. Groundhog Mountain contains samples of types of old wooden fences. Although many people treat the parkway as the experience, Ranger Peter S. Givens, interpretive specialist, says, "It's a window to those little communities alongside it where people should browse around the restaurants and craft shops. That's part of why the parkway is here."

Location: South-central Virginia beginning at Roanoke.

Route numbers: There is no route number. The Blue Ridge Parkway is measured with cement markers or mileposts (MP), and distances and attractions are noted in tenths of a mile.

Travel season: Travel is heaviest on weekends during the summer months and in mid-Oct when autumn leaf colors of oak,

hickory, tulip, buckeye, and ash trees are at their most brilliant with fir and spruce providing a constant coniferous background. As they occupy different elevations, the leaves don't turn at the same time offering a cascade of colors. However, the blooming rhododendrons, tulip trees, serviceberries, and dogwoods make spring a wonderful time to visit, too. The parkway is open all year, although some portions may be closed temporarily during winter storms or during times of icing, fog, and snow.

Camping: Camping is available from around May 1 through the end of Oct at Rocky Knob. You can also camp at Fairy Stone State Park, about 24 miles from the exit at Tuggle Gap, MP 165.3.

Services: Gasoline, restaurants, motels, and hotels are abundantly available in Roanoke. Gasoline is not available along the route. A restaurant at Mabry Mill is the only food service along this part of the parkway.

Nearby attractions: The Roanoke area has several points of interest; these are described in Route 9. The towns of Floyd and Galax are famed for their mountain music.

For more information: Blue Ridge Parkway, (540) 767-2492, nps.gov/blri; Virginia's Blue Ridge, (540) 342-6025, visit vablueridge.com; Roanoke Visitor Information, (540) 342-6025, visitroanokeva.com; Blue Ridge Music Center, (276) 236-5309, blueridgemusiccenter.org.

The Route

This 97-mile route follows the Blue Ridge Parkway south from Roanoke to the North Carolina border. The Blue Ridge Parkway is a ridgetop road that stretches 469 miles along the crest of the southern Appalachian Mountains linking

Blue Ridge Parkway South

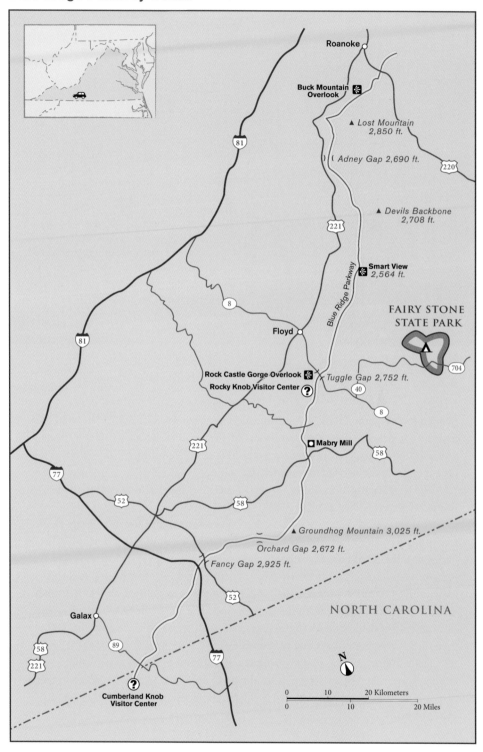

Roanoke

Buck Mountain
Overlook

81

▲ Lost Mountain
2,850 ft.

)(Adney Gap 2,690 ft.   220

▲ Devils Backbone
2,708 ft.

221

Smart View
2,564 ft.

Blue Ridge Parkway

FAIRY STONE
STATE PARK

8

Floyd

704

Rock Castle Gorge Overlook
Rocky Knob Visitor Center

⟨ Tuggle Gap 2,752 ft.

81

40

8

221

■ Mabry Mill

58

77

52

58

▲ Groundhog Mountain 3,025 ft.

Orchard Gap 2,672 ft.

Fancy Gap 2,925 ft.

52

NORTH CAROLINA

Galax

89

N

58

77

221

?
Cumberland Knob
Visitor Center

0   10   20 Kilometers

0   10   20 Miles

Even on a rainy day, there's peace and serenity along the Blue Ridge Parkway.

Shenandoah National Park in Virginia and Great Smoky Mountains National Park and the Cherokee Indian Reservation in North Carolina. Because of the terrain and winding roads, you are best served not using GPS routing for directions. Pick up a map from an information center or online.

The northern section of the Virginia portion of the parkway is described in Route 9.

This section of the route follows the high eastern rim of the Blue Ridge escarpment past farms, woods, and small towns. Much of the land bordering the parkway is leased to farmers or privately owned, with crops growing almost to the right-of-way. The farms alternate with open areas and lush forests of pines and hardwoods. Old rail fences line the road in many places, with century-old log cabins and modern farmhouses in the background. The road climbs to the top of the escarpment for distant views of the Piedmont and Appalachian Mountains and then dips through low gaps and broad valleys.

The winding, 2-lane, paved road has a speed limit of 45 miles per hour although you may want to drive more slowly to enjoy the views. Or others in front of you may want to drive more slowly. Be patient and appreciate Mother Nature at her finest.

Frequent scenic turnouts or overlooks are noted with a sign indicating it is coming up and whether it's on the right or the left. The overlook should appear within a quarter mile of the sign. An apology is extended if a sign is missing; parkway staff are at work to replace those that go missing. Once you pull into the overlook, you'll see a sign with the name of the overlook, what you're looking at, elevation, and any other interesting facts.

Some of the overlooks only provide forest vistas rather than the details the designers had in mind in the 1930s and '40s. Sometimes trees encroach between the regular cutbacks made on public land, but other trees may be on private land where nothing can be done about them.

Senator Harry F. Byrd (D-VA) suggested the creation of the parkway to President Franklin D. Roosevelt in the early 1930s. Construction started in 1935 and wasn't complete until 52 years when the last 7-mile section, around Grandfather Mountain (near the Linn Cove Viaduct) in North Carolina, was completed in 1987. The parkway was designed to harmonize with the natural beauty of the mountains and to preserve the historical and cultural features of the area, long a home to mountain farmers and hunters. The popularity of the route probably far exceeds anything Senator Byrd envisioned: More than 15 million people visited some portion of the parkway in 2012, making it the most visited site in the National Park System.

The Blue Ridge Parkway is maintained by the National Park Service. All plants and animals are protected. There is no fee, and you can enter and leave the parkway at numerous intersections. Commercial vehicles are not permitted. Pets must be on a leash or in your arms in public areas.

Roanoke to Smart View

The route starts outside Roanoke at MP 121.4 at the junction of US 220 where Route 9 ends. If you haven't visited the Roanoke area or taken Route 9, you may want to refer to it for points of interest in **Roanoke** and north along the parkway in the Roanoke area. Other access roads between Roanoke and the parkway are VA 24 at MP 112 and US 460 at MP 105.

Head south on the parkway, along the valley of the Roanoke River. At the **Buck Mountain Overlook,** MP 123.2, a 0.5-mile trail leads to the summit and a scenic, albeit urban, view of southern Roanoke.

Then begins the long climb up the Blue Ridge escarpment. Several turnouts provide views of the Roanoke Valley. Perhaps the best is at **Lost Mountain** or the Roanoke Valley Overlook, MP 129.9, where in one direction you can see the spine of the Blue Ridge, and in the other, the parallel ridges of the Valley and Ridge province. Nobody seems to know why this peak is called Lost Mountain. The mountain isn't lost, just the reason for its name.

In the frequent open areas are fields where cattle and horses graze. Farmers till the rolling fields planted in corn, soybean, oats, and other crops with their homes, silos, and barns nearby. Timeless dirt roads, looking much as they did 100 years ago, parallel and cross the parkway, perhaps leading you to envision couples holding hands in a horse and carriage.

In other places forests of pine, oak, hickory, and birch surround the roadway, along with thick growths of flame azaleas, rhododendrons, dogwoods, geraniums, and mountain laurel. The result is a feeling that the parkway belongs here, that it fits in with the scenery and history of this peaceful land.

The **Smart View Recreation Area,** MP 154.5, has picnic grounds by a small pond. A short trail takes you to an 1890s log cabin where you'll see "a right smart" view. The 1-room cabin itself, with its rough-cut logs, garden, and nearby spring, is typical of many mountain dwellings and was lived in until the 1920s. The Park Service suggests an early May visit when the dogwoods are in bloom.

Tuggle Gap to Mabry Mill

At **Tuggle Gap,** MP 165.3, VA 8 leads 6 miles north to **Floyd,** long famed as a mountain music center. (See information about the Blue Ridge Music Center at MP 213.) The parkway actively participates in these music programs, helping to preserve this cultural and entertaining heritage.

VA 8 also leads east 24 miles from Tuggle Gap to **Fairy Stone State Park.** The "fairy stones" are twinned crystals of the mineral staurolite, which intersect to form a cross. No fairy story, however, was a 50-pound channel catfish caught in the park's lake. The park also features a campground, swimming, and boating.

Back on the parkway, when you approach the **Rocky Knob Visitor Center,** you'll see rocks along the road standing almost straight up around MPs 167–69. They reminded some old-timers of the fins on the back of a fish. So these are known as **The Fins:** Actually they are erosional remnants of schist and gneiss rocks that were folded almost vertically.

At MP 168.8 is an imposing view of **Rock Castle Gorge.** You can hike into the gorge on a strenuous, 7-mile loop trail or just stretch your legs on several shorter walks. The **Rocky Knob Recreation Area** also has a campground, rental cabins, and ranger-led programs. The cabins, and much of the roads and trails, were built by youths enrolled in the Civilian Conservation Corps, a government program that provided employment during the Depression.

Mabry Mill, MP 176.1, is the best-known and probably most frequently photographed spot on the entire parkway. It was built by E. B. Mabry in 1910 and remained in operation as a gristmill, sawmill, and blacksmith shop until 1935. Mabry left the coal mines of West Virginia in 1908 to work as a blacksmith. As his

Beautiful old rustic Mabry Mill in spring with rhododendrons blooming
©JUDY KENNAMER/SHUTTERSTOCK.COM

fortunes increased, he built the mill where he ground meal and sawed logs for his mountain neighbors.

The waterwheel still turns and the mill still grinds today. You can sample the output with purchases of mill-ground cornmeal and buckwheat. Other exhibits show pioneer workshops of tanners, blacksmiths, shoemakers, and other crafts-people. During summer and fall, frequent demonstrations bring to life old-time skills. A gift shop and restaurant are nearby.

Groundhog Mountain to Cumberland Knob

At **Groundhog Mountain,** MP 188.8, a lookout tower fashioned like a tobacco barn provides a 360-degree view. And if you've been wondering about the differ-ent types of wooden fences you've been seeing, look closely at the three kinds dis-played here: snake, buck, and post and rail.

At **Orchard Gap,** MP 193.7, several trees from an old apple orchard are still standing. Others have been replaced by a cluster of houses. Many old graveyards, big and small, are scattered through the woods and hills. Some are abandoned, while others are tended with care and reverence by present-day descendants.

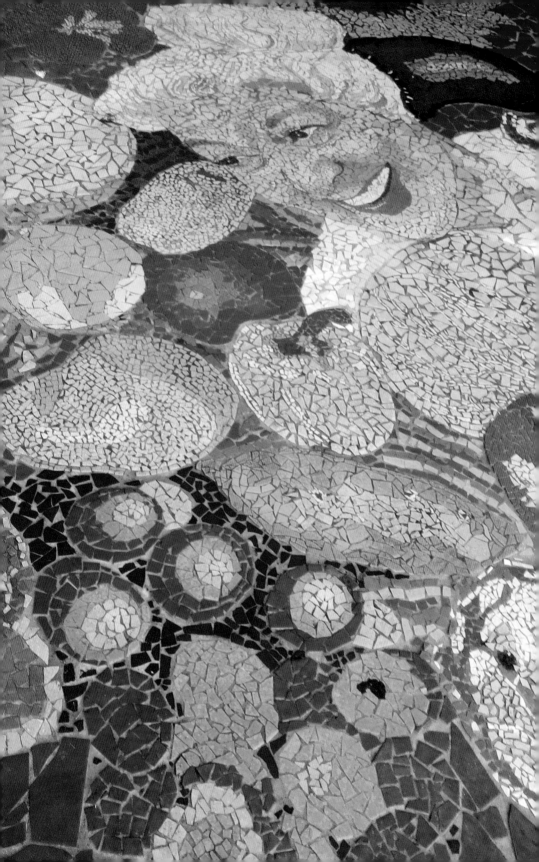

Most are hidden from the route, tucked away in hollows. Some headstones are a simple rock slab with a knife-scratched inscription and some are more elaborately sculpted memorials. A graveyard of the simple kind can be seen at MP 196.8.

The **Blue Ridge Music Center** at MP 213 celebrates the music and musicians from this area with a museum and an outdoor amphitheater. It was established by the US Congress in 1997, and the visitor center provides an indoor interpretive center that highlights this unique American musical culture. There's information for your mind, and trails provide stimulation for your body. Check the website for information about opening times, events, and the trails.

The last exit in Virginia is for VA 89 at MP 215. The town of **Galax** lies 7 miles north on VA 89. Galax is another famed center for mountain music. You can hear those fiddles playing almost any weekend, with the music building to a crescendo the second weekend each August when the town overflows with both people and music for the **Old Fiddlers' Convention.** This has been an annual event since 1935.

You leave Virginia and enter North Carolina at MP 216.9. The boundary was first surveyed in 1749 by a party that included mapmaker Peter Jefferson, Thomas Jefferson's father.

The **Cumberland Knob Visitor Center,** with trails to Cumberland Knob, is just a little bit farther down the road, at MP 217.9. The visitor center and 12 miles of drive south of here opened in 1936; it was the first completed section of the parkway.

From here, you can reverse direction and go north into Virginia, or continue on the Blue Ridge Parkway into North Carolina.

Newly created mosaics welcome shoppers to the downtown Roanoke market area.

11

Fredericksburg & Spotsylvania Battlefields

A Civil War Tour

General description: This is a 40-mile, historical route through four Civil War major battlefields preserved in the Fredericksburg and Spotsylvania National Military Park. The route covers the Fredericksburg Battlefield on the outskirts of Fredericksburg, and the Chancellorsville, Wilderness, and Spotsylvania Court House battlefields west of Fredericksburg. The region is one of flat or gently rolling land with a mixture of open fields and hardwood, second-growth forests.

Special attractions: The Civil War battlefields themselves are the main points of interest, with their maps, exhibits, explanations, and tours.

Location: The battlefields and route are both in Fredericksburg and west of town within a 15-mile radius. Fredericksburg is in eastern Virginia about 50 miles south of Washington, DC, and 60 miles north of Richmond on I-95.

Route numbers: US Business 1; VA 638, 636, 208, 613, 621, 3, 610, and 20; and several local roads within the battlefields.

Travel season: All year.

Services: Motels, restaurants, and gasoline are available in Fredericksburg and along VA 3 west of Fredericksburg.

Nearby attractions: Fredericksburg, George Washington's hometown for many years, has numerous restored colonial buildings.

For more information: Fredericksburg Department of Economic Development and Tourism, (540) 372-1216 or (800) 260-2646, visitfred.com; Fredericksburg Welcome Center, (540) 786-8344, virginia .org; Economic Development Spotsylvania County, (540) 507-7210, spotsylvania.org; Battle of Fredericksburg Visitor Center, (540) 373-6122, nps.gov/frsp; Chancellorsville Battlefield Visitor Center, (540) 786-2880, nps.gov/frsp; History of Wilderness and Spotsylvania, (540) 373-6124, nps.gov/frsp; John J. Wright Educational and Cultural Center, (540) 682-7583, jjw museum.org.

The Route

This 40-mile loop tours the four battlefields—Fredericksburg, Chancellorsville, Wilderness, and Spotsylvania Court House—preserved in the Fredericksburg and Spotsylvania National Military Park in Fredericksburg and vicinity. The route begins and ends in Fredericksburg and extends west of the city about 15 miles. The country outside the city is gently rolling with a mixture of open fields and farms, hardwood forests, rural houses, and suburban housing.

To make the route as scenic as possible, the battlefields are not visited in chronological order, and the route varies from the self-guiding tours set up by the

Fredericksburg and Spotslvania Battlefields

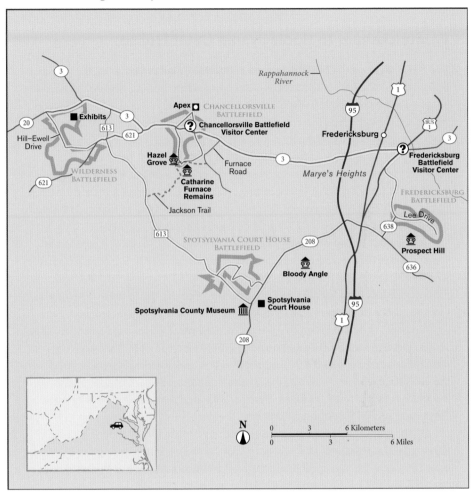

National Park Service, which pass through several shopping mall areas. If you are a Civil War buff whose main interest is history and battle strategy, you will probably prefer to follow the detailed, more direct, and less scenic, route laid out by the Park Service.

Fredericksburg, home of University of Mary Washington, has many restored colonial homes, including 300 original buildings constructed before 1870. More than 100 predate the Civil War. Fredericksburg was also the hometown of the Washington family, including George, his mother, sister, and brother; some restored buildings were Washington family residences. Fredericksburg is also the starting point for Route 12, the Northern Neck, and is described in more detail in that route.

Fredericksburg to Spotsylvania Court House

The route begins at the **Fredericksburg Battlefield Visitor Center** on the outskirts of the city. At the start of the Civil War the town was a bustling port on the Rappahannock River with a population of about 5,000. Its prime location, halfway between the federal capital at Washington, DC, and the Confederate capital at Richmond, made it a strategic Civil War target for both sides. Over a 2-year period more than 600,000 men fought here in four major battles; more than 100,000 died.

The visitor center features audiovisual programs, exhibits, detailed maps, battle tour information, and publications. A small fee is charged for the 20-minute film. Outside the visitor center you can walk up the short hill to **Mary's Heights,** now a national cemetery for 15,000 Civil War soldiers.

In the **First Battle of Fredericksburg,** December 11–13, 1862, Confederate General Robert E. Lee successfully fought off the invading federal troops. This battle gave Lee his most one-sided victory of the war, with a high price: 12,000 Union and 5,000 Confederate troops died in this conflict, prompting Lee to make his famous remark, "It is well that war is so terrible—else we should grow too fond of it."

To begin the actual route, turn right on Business US 1 as you leave the visitor center. Go about a half-mile and turn left on Lee Drive to enter the battlefield. For 4 miles the route follows the 7-mile, sinuous line of Confederate trenches dug for the 1862 engagement. Although the area surrounding the park is now urbanized, the route passes through hardwood groves with abundant rhododendron bushes. Exhibits at several turnoffs help interpret the site.

At the stop sign cross VA 638 and continue on Lee Drive. It dead-ends at a parking area at **Prospect Hill,** where the federal troops broke through the Confederate line. You can also see the 20-foot-high **Southern Memorial Pyramid** built after the war to be visible from the adjacent railroad.

Turn around and retrace your steps about 2 miles to the stop sign. Turn left on VA 638, go less than a mile, and turn right on VA 636. VA 636 meanders through suburbia, crossing US 1, to a traffic light at VA 208, also known as Court House Road. Turn left on 4-lane VA 208 toward Spotsylvania Court House.

The houses soon thin out, replaced by woods, cattle farms, and barns as you drive over gently rolling ground. About 4 miles from the traffic light, you pass a narrow road on the right. This is the exit for the one-way loop through the **Spotsylvania Court House Battlefield;** you will pass this spot again after touring the battlefield.

Turn left on Business VA 208 for the Historic District, on the left, and, just before the town of Spotsylvania Court House (sometimes known simply as Spotsylvania), is a Confederate cemetery holding the remains of about 570 Confederate soldiers killed in the fighting around Spotsylvania. The town is known as the "Crossroads of the Civil War" and has several historic spots to visit.

Confederate cemetery headstones
©STEVE HEAP/SHUTTERSTOCK.COM

TO THE CONFEDERATE DEAD

VA 208 ends in town at a T-intersection with VA 613. Turn right and go approximately 0.5 mile and turn right again onto Old Battlefield Boulevard. The **John J. Wright Educational and Cultural Center, the Historic Courthouse, Old Jail,** and **Spotsylvania Museum** are historic attractions here.

When you leave the museum, turn right on VA 613 and continue past the intersection with VA 208. Turn right in about a mile at the entrance to the **Spotsylvania Court House Battlefield** and go to the exhibit shelter on the left. The **Battle of Spotsylvania** took place in May 1864, after the stalemate at the Wilderness Battlefield a few days earlier. (You will pass through the Wilderness Battlefield later on this route.) Spotsylvania Court House was a 14-day fight ending in defeat for Lee and the Confederate troops. It was a major step in Grant's drive south leading to Lee's surrender at Appomattox less than a year later. (Route 16, Lee's Retreat, covers this final Civil War campaign.) Maps and displays help explain the complex military maneuvers during the 2-week battle. The exhibit shelter is also the starting point for a 7-mile walking tour of the battlefield.

From the exhibits continue for about a mile to the parking area at the **Bloody Angle,** scene of some of the most ferocious fighting of the entire war. During a 23-hour battle May 12–13, 1864, Grant's troops captured 20 cannons and most of a Confederate division. In brutal, face-to-face engagement, men fired at point-blank range and slaughtered each other with bayonets and clubs. During the intense fighting, an oak tree 22 inches in diameter was cut down by the deadly hail of small-arms fire.

The Bloody Angle today consists of rolling, pastoral fields and quiet woods. A few Confederate trenches and interpretive signs are the only reminders of its savage history where more than 20,000 soldiers died. From the parking lot you can cover the entire battlefield in a 30-minute walking tour; folders are available at the site.

The route through the battle area winds past woods and open fields. Spurs lead to the trenches at **Lee's Final Line** and the site of several houses used as headquarters during the battle. The road curves and leads to **East Angle** for another view of Bloody Angle.

Sporadic fighting continued at Spotsylvania until May 21, 1864, when Grant pulled his troops out and began his drive south, toward Richmond, Petersburg, and the war's end at Appomattox.

Past East Angle the road becomes one-way. Follow it under overhanging trees to the stop sign at VA 208. Turn right on VA 208. This is the part of the route that is repeated. Follow VA 208 to the T-intersection at VA 613 in the town of Spotsylvania Court House. Turn right. Continue straight on VA 613 this time, past the entrance to Spotsylvania Court House Battlefield.

Chancellorsville and Wilderness Battlefields to Fredericksburg

Follow winding VA 613 through wooded glens for about 7 miles and turn right at the intersection with VA 621, known in Civil War days as the Orange Plank Road. VA 621 ends in about 2 miles at 4-lane VA 3. Turn right on VA 3 for 1 mile and turn left into the visitor center at the entrance to **Chancellorsville Battlefield.**

Maps and detailed battle descriptions are available at the visitor center. The **Battle of Chancellorsville** in May 1863 was the South's greatest victory, when Lee defeated Union General Joseph Hooker by a brilliant flanking attack. During the battle Confederate General Thomas Jonathan "Stonewall" Jackson, returning from the front, was mistakenly shot by his own troops. Jackson's left arm was amputated below the shoulder, and he was so weakened by his wounds that he developed pneumonia and died a few days later. His arm is supposedly buried beneath a low stone monument behind Ellwood Manor at the Fredericksburg and Spotsylvania National Military Park. The rest of him is buried in the Stonewall Jackson Memorial Cemetery, under a statue of him surround by wrought-iron fencing, in Lexington, Virginia.

When you leave the visitor center, follow the one-way road through stands of redbud and rhododendron to the **Apex,** site of Hooker's last line. Turn right on VA 610. At the stop sign at VA 3, VA 610 passes the site of the Chancellorsville Inn, a popular pub and meeting place before the Civil War, and used as headquarters by General Hooker.

Cross VA 3 and go about a mile on VA 610 to unnumbered Furnace Road. Turn right on Furnace Road, which follows the route of **Jackson's Flank March.** Soon you come to the **Catharine Furnace Ruins,** site of an early 19th-century iron foundry. Although closed before the Civil War, it was reopened to manufacture Confederate munitions. On the morning of May 2, 1863, Confederate General Stonewall Jackson's corps began a roundabout all-day march to the Union army's right flank, which would end in a Confederate victory in the Battle of Chancellorsville. As his men crossed over a ridge near Catherine Furnace, Jackson became aware that they were being watched by the enemy from the high ground at **Hazel Grove.** Ordering a regiment to be detached, he instructed it "to guard the flank of the column in motion against a surprise, and call, if necessary, upon any officer whose command was passing for reinforcements." The furnace, although protected that day, would be destroyed by federal troops in 1864.

Turn right at Catharine Furnace. Bear left at the intersection, passing the cannons at Hazel Grove. Because trees and heavy underbrush covered much of the area, artillery was infrequently used. At the open ground in Hazel Grove,

Confederate troops took over the area from retreating federals and opened fire on the Northern troops.

Across the highway from the Chancellorsville Visitor Center, turn left on VA 3. Go about 2 miles and turn left on VA 20, which enters the **Wilderness Battlefield.** Drive about 1.3 miles to the exhibits for a detailed explanation of this encounter.

The **Battle of the Wilderness,** in early May 1864, was the first time Grant and Lee met in combat. It ended in an apparent stalemate. The battle gets its name from the thick underbrush and dense thickets that obscured views for both troops. In the heavy woods, confused troops could not tell friend from foe. Inexperienced and frightened soldiers fired at the slightest provocation, real or perceived, and many soldiers were killed by their own side. Muzzle flashes from the guns set the woods on fire, resulting in severe and often fatal burns on both sides. A 2-mile-loop walking trail from the shelter traverses much of the battle area, with several views of earthworks constructed by Union soldiers.

Continue down VA 20 for a few hundred feet when you leave the shelter, and turn left on Hill-Ewell Drive. You will notice numerous Confederate trenches beside the road. Turn left at the stop sign at VA 621.

Although the Battle of the Wilderness was a draw, Grant and Lee met again a few days later at Spotsylvania Court House 8 miles to the south, already described in this route. The route continues on VA 621 to the stop sign at VA 3.

Turn right on VA 3, passing the Chancellorsville Visitor Center again and leaving the battlefield area. Follow VA 3 about 10 miles to Fredericksburg. The last few miles pass by several malls and shopping centers. Cross I-95 and proceed into Fredericksburg.

This chimney is all that remains of Catharine Furnace, a Confederate munitions plant, which was destroyed by Union troops in 1864 during the Battle of the Wilderness.

12

Northern Neck

Fredericksburg to Reedville

General description: The Northern Neck is the stretch of land extending east of Fredericksburg between the Rappahannock and Potomac Rivers. From Fredericksburg this 70-mile route follows the shoreline of the wide tidewater Potomac, past several stops of historical, scenic, and ecological interest, to end at Reedville, a fishing village on the shores of Chesapeake Bay. Along the way you'll pass through gently rolling farmland and woods, with frequent views of inlets and bays. Beach walking, historic mansions, and old fishing villages may all be of interest.

Special attractions: Historic sites include the George Washington Birthplace National Monument (and the Memorial House constructed in 1931), the birthplace of James Monroe and Stratford Hall, and the aristocratic mansion of the Lee family and birthplace of Robert E. Lee. At Westmoreland State Park are swimming, canoeing, kayaking, camping, and picnicking along the Potomac. Beach walks give striking views of the Horsehead Cliffs and the opportunity to search for fossil whale bones and sharks' teeth. At both Westmoreland and Caledon State Park, you have a chance to see bald eagles. As you approach Chesapeake Bay, you can ride on a free two-car ferry in Lancaster or Northumberland Counties and visit the fishing villages of Kinsale and Reedville, debarkation point for several popular boating trips to Smith and Tangier Islands in the Chesapeake Bay islands.

Location: East-central Virginia. The route starts in Fredericksburg near exit 130 of I-95, about 45 miles south of Washington, DC, and concludes in Reedville on the shores of Chesapeake Bay.

Route numbers: The main route follows US 360, VA Business 3, 218, 205, 3, 202, 604, 640, 646, 644, and 657. Side trips, mostly short spurs to points of interest, follow VA 696, 205Y, 204, 347, 214, and 203.

Travel season: All year. The hardwood forests are very colorful in autumn; spring brings flowering dogwood and other plants. Summer is the heavy travel season, and crowds can be expected on weekends at some beaches and attractions. Snow is rare; the bare winter trees provide long views not visible when leaves are on the trees. However, some attractions have reduced hours in winter.

Camping: Westmoreland State Park has a variety of campsites, many with RV hookups, and Civilian Conservation Corps–era cabins. Belle Isle State Park in Lancaster County on the Rappahannock River also has RV campsites. Private campgrounds are available in Fredericksburg, Colonial Beach, Coles Point, Warsaw, and Reedville.

Services: Motels, restaurants, and gasoline are available in Fredericksburg, Colonial Beach, Montross, Warsaw, Kilmarnock, and most villages along the route.

Nearby attractions: Menokin, the home of Francis Lightfoot Lee, signer of the Declaration of Independence, is located outside of Warsaw and has hiking trails to Cat Point Creek. Historic Christ Church in Weems, outside of Irvington, is an excellent example of a well-preserved colonial church. Morattico Waterfront Museum interprets the story of the Chesapeake Bay watermen within a 1901 general store. The wineries along the Chesapeake Wine Trail offer historic sites along with wine tastings and gift shops. Route 11, Fredericksburg and Spotsylvania Battlefields, is a Civil War tour.

Northern Neck

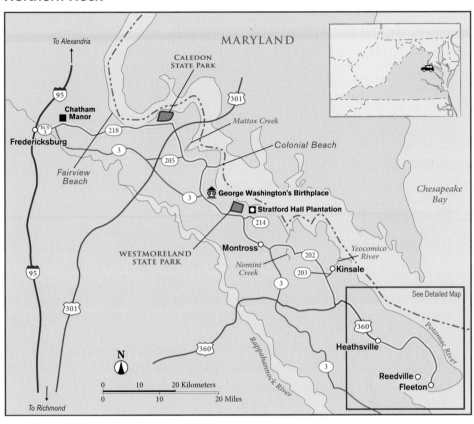

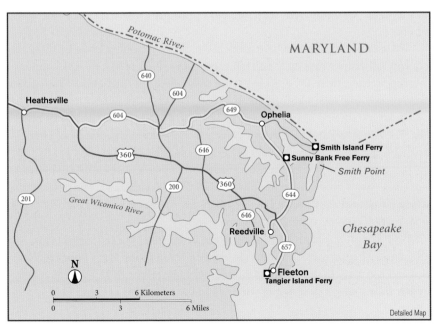

Detailed Map

For more information: Northern Neck Tourism Commission, (804) 333-1919, northernneck.org; George Washington Birthplace National Monument, (804) 224-1732, nps.gov/gewa; James Monroe Birthplace, (804) 214-9145, monroefoun dation.org; Stratford Hall, (804) 493-8038, stratfordhall.org; Menokin, (804) 333-1776, menokin.org; Morattico Waterfront Museum, morattico.org; Reedville Fishermen's Museum, (804) 453-6529, rfmuseum.org; Caledon, Westmoreland and Belle Isle State Parks, dcr.virginia.gov; Coles Point, (804) 472-4011, colespointmarina.com; Chesa peake Bay Wine Trail, (804) 435-6092, chesapeakebaywinetrail.com; Colonial Beach, (804) 224-7181, colonialbeachva .net; The Inn at Montross, (804) 493-8624, theinnatmontross.com.

The Route

The Northern Neck east of Fredericksburg is a peninsula running generally north-west to southeast, bordered by the Potomac River to the north and the Rappahan-nock River to the south as they feed into Chesapeake Bay. From Fredericksburg, it stretches southeast some 70 miles to the shores of the bay. The Virginia Indians fished, farmed, and hunted here for centuries before European exploration and settlement.

In the early 1600s explorer John Smith sailed up both the Potomac and Rap-pahannock Rivers. White settlers soon followed, to the detriment of the Virginia Indians, many of whom quickly succumbed to European diseases and firearms, while the white settlers flourished. The flat, rich farmland, moderate climate, and access to ocean travel made the area a major stop for trading ships during colonial days, and the Northern Neck soon became a most prosperous region in the new continent.

The families who settled here produced many outstanding leaders. Along the way you will visit or pass by the birthplaces of several signers of the Declaration of Independence, three US presidents, the commander in chief of the Confederate army, plus several lesser-known notables.

Today nature and beauty are as important to the Northern Neck as its his-tory. The two rivers and their scenic cliffs provide water recreation of all kinds, fossil hunting, and a home for bald eagles and other birds. The land's gently roll-ing, sandy surface supports extensive hardwood forests and open fields alternating with small towns, many looking much as they did 200 years ago. The peninsula's eastern end lies along Chesapeake Bay where the economy is based on nearly equal parts of commercial fishing and recreation.

Before or after this route, you may want to see some of Fredericksburg's attractions. The town was an important port in colonial and Revolutionary War days and has more than 300 original buildings built before 1870; more than 100 predate the extensive destruction wrought on the town during the Civil War.

Marinas line the shores along the coast of the Northern Neck

Places of interest in Fredericksburg include the Hugh Mercer Apothecary Shop, restored to its 1771 elegance, and the Rising Sun Tavern, the town's social and political gathering place, built by George Washington's younger brother, Charles. Fredericksburg was hometown in later years to the Washington family, including George, his mother, sister, and brother. Current residents like to claim that "George Washington slept in many places, but he lived here." The town is also the starting point for Route 11, Fredericksburg and Spotsylvania Battlefields.

Fredericksburg to Colonial Beach

To begin the route, from downtown Fredericksburg take VA Business 3 east across the Rappahannock River bridge. Turn left a few hundred yards beyond the bridge on VA 218.

As the road climbs steeply from the river bottom, you pass the entrance on the left to **Chatham Manor,** a unit of Fredericksburg and Spotsylvania National Military Park. The mansion, which was used as a command post and hospital during the Civil War, has a sweeping view of Fredericksburg and the Rappahannock River.

View of the Potomac River from Colonial Beach
©DASHINGSTOCK/SHUTTERSTOCK.COM

A designated Virginia Byway, 2-lane VA 218 curves its way gently up and down through pines and open fields. About 12 miles from Fredericksburg, turn left on Fairview Drive which leads in about a mile to **Fairview Beach,** a small swimming and picnic area on the banks of the Potomac River. The Potomac here is a tidewater estuary with the Maryland shore visible about 2 miles across the water.

Retrace your route back to VA 218 and turn left. Eight miles on the left is **Caledon State Park**, a National Natural Landmark known for old-growth forest and summer home to one of the largest concentrations of American bald eagles on the East Coast. They in turn attract a huge birder population that is fascinated and entertained by the visiting eagles. Although some eagles are year-round residents, they are most numerous during the spring and summer nesting season along the Potomac's shores when fish are readily available. From October through March, you can hike the 3.5-mile, self-guided **Boyd's Hole Trail** at Caledon State Park, which leads to the Potomac and provides a good chance to see some resident eagles. The trails are open all year, but access to marshes, some trails, and areas along the Potomac may be restricted to protect the eagle habitat. Owl Prowling and Eagle Tours are offered year-round. The park also has a small visitor center with bald eagle exhibits and restrooms. Several picnic tables are adjacent to the parking area.

Continue on VA 218, bearing left where it is joined by VA 206. Stay on VA 218 and cross 4-lane US 301. In a few miles you cross picturesque Machodoc Creek, one of several tidewater inlets.

James Madison, our country's fourth president, was born a few miles to the south in 1751; also nearby is the house where John Wilkes Booth was killed when he fled from Washington, DC, after assassinating President Abraham Lincoln.

VA 218 and this Virginia Byway section end at the junction with VA 205. Go left on VA 205. In the resort town of **Colonial Beach,** turn left on VA 205Y to reach the beach, the second-longest public beach in the state. If you walk along the beach and look left, you may see the 1.7-mile-long Harry W. Nice (US 301) bridge across the Potomac River about 5 miles upstream.

Colonial Beach to Washington's Birthplace

Retrace VA 205Y to VA 205 and go left. Less than a mile from town you pass the **birthplace of James Monroe,** where there is a monument and small visitor center dedicated to our fifth president. The unpaved dirt turnout, marked by a simple sign and small obelisk, are a sharp contrast to the extensive and detailed memorials to George Washington and Robert E. Lee you will pass later on the route.

James Monroe was born here in 1758 and left when he was 16 to enter William and Mary College. He served in the Revolutionary War and then held a variety of government positions, including a brief term as governor of Virginia. In 1816 he was elected US president, serving two terms. He is best known for the Monroe Doctrine, which declared that the Americas were no longer open to colonization by foreign countries. Unfortunately, there are no remnants of the Monroe family home.

The route crosses a short causeway over Mattox Creek, another tidal inlet. A mile beyond that, VA 205 ends at the traffic light and junction with VA 3. Turn left (south) on VA 3.

The next 10 miles along VA 3 may be slow driving—not on account of traffic, but because the scenery is worth enjoying.

Turn left on VA 204 to visit **George Washington Birthplace National Monument.** This memorial preserves Washington's birthplace. He was born here February 22, 1732, into a family of prosperous planters and farmers. Although no original buildings survive, modern reconstructions of a memorial house, kitchen house, dairy, and other farm buildings help to give a sense of genteel Tidewater colonial farm life.

Slaves helped raise the main crops of tobacco, corn, and wheat. They also worked at growing other vegetables and raising farm animals for meat and hides. The location on the banks of Popes Creek, at its outlet into the Potomac River, gave access to the river highway and outside world.

As you drive onto the grounds, you are greeted by a miniature Washington Monument. The visitor center overlooks Popes Creek and is surrounded by spacious groves of mature hardwood trees. Costumed interpreters demonstrate colonial farming techniques and domestic tasks, from tobacco cultivation to soap making. The area also includes a family burial ground, picnic area, and short nature trail.

Throughout his life Washington was drawn to the Virginia side of the Potomac River, and he returned to this area whenever his busy career and obligations permitted. His mother, Mary Ball Washington, was born in Lancaster County, and Washington lived at Popes Creek for the first two and a half years of his life, at which time his father moved the family up the Potomac to what is now known as Mount Vernon. He also lived at Popes Creek frequently during his early teen years, when the area was farmed by his half-brother, Augustine. For most of his working life Washington's home was in Fredericksburg; the city, as we have seen, claims to be Washington's hometown. His retirement years were spent at Mount Vernon (Route 3).

Washington always considered himself to be a farmer and planter first; his other occupations—surveyor and soldier, politician and president—were temporary interruptions in his chosen field. The site is open all year.

Washington's Birthplace to Reedville

Return to VA 3 and turn left. In a few miles you come to VA 347 and the entrance to **Westmoreland State Park.** Most of the park is set on top of the 40-foot-high Horsehead Cliffs on the Potomac. Be sure to drive down the mini-canyons to reach the shore area, where you can walk along the beach and search for fossil shark teeth, whale bones, shells, and other marine animals.

The fossils are found in unconsolidated sediments of gravel, sand, silt, and clay that dip gently to the east. Similar deposits are found throughout the Northern Neck. The sediments here were deposited about 12 million years ago during the Miocene epoch. At that time the eastern margin of North America was still covered by the Atlantic Ocean; the ancestors of today's rivers and streams dumped large amounts of debris from the eroding Appalachian Mountains into the shallow waters. The better-known and somewhat higher Calvert Cliffs area across the Potomac in Maryland has similar deposits and fossils.

The Reedville Watermen's Museum pays tribute to the watermen's way of life over the decades and centuries.

Westmoreland State Park also features canoeing, kayaking, fishing, swimming, picnicking, and camping in season, and several short hiking trails. A Discovery Center houses numerous exhibits, including representative fossils. A fee is charged during the warmer months.

Return to VA 3 and again turn left, traveling a few miles to VA 214 and the entrance to **Stratford Hall,** home of the Lees of Virginia and Confederate General Robert E. Lee's birthplace. Stratford Hall was built in the late 1730s by Thomas Lee, a successful planter. It was also home to Thomas Lee's eight children. Two sons, Richard Henry Lee and Francis Lightfoot Lee, were the only brothers to sign the Declaration of Independence.

Their cousin, "Light Horse Harry" Lee, who also lived at Stratford Hall, was a friend of George Washington, a Revolutionary War hero, governor of Virginia, and father of Robert Edward Lee, who later became the Confederate army's leading general.

The Georgian-style brick manor, with its twin, imposing clusters of chimneys, has been carefully restored and maintained. The Great Hall in the center has been designated one of the most beautiful rooms in America. Visitors can

Eating area at State Park in Montross
©ANDREA CATENARO/SHUTTERSTOCK.COM

see the bedchamber where Robert E. Lee was born. A nonprofit organization, the Robert E. Lee Memorial Association, Inc., maintains the plantation, including a working farm and farm animals, outbuildings, and operating water-powered grist-mill. Several short hiking trails allow you to visit the shoreline and walk through the woods. Admission is charged. A restaurant, visitor center, and gift shop are located on the grounds, and the **Inn at Stratford Hall** has guesthouses for over-night stays.

Once more, return to VA 3 and turn left. At Court House Square in **Montross,** is the old courthouse, originally built in 1707 and now used for special events. Across the street from the courthouse is the **Westmoreland County Museum,** which houses a life-size portrait of William Pitt and other historical exhibits.

Just past Montross at the intersection of VA 3 and VA 202, go left on VA 202. You soon cross **Nomini Creek,** one of many small tidewater creeks here. The country here is flatter and more open, with less woods and more farmland. Numerous small creeks have cut channels into the unconsolidated sediments, causing many 10- to 15-foot dips in the road.

Turn left on VA 203 for a short jaunt to **Kinsale** on the Yeocomico River. In the early 1700s this busy port was responsible for shipping almost one-third of the entire colony's products. The route winds down Steamboat Hill to the still-active wharf. A small, free museum, open during the warmer months, describes the port's early days and its later rise to prominence as a steamboat terminal for voyages to Baltimore and Washington, DC.

Return to VA 202 and turn left. At the intersection with US 360, turn left. US 360 is primarily a 3-lane highway, with occasional 4-lane stretches. The town of **Heathsville** has several restored old buildings including **Rice's Hotel/Hughlett's Tavern**, built in 1795, and a jail (1844), and a courthouse (1851). Other buildings around the tavern exhibit heritage trades performed by active guilds, such as blacksmithing, spinning and weaving, quilting and woodworking.

Continue left on US 360 to leave Heathsville. Stay to the left to keep on US-360 (Northumberland Highway) for nearly 8 miles. Turn left onto Hacks Neck Road and then right onto Folly Road. When you reach Ophelia, turn right onto Ferry Road, aiming toward Sunny Bank Ferry.

One of the state's last free ferries. The 4-car ferry carries you across the Little Wicomico River. Maintained by the Virginia Department of Transportation (VDOT), the ferry runs year-round 7 a.m. to 7 p.m. during daylight hours only. It does not operate on Sunday or during unusually high or low water. (If the ferry is not running, turn around. Backtrack to Ophelia and past it to VA 604 and turn left on VA 604; turn left again on US 360 and follow it to its end in Reedville.)

After the ferry ride, continue on VA 644. At the stop sign on the outskirts of Reedville, turn left on VA 657. To the right, across the waters of Cockrell Creek, you will see the town of Reedville. Follow VA 657 a few miles to **Fleeton.** As you approach town, a sign proclaims that 89 inhabitants and 17 dogs welcome you; the numbers are crossed out and changed whenever there is an addition or subtraction.

The harbor at Fleeton has views of a lighthouse and Chesapeake Bay. The town is primarily laid out in a square with one side facing the bay. Drive around the block to reverse direction, and follow VA 657 back to the intersection with VA 644. Follow VA 644 to US 360 and turn left in Reedville, on the opposite shore of Cockrell Creek, to the route's end.

Reedville was established after the Civil War as a fishing port for menhaden, a small fish now used as a source of fish oil. The fish brought prosperous times to the town and one of the highest per capita incomes in the country in the late 1800s. Wealthy ship captains built rows of Victorian mansions that today line portions of Main Street. Many residences still have widows' walks, small, open porches on the roof where anxious wives scanned the sea hoping to spot their husband's ship returning to port.

View of Tangier Island at dawn
©DAVID KAY/SHUTTERSTOCK.COM

In town is the **Reedville Fishermen's Museum,** open during the warmer months. It tells the story of the menhaden (fish), which are still caught and processed here. The museum also has boatbuilding workshops and displays a Chesapeake Bay skipjack, *Claud Somers,* a workboat, or deadrise, *Elva C.,* and a replica of the John Smith shallop, or sailing barge, *Spirit of 1608.* Nearby are the terminals for the popular tour boats to **Tangier Island,** an old fishing village in the middle of Chesapeake Bay, and to **Smith Island** in the Maryland portion of the bay.

13

Eastern Shore

Maryland Line to Kiptopeke

General description: The Eastern Shore of Virginia is the sandy peninsula between Chesapeake Bay and the Atlantic Ocean. It is a unique blend of land, marsh, and water, known for beaches, historic villages, NASA rockets, seafood, and unique bird and animal life. This 100-mile route covers the peninsula from the Maryland border on the north to the southern tip, meandering back and forth from the Atlantic side to the Chesapeake Bay side. With a little planning you can watch the sunrise over the Atlantic and just a few miles to the west watch the sunset over the Chesapeake on the same day. It's also "country" enough that you'll sometimes find places based on mile markers rather than street addresses.

Special attractions: Chincoteague National Wildlife Refuge and Assateague Island National Seashore make up one of the few unspoiled stretches along the Atlantic shore and are known for birds, beaches, marshlands, ponies, deer, and other features. These provide an interesting contrast with the space and rocket exhibits of NASA. There are numerous little historic towns, sandy beaches, and inlets, with numerous opportunities for boat trips and bird-watching along both Chesapeake Bay and the Atlantic Ocean.

Location: The Virginia portion of the peninsula bordered by Chesapeake Bay and the Atlantic Ocean in the extreme northeast part of the state.

Route numbers: US 13 and Business 13 and more than a dozen numbered state roads, many of which also have local names. Whenever possible, the route is parallel to but stays away from US 13. It's easy enough to navigate back to it should you have a hunger or bathroom emergency.

Travel season: The route can be followed all year long. Bird-watching is excellent all year, and it can be particularly interesting during the spring and autumn migrations when large flocks and occasional rare species are seen. Brilliant autumn leaf colors—mostly maple, oak, and poplar—occur most years. The famous pony roundup the last week of July at Chincoteague attracts enormous crowds; summer crowds at Chincoteague are huge.

Camping: Camping is available at Assateague Island National Seashore near the northern end of the route, and at Kiptopeke State Park near the southern end.

Services: Gasoline, restaurants, and motels are available along US 13 and in the larger towns.

Nearby attractions: Just north of the route is the Maryland portion of Assateague Island National Seashore and Maryland's Assateague State Park and resort beaches. Connecting at the south end of the route are the Chesapeake Bay Bridge-Tunnel, Route 14, and the Norfolk and Virginia Beach areas.

For more information: Eastern Shore of Virginia Tourism Commission, (757) 787-8268, esvatourism.org; Northampton County Chamber of Commerce, (757) 678-0010, northamptoncountychamber.com; Wallops Flight Facility, (757) 824-2050, nasa.gov/centers; Museum of Chincoteague Island, (757) 336-6117, chincoteaguemuseum .com; Eastern Shore Railway Museum, (757) 665-7245, parksley.com; Barrier Islands Center, (757) 678-5550, barrier islandcenter.com; Brownsville Seaside Farm, (757) 442-3049, virginia.org; Chatham Vineyards, (757) 678-5588, chathamvine yards.net; Eastern Shore of Virginia National Wildlife Refuge, (757) 331-3425, fws.gov.

Eastern Shore

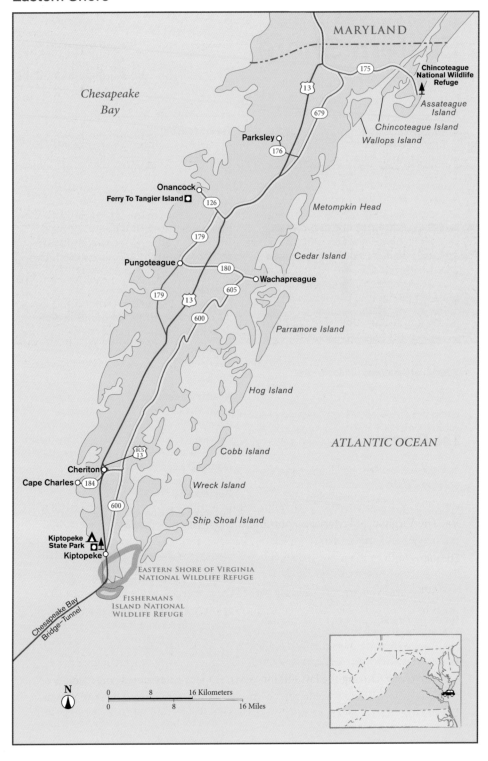

MARYLAND

Chesapeake Bay

Chincoteague National Wildlife Refuge

Assateague Island

Chincoteague Island

Wallops Island

Parksley

Onancock

Ferry To Tangier Island

Metompkin Head

Pungoteague

Wachapreague

Cedar Island

Parramore Island

Hog Island

ATLANTIC OCEAN

Cobb Island

Cheriton

Cape Charles

Wreck Island

Ship Shoal Island

Kiptopeke State Park

Kiptopeke

EASTERN SHORE OF VIRGINIA NATIONAL WILDLIFE REFUGE

FISHERMANS ISLAND NATIONAL WILDLIFE REFUGE

Chesapeake Bay Bridge-Tunnel

N

| 0 | 8 | 16 Kilometers |
| 0 | 8 | 16 Miles |

Bird watching at The National Wildlife Refuge in Chincoteague as a Snowy Egret flies over a marsh.

©DMVPHOTOS/SHUTTERSTOCK.COM

The Route

The Delmarva Peninsula, comprised of portions of Delaware, Maryland, and Virginia, lies between Chesapeake Bay on the west and the Atlantic Ocean on the east. The word "Delmarva" is an abbreviation for the three state names: Del-Mar-Va. The Virginia and Maryland portions are known as the Eastern Shore. From the Maryland/Virginia border, the Virginia part of the Eastern Shore stretches 70 miles south to the mouth of Chesapeake Bay and the Chesapeake Bay Bridge-Tunnel (Route 14).

Wherever you are in Virginia's part of the Eastern Shore, you're within 10 miles of water. The side facing the Atlantic is known as the Seaside; the Chesapeake side is the Bayside.

The land of the Eastern Shore consists of beach deposits and similar offshore loose sediments—mostly sand and mud—left when sea levels were higher than they are today. During the last million years, sea levels fluctuated considerably so that the Eastern Shore was alternately dry land and then covered by shallow seas. During one glacial epoch, so much water was tied up in glacial ice that sea level

was about 450 feet below the current level and the Atlantic shoreline was 60 miles to the east. At that time the major rivers that now form Chesapeake Bay—the Potomac and the Susquehanna—flowed in deep channels to the ocean.

When the last continental glaciers melted some 10,000 years ago, sea levels rose to about the present level, flooding the river valleys and forming Chesapeake Bay as we know it today. The river valleys of what are now the lower James, York, Rappahannock, Potomac, and other rivers that flow into Chesapeake Bay were also flooded, making Chesapeake Bay into the largest estuary in the US.

As with all estuaries, the bay is fed by fresh rivers, streams, and creeks but becomes salty as it meets the Atlantic. There are varying degrees of brackish water in between as the tide and rivers flowing into it change, with corresponding changes in salinity. A slow-moving hurricane or heavy rains can upset the balance as much as a year of little precipitation. Pollution is a constant concern and battle, with parking lot runoff (instead of absorption) as much a problem as lawn and farmland fertilizer deposits. Invasive plants, fish, and diseases also affect the health of the bay and its inhabitants.

The mild climate, abundant food, and level, sandy farmland of the Eastern Shore attracted Native Americans long before the first European settlers arrived in the early 1600s. Despite the long history of human habitation, the Eastern Shore is known today for its miles of unspoiled beaches, marshlands, and wildlife preserves—particularly Chincoteague National Wildlife Refuge and Assateague Island National Seashore—plus historic fishing villages, small towns, and the rockets of Wallops Island.

This 100-mile route can be completed in one day, if you aren't lured into exploration of the bay and the ocean, the beaches and marshes, the birds and other wildlife, and the quaint towns and other attractions.

The route begins at the Maryland-Virginia border on 4-lane US 13 (Charles M. Lankford Memorial Highway) which follows the high ground 35 to 45 feet above sea level down the middle of the peninsula. The route meanders back and forth from the Seaside to the Bayside, tracing the 2-lane roads when possible. Although the side trips may make the driving directions appear complicated because of the many route numbers, road signs will help you to easily find the next town or point of interest. If most of your normal driving life is spent on interstate or divided-limited access highways, you're in for a treat even if you're just taking US 13 and not stopping to see some of the sights on either side of the road. There is no freeway over here. The route passes through a number of little towns as you're driving through history on a road that hasn't changed that much

A wild Chincoteague pony grazing on the Barrier islands
©JORGE MORO/SHUTTERSTOCK.COM

since it became a divided highway. Yes, it carries a huge amount of traffic, and one can consider it a moving window on rural life.

The route ends at the southern tip of the peninsula at the Chesapeake Bay Bridge-Tunnel at the mouth of Chesapeake Bay across from Norfolk and Virginia Beach and the starting point for Route 14.

Maryland/Virginia Line to Chincoteague

From the Maryland border on US 13, you pass through Accomack County, with its flat, sandy farmlands, mixed pine and hardwood forests, plus numerous gas stations, restaurants, and other commercial developments. The 2012 estimated population was just over 33,000, an increase of less than 0.5 percent since 2010, which equates to about 74 people per square mile.

Turn left on VA 175, at the well-marked signs to Chincoteague.

This 2-lane road quickly leaves the commercial bustle of US 13 behind. In 5 miles the road curves to the left and passes an airport runway, part of the federal **Wallops Flight Facility** of the **National Aeronautics and Space Administration (NASA).** On the right is the NASA Visitor Center, unmistakable with the numerous rockets, launchers, and associated space equipment displayed in front. The self-guided tour inside the visitor center includes scale models of satellites, aircraft, and space vehicles, a moon rock, a space suit, and numerous other exhibits. Because you will retrace this part of the route, you can visit NASA now or later, when you return from Chincoteague.

Wallops Island is used for small launches, some by private enterprise; since its inception in 1945 it has sent more than 14,000 rockets and satellites into space. This is a much smaller operation than Florida's Kennedy Space Center, and it's not nearly as conveniently accessible. That's great news because it means it's not nearly as crowded and there's more room for you to explore as much as you want for as long as you want. Since the shuttle program was canceled, the launches from here will deliver supplies to the *International Space Station.* You can watch launches from the visitor center or via webcast.

Driving east from the NASA facility, VA 175 soon curves to the right and becomes a 4-mile causeway over tidal flats, salt marshes, and water. A bridge over the Chincoteague Channel leads you to **Chincoteague Island** and the town of Chincoteague (Indian name for "pretty land across the water"), a pleasant resort town with numerous motels, bed-and-breakfast homes, and shops. The town also has several outstanding seafood restaurants where you can experience the culinary delights of Chesapeake's famed blue crabs and other sea dishes.

Follow VA 175 through town, turning left on Main Street and then right several blocks later on Maddox Boulevard. You pass the **Museum of Chincoteague**

View of the Eastern Shore
©JOMO333/SHUTTERSTOCK.COM

Island, known for its displays about life on the island from prehistory to the present. Look for woolly mammoth fossils, shell fossils, and an 1866 first-order Fresnel lens that lights and keeps the current Assateague Lighthouse light company. Fire engine buffs will delight in the 1880 volunteer fire company hand pumper. The museum is open Tues through Sun Memorial Day through Labor Day and Fri, Sat, and Sun the rest of the year.

Cross another short causeway over the Assateague Channel and you arrive at the entrance station to **Assateague Island National Seashore** and **Chincoteague National Wildlife Refuge**. The area is administered jointly by two federal agencies of the US Department of the Interior: the National Park Service (Assateague Island National Seashore) and the Fish and Wildlife Service (Chincoteague National Wildlife Refuge). A nominal admission fee is charged. Please note that pets are not allowed on the seashore or refuge, even if they are kept in the vehicle.

The area was established as a wildlife refuge in 1943 to protect the winter feeding grounds of thousands of migratory waterfowl. The entire Atlantic coast of

the Eastern Shore, including Chincoteague, lies along the Eastern Flyway, a primary migration route. During spring and fall, millions of birds and hundreds of birders converge on the refuge. At any time of year, you will see numerous herons, egrets, and other wading birds. Shorebird populations, including terns, gulls, and sandpipers, reach their peak in July and August; the thickets and forests are home in summer to numerous warblers and other passerine birds. More than 300 species of birds have been spotted in the refuge.

Even a short visit should allow you to see two kinds of deer (Virginia whitetail and the smaller sika elk), an old lighthouse, mile-long stretches of pristine beach, rolling surf, dunes, and quiet marshlands. In addition to birds, the refuge protects several endangered species, including the Delmarva Peninsula fox squirrel, and the nesting grounds of the piping plover.

You may want to walk or hike along the **Wildlife Trail** or attend a naturalist's talk. Longer hikes away from the developed portions will take you into unspoiled wilderness. Boat trips through the barrier islands and guided wildlife tours are available. Rangers at the entrance station and visitor center can help you plan your visit.

The area's many outstanding features and attractions are often overshadowed by its wild horses, made famous by Marguerite Henry's best-selling children's book, *Misty of Chincoteague*. The widely publicized **pony roundup and swim** are held the last Wednesday of July. Surplus horses are corralled for the occasion and are sent out to swim (safely) across the channel from Assateague Island to Chincoteague Island to be auctioned. In 2012, 67 ponies were sold for an average price of $1,442.16. The high bid was $7,200 and the low bid was $400. Proceeds benefit the Chincoteague Volunteer Fire Department. This event attracts huge crowds and the heaviest traffic of the year.

Chincoteague to Kiptopeke

When you leave the Chincoteague area to continue the route, head west on VA 175, retracing the route over the causeway and past the NASA Visitor Center and airport. Just beyond the air base, turn left on VA 798, Atlantic Road. In a few miles the route number changes to VA 679, but remains Atlantic Avenue, eventually changing to Metompkin Road. VA 679 changes its name again to Fox Grove Road just before the stop sign and intersection with US 13. Cross over the median of 4-lane US 13 and turn left onto the highway.

Assateague lighthouse during the summer season
©MARY TERRIBERRY/SHUTTERSTOCK.COM

Wachapreague pier

Railroad buffs will want to take a side trip to the **Eastern Shore Railway Museum** in the old train station at **Parksley.** The town and museum are a few miles off US 13 to the west on VA 176. The museum features several old railcars and railroad exhibits, including a post office car, a 1947 dining car (with galley), a couple of cabooses, a 1927 Pullman Diplomat, and other items that are sure to kindle fond memories or cause lots of questions from youngsters. Enough local shops and Victorian homes have survived time and tide to warrant the town being considered "quaint" with the "look of a model train village come to life." The **Accomack-Northampton Antique Car Museum** and **Civil War Monument** are nearby.

From Parksley, take Bennett Street toward Dunne Avenue, turning left onto VA 316 S (Greenbush Road) for almost 6 miles. Turn right onto VA 126 W (Fairgrounds Road) for 1.4 miles, then right onto Market Street into **Onancock.**

The town's name comes from Indian for "foggy place," and it's on the Bay-side. Go through town to the wharf and small, picturesque harbor. The wharf is the terminal for the ferry to **Tangier Island,** a lovely unspoiled village in the bay, barely a square mile in land area, accessible only by boat. It's thought that the Pocomoke Indians spent at least summers on the island, long before the English settled in the area. The ferry runs May through September and operates on a first-come, first-boarded basis.

When you leave Onancock, take Market Street toward Crockett Avenue, for 2 miles, then continue on to W. Main Street for 1.3 miles. Take VA 789 (Locust-ville Road) for 2.6 miles and turn right on to VA 605 (Drummondtown Rd) for 3.5 miles. Staying on Route 605 puts you on Curtis Street for a minute, then it's a right onto Finney Street and a left onto Main Street.

You're now in **Wachapreague** ("town by the sea") on the Seaside. The town, which calls itself the "Flounder Capital of the World," is known for its many charter-fishing and sightseeing boat tours. It's as picturesque a boating town as you could imagine, and if the boats have left by the time you arrive, you can still take pictures of seagulls taking their stand on the numerous pilings.

The salt flats, inlets, and barrier islands parallel the shore and stretch for miles into the Atlantic, giving Wachapreague a feeling of openness and gran-deur. Most of these remote islands are owned in part or entirely by The Nature Conservancy and make up the **Virginia Coast Reserve,** which stretches 75 miles from Chincoteague and Wallops Island to Cape Charles at the southern tip of the peninsula.

From Wachapreague, head west on VA 180 West (Main Street) toward Cen-ter Street for about 3 miles. Turn left onto VA 600 (Seaside Road) for about 13 miles until a right onto Mill Street and a right on US 13 North.

You're now in **Nassawadox,** home of the **Barrier Islands Center** (you should be between mile markers 90 and 91). It's set in three buildings that were constructed in 1725, the 1880s, and 1910. Within this history museum and cul-tural center, you should be able to learn everything you want to know about the 23 barrier islands that protect the peninsula from the Atlantic. Check the 7,500-plus artifacts they've gathered; the oral histories they've collected that explain what life was like 70, 80, and 90 years ago; or learn why the low-lying marshes are such a wonderful place for hunting and fishing. Two documentaries have been produced that have aired on PBS, and a children's book about the Hog Island sheep has been published. The sheep are an endangered species that used to roam and forage on the islands.

From here, take US 13 North for a wee bit, turn right onto Rogers Drive and then another right in 0.2 mile with a slight zigzag right and left and you're back on

VA 600 South (Seaside Road). Take it 5 miles to CR 627 (Machipongo Drive) for 1 mile, then a right onto CR 626 and then back north onto US 13.

For a little break, stop at **Chatham Vineyards,** owned and operated by the Wehner family on a farm that has been worked for 4 centuries. Using a high-density, European-style planting, they grow 32,000 chardonnay, merlot, cabernet franc, cabernet sauvignon, and petit verdot vines on 25 acres. Oenophiles should check the website for special events. As you'd expect, you can have a complimentary tour and wine tasting, or you can schedule a winery kayak tour ("Paddle Your Glass Off").

To continue the route, turn around and follow VA 180 about a half-mile to VA 605. Turn left on VA 605, passing through more farmlands and pine forest. In 4 miles turn right on VA 182. After crossing some tidal flats, turn left at the intersection with VA 600, a Virginia Scenic Byway.

Tranquil VA 600 passes by woods and farms with occasional views of the bays and offshore islands along the Atlantic side to the left. VA 600 parallels busy US 13 a few miles to east.

Continue on VA 600 about 15 miles to VA 639, turn right and follow it to the intersection with Business 13, Bayside Road, in Cheriton. Turn left on Business 13. At the traffic light at US 13, go straight, crossing US 13. The highway number changes to VA 184, Stone Road.

Follow VA 184 to the town of **Cape Charles** on the Bayside. As you approach town, be sure to admire the water tower cleverly painted when it was designed in 1992 (and repainted in 2013), to resemble the old Cape Charles lighthouse. At one time Cape Charles was the largest town on the peninsula and the southern terminal of the New York, Philadelphia & Norfolk Railroad. Coal from the mines in the mountains of Virginia and West Virginia was the main cargo. The coal was shipped by rail to Newport News on the southern edge of Chesapeake Bay, transported on barges to Cape Charles, and then up the peninsula to Philadelphia, New York, and other cities along the northeastern seaboard.

You can walk out on the pier or jetty that extends several hundred yards into the water. The town has the only public beach on the peninsula so feel comforted that under normal circumstances the waves just gently lap the shore and your wiggling toes. Consider staying until the spectacular sunset over the bay.

When you leave Cape Charles, retrace your steps back to VA 600: Follow VA 184 to US 13 and Business 13. Turn right on VA 639 in **Cheriton.** At the first intersection with VA 600, turn right (south) to continue the route.

The peninsula is only a few miles wide at this point, giving you occasional views of the barrier islands, bay, and inlets. Almost at the southern tip is the **Eastern Shore of Virginia National Wildlife Refuge,** where, during the fall migration, millions of songbirds, monarch butterflies, and thousands of raptors gather

Cape Charles with the Cape Charles Lighthouse in the background
©JOMO333/SHUTTERSTOCK.COM

like an annual convention before continuing south. To visit this wildlife refuge and see some of the 406 species found there, turn in at the well-marked sign where VA 600 makes a 90-degree turn to the right about 7 miles from Cheriton. The refuge has a visitor center and some short hiking trails, with birds being the biggest attraction. The varied habitat supports a large number of species. Check at the visitor center for information.

When you leave the Eastern Shore of Virginia National Wildlife Refuge, turn left on VA 600. That road ends in about a half-mile at US 13. Turn left on US 13 and continue about a mile to the end of the route at the Chesapeake Bay Bridge-Tunnel, Route 12.

For a visit to **Kiptopeke State Park,** turn right (north) on US 13 at the stop sign at the end of VA 600. The park is a few miles north on US 13. Turn left into the park entrance on the Bayside. The park is the site of the old ferry terminal used before the Chesapeake Bay Bridge-Tunnel was built. The park

Chesapeake Bay blue crabs waiting to be steamed

has a campground and features nature walkways through the dunes and sandy shores, with excellent bird-watching. A recent seasonal visitor is a set of four giant white Adirondack chairs, each painted with a letter spelling love. It's part of the LOVE work project that has the Virginia Love logo presented in various manifestations.

14

Chesapeake Bay Bridge-Tunnel

Water, Sun & Sky

General description: The Chesapeake Bay Bridge-Tunnel is a 23-mile route across the mouth of Chesapeake Bay where it meets the Atlantic Ocean. This highway complex traverses trestles, causeways, bridges, man-made islands, and tunnels to connect the rural farmlands and the southern tip of the Delmarva Peninsula on the eastern shore of the bay with the Hampton Roads area on the western shore. The bridge-tunnel goes in a north-south direction; however, references are often made to the eastern (northern) and western (southern) shores. The Chesapeake Bay Bridge-Tunnel should not be confused with the Chesapeake Bay Bridge (William Preston Lane Jr. is the official name) farther north that crosses the upper bay between Annapolis and Kent Island.

Special attractions: The spectacular views from the bridges and trestles of the open Atlantic and Chesapeake Bay, as you are suspended between sky and water could make you think you're somehow in a flying submarine. A stop at the restaurant and fishing pier 4 miles out at sea (from the western shore) on one man-made island gives you the opportunity to walk out to the water's edge to look at oceangoing vessels and seabirds from the best avian viewing place in Virginia.

Location: Southeast Virginia between Hampton Roads and the Eastern Shore (Delmarva Peninsula).

Route numbers: US 13.

Travel season: The highway is open all year. There are occasional fog, high winds, and rare winter snow that can affect traffic. Winter is the best time of year to view seabirds and humpback whales

Camping: At the northern end (Eastern Shore) of the bridge-tunnel, camping is available at Kiptopeke State Park; the park has 47 tent sites; 54 sites with electric and water hookups; 32 with electric, water, and sewer; 7 rental RVs; 1 yurt; and 5 camping lodges. At the southern end (Western Shore) of the route, First Landing State Park in Virginia Beach has more than 200 campsites including 107 with electric and water, 81 standard, and 22 for groups, with 20 cabins. Several private campgrounds provide a variety of accommodations in the Hampton Roads area.

Services: The bridge-tunnel has a restaurant and gift shop on Island 1 (the closest to Hampton Roads). Gasoline is not available on the bridge-tunnel. Emergency road service is provided along the entire bridge-tunnel with call boxes every half mile. Gasoline, motels, hotels, and restaurants are available at either end of the route.

Nearby attractions: The northern end of this route is the end point for the Eastern Shore (Route 13). At the southern end of the route are the beaches of Virginia Beach, Cape Henry Lighthouse, and the many attractions of the Norfolk area, including tours of the massive Norfolk Naval Air Station.

For more information: Chesapeake Bay Bridge-Tunnel, (757) 331-2960, cbbt.com; Virginia Fisherman Identification Program, (800) 723-2728, mrc.virginia.gov/FIP.

Chesapeake Bay Bridge–Tunnel

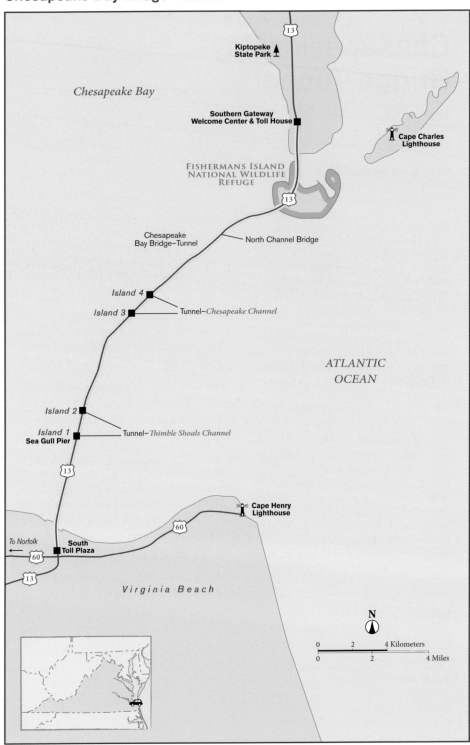

Chesapeake Bay

Kiptopeke
State Park

Southern Gateway
Welcome Center & Toll House

Cape Charles
Lighthouse

FISHERMANS ISLAND
NATIONAL WILDLIFE
REFUGE

Chesapeake
Bay Bridge–Tunnel

North Channel Bridge

Island 4

Island 3

Tunnel–*Chesapeake Channel*

ATLANTIC
OCEAN

Island 2

Island 1
Sea Gull Pier

Tunnel–*Thimble Shoals Channel*

Cape Henry
Lighthouse

To Norfolk

South
Toll Plaza

Virginia Beach

N

| 0 | | 2 | | 4 Kilometers |
| 0 | 2 | | 4 Miles |

Virginia Beach side, Bay Bride in the background
©JOMO333/SHUTTERSTOCK.COM

The Route

This 23-mile route follows US 13 across the Chesapeake Bay Bridge-Tunnel at the mouth of Chesapeake Bay and connects the Eastern Shore of Virginia with the Hampton Roads area. The bridge-tunnel has more than 12 miles of low-level trestles, two 1-mile tunnels, almost 2 miles of causeway, two bridges, and four man-made islands (each a little more than 5 acres). Throw in 5.5 miles of approach roads and it's the earth's longest bridge-tunnel complex. Of the nine others around the globe, two are the Hampton Roads Bridge-Tunnel and the Monitor-Merrimac Memorial Bridge-Tunnel, both at Hampton Roads.

The mouth of Chesapeake Bay is one of the busiest maritime areas in the world, and you see a lot of its activity from the bridge-tunnel. At any time, you might spot aircraft carriers, battleships, submarines, and other military vessels. You can also see freighters carrying coal, cars, fuel, food goods, and other cargo to Baltimore and other ports along the bay. Oh, and you can also see pleasure craft, from sailboats to cruise ships.

Early travelers going to or from the Eastern Shore had to travel overland through parts of Maryland from the north or use some kind of water transport from the west and south. Since colonial days, private ferry boats provided the main means of access, and as automobile travel grew in the 1900s, a vehicle-carrying ferry became an integral link on US 13.

In the 1950s it became apparent that the ferry system was obsolete. Originally, bridges were considered instead of tunnels for the shipping channels, but US Navy officials objected because bridges, no matter how tall, would restrict the height of naval vessels passing under them, and sabotage to the bridges could block the water passage completely. Also, the distance between the two points of land is almost as great as the English Channel.

The Virginia legislature appointed a commission to study the construction of a bridge-tunnel and the original 2-lane highway was open to traffic on April 15, 1964. By this time, seven ferries were making 90 one-way crossings a day, each taking 85 minutes, making it the world's busiest ferry system. Five boats were sold to the Cape May–Lewes Ferry connecting Cape May, New Jersey, with Lewes, Delaware. In 1965, the complex was selected as one of the "Seven Engineering Wonders of the Modern World," and in competition with more than 100 other projects, it was recognized by the American Society of Civil Engineers as an "Outstanding Civil Engineering Achievement."

In 1987, the Chesapeake Bay Bridge-Tunnel was officially named the Lucius J. Kellam Jr. Bridge-Tunnel. Kellam was chairman of the original tunnel commission and its predecessor, the ferry commission, from 1954 to 1993, and it was his foresight and leadership that helped make the structure a reality.

As traffic increased, plans were made to construct a parallel causeway to make a 4-lane roadway, and those lanes were opened in 1999. The tunnels, however, are still single lane with hopes for expanding to 4 lanes by 2030.

Allow 45 minutes for the actual driving and then add time for fishing, birding, eating, and souvenir shopping.

Besides being a scenic route, it's estimated that motorists save 90 minutes (or more, depending on traffic) when they drive the CBBT than if they use I-95 from Wilmington, Delaware, and points north heading toward Virginia Beach, the Outer Banks of North Carolina, and other points south (or vice versa).

The toll for passenger cars (including pickup trucks, panel trucks, station wagons, motorcycles, and minibuses/vans with seating for 15 or fewer people) in 2013 is $12. It's only $5 for the return trip if you make it within 24 hours and if you have your receipt. Overhead clearance is 13'6". Because of weather conditions, certain vehicles may be prohibited from using the bridge-tunnel. Text Followthegulls to 40404 to receive CBBT updates or sign up for updates at 511Virginia.org.

You may use your E-ZPass (ezpassva.com) with the two left lanes, each direction, dedicated E-ZPass lanes for cars and pickup trucks. Bicycles are not allowed. However, if you call ahead, they will provide a shuttle for you and your bike for $12.

A free MP3 driving tour is available on the CBBT website. The southbound recording is 18 minutes and the northbound one is 20 minutes. Each should be started just past the toll booth. They include a history of the bridge-tunnel, remarkable facts about the engineering, and some interesting notes along the way. Pause points are incorporated so you can time it with your travel.

Southern Gateway Welcome Center and Toll Plaza

Our route begins at US 13 at the **Southern Gateway Welcome Center and Toll Plaza** approach to the bridge-tunnel. Pay your toll, and then stop by the scenic overlook on your right where you can take pictures to your heart's content and scan the bay through viewing machines. A parking lot accommodates cars, recreational vehicles, and buses. This is a good time to take care of any foreseeable emergencies as the overlook has restroom facilities, telephones, and vending machines.

Back in your car, you'll be driving on the newer lanes of the complex. You'll cross the Fisherman Inlet Bridge that provides a 40-foot vertical clearance for boats using the Intracoastal Waterway.

That spot of land, a barrier island that is growing rather than eroding is **Fishermans Island National Wildlife Refuge.** It supports diverse colonies of nesting waterbirds, including several species of gulls, terns, herons, and ibis. Almost 300 species of birds have been identified on the refuge. However, to protect the birds, the refuge can be visited only by special permit, and stops are not allowed. While keeping your eyes on the road, you and your passengers may notice osprey nests and catch sight of American bald eagles.

Open water beckons on the trestle beyond Fishermans Island. To the right (west) lies miles and miles of Chesapeake Bay; to the left (east) is the Atlantic Ocean. In a few miles you cross the **North Channel Bridge;** 75 feet above water that's as much as 100 feet deep. This bridge provides an extraordinary view of the vast miles and miles of water while small craft and fishing trawlers going to and from the Eastern Shore pass underneath the span.

As you drive down the far side of the bridge, you can see the highway, islands, and tunnel portals stretching to Norfolk and the southern shore about 15 miles ahead.

Island 4

In a few miles you come to the first of four man-made islands built on tons of rocks that were carried by barge to the site. (This island is actually Island 4, because the islands are numbered from south to north.) The islands provide approaches to the tunnels and house the ventilation equipment.

At **Island 4** the route enters the mile-long **Chesapeake Channel Tunnel** which allows shipping traffic to and from Chesapeake Bay to pass overhead.

The islands are the best places in Virginia to observe seabirds. These rock piles provide abundant feeding grounds for fish, shellfish, and other aquatic life, and these in turn attract diving sea ducks and other birds.

Birders (and the curious) can stop on the islands if they obtain written permission in advance. Write or call the Chesapeake Bay Bridge and Tunnel District before your trip, and they will send you written permission and instructions to stop at the other islands. (See the Appendix for the address and phone number. Allow the district office at least 2 weeks to receive and process your request.) Do not stop without permission; you will receive a ticket and fine.

Bird life is most abundant in the winter months. Waterbirds include all three species of scoters, plus many other ducks and gulls. Snow buntings, ruddy turnstones, and double-crested and great cormorants are commonly seen. The birding is best when the weather is at its worst: during January and February after a hard freeze has iced over the tidal creeks and inlets of the mainland.

Islands 3 & 2

You emerge from the Chesapeake Channel Tunnel at **Island 3,** about the halfway point on the route that continues over low-level trestles for several miles to **Island 2,** the portal for the **Thimble Shoals Channel Tunnel.** This channel is the main shipping lane for the US Navy Atlantic fleet and the ports at Norfolk, Portsmouth, Newport News, and Hampton.

Island 1

When you exit from the Thimble Shoals Channel Tunnel, make a sharp right turn at the sign to visit the public facilities, including the wheelchair-accessible **Sea Gull Pier** that extends 625 feet into Chesapeake Bay. It has expansive views of the Norfolk–Virginia Beach shoreline 4 miles away. The pier is open 24 hours a day, all year, and can be crowded on summer weekends when local anglers try their luck at catching bluefish, croaker, rockfish, trout, flounder, shark, and other species. A certified weighing station and fish-cleaning stations are provided. Although you don't need a license, you must register with the Virginia Fisherman Identification Program annually.

The only island normally open to the public is this last one on our trip. You can eat, enjoy birding, watch the ships navigate into and out of the bay, and see exhibits on the construction of the bridge-tunnel and the history of the US Navy on the bay. A special delight is spotting the local dolphins frolicking in the waters and during the winter you can often see humpback whales. The large ships anchored nearby are waiting to enter Hampton Roads to load or unload cargo.

Cape Henry Lighthouse, Virginia Beach
©SUSIE PRENTICE/SHUTTERSTOCK.COM

Full-service and grab-and-go dining is available for breakfast, lunch, and dinner at the **Chesapeake Grill** restaurant, with indoor and outdoor (weather permitting) dining options. Gifts and souvenirs may be purchased at the **Virginia Originals** shop. Oh, and sunsets and sunrises over the water can be spectacular.

As you leave the pier, turn right onto the roadway toward the distant shore. Ahead, Norfolk is to the right and Virginia Beach to the left. From the pier it is about 4 miles over causeways to the end of the route at the **South Toll Plaza,** located halfway between Norfolk and Virginia Beach.

You should have your next destination in mind as you leave the toll plaza. Well-marked signs will direct you to connecting roads and interstates, including I-64, I-264, I-564, I-664, US 13, US 17, and US 60, and the surrounding cities of Norfolk, Virginia Beach, Portsmouth, Hampton, Newport News, and Williamsburg.

15

Goshen Pass & Lake Moomaw

Lexington to Covington

General description: This is a mountain route west of Lexington with a variety of scenic and historic sites. It passes the Virginia Horse Center and goes by the steep cliffs and rushing streams of Goshen Pass in Jefferson National Forest. From there, it heads down the valley of Bath County, past numerous hot springs and spas, including the well-known Omni Homestead Resort. Other features include Falling Spring Falls, first described by Thomas Jefferson, and imposing Gathright Dam and Lake Moomaw in the heart of Jefferson National Forest. The route is almost 75 miles long and ends at Covington.

Special attractions: Virginia Horse Center, Wade's Mill, Goshen Pass, Lake Moomaw, the Jefferson Pools, Omni Homestead Resort, Garth Newel Music Center, and Falling Spring Falls.

Location: West-central Virginia. Lexington is at exit 55 off of I-64 or exit 188 of I-81.

Route numbers: US 11 and 220; VA 39, 640, 687, and 600; and local Forest Service roads.

Travel season: The route can be followed at any time of year; with roads closed occasionally by snow during the winter months or sudden large rainstorms at other times. Summer and fall are the most popular travel seasons. Spring brings the colorful blossoms of redbud, rhododendron, dogwood, and other flowering plants, while in autumn the changing leaves bathe the hillsides in yellow, orange, and red.

Camping: On the route itself, Lake Moomaw in Jefferson National Forest has several hundred tent campsites scattered around the lake and forest; some are wilderness sites, but most are equipped with showers and electricity. Nearby, off the route, Douthat State Park has 87 campsites, many with all the amenities, that can accommodate everything from tent campers to motor homes. Two private campgrounds near Natural Bridge have about 300 campsites, most with full hookups.

Services: Motels, restaurants, and gasoline can be found in Lexington and Covington at either end of the ride. Lodging, meals, and gasoline are available throughout Bath County where accommodations range from the sumptuous Omni Homestead to simple motels at Warm Springs, particularly at Garth Newel. There are dozens of bed-and-breakfast establishments in the county. Nearby Douthat State Park has 32 rental cabins and 6 lodges.

Nearby attractions: Douthat State Park, nestled between mountain ridges, features camping, hiking, fishing, and boating. Heavily advertised Natural Bridge, south of Lexington on US 11, is a 215-foot-high limestone arch.

For more information: Lexington & the Rockbridge Area Tourism Development, (540) 463-3777 or (877) 453-9822, lexingtonvirginia.com; Bath County, (540) 839-7202, discoverbath.com; Garth Newel Music Center, (540) 839-5018, garth newel.org; Jefferson Pools, (540) 839-7741, discoverbath.com.

Goshen Pass and Lake Moomaw

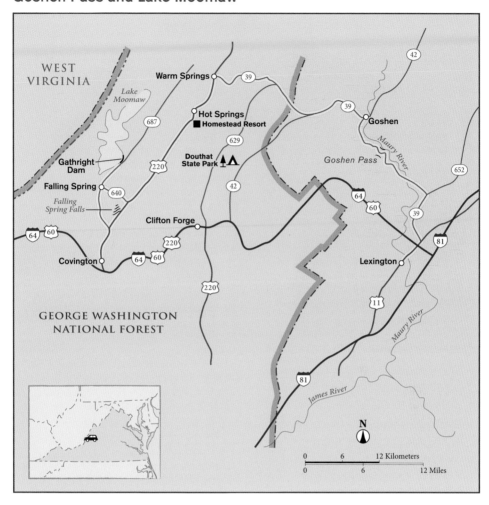

The Route

The route starts in downtown Lexington, a beautiful and historic cultural center. After leaving Lexington, you soon pass the Virginia Horse Center, where equestrian events are held year-round, and enter Goshen Pass in Jefferson National Forest, known for its steep rock cliffs that rise abruptly from the banks of the Maury River. The route then traverses Bath County, where hot springs and spas have been popular since colonial days, including those at Omni Homestead Resort, a well-known resort. Other features include Falling Spring Falls and Gathright Dam at Lake Moomaw in the heart of the national forest. The route ends in Covington.

Lexington is home to both Washington and Lee University and the Virginia Military Institute. These two institutions sure do present an architectural contrast:

Stonewall Jackson House in Lexington
©CAROLYN M CARPENTER/SHUTTERSTOCK.COM

Washington and Lee's stately colonial and federal-style buildings, reminiscent of Virginia's genteel traditions, sit across from VMI's angular and sober gothic constructions.

Well-known military figures have been associated with both schools. Confederate General Robert E. Lee assumed presidency of Washington and Lee (then known as Washington College) 6 months after the Civil War ended at Appomattox. Before the Civil War, Confederate General Stonewall Jackson instructed VMI students in the tactics and strategy of battle. General George C. Marshall, who fought in both World War I and World War II and later devised the Marshall Plan to rehabilitate Europe, graduated from VMI.

The visitor center downtown can provide you with suggestions for and directions to other nearby attractions, including the Stonewall Jackson House, the George C. Marshall Museum, Lee Chapel, and VMI Museum. If you tire of military exhibits, visit the Cyrus McCormick Farm, maintained to look much as it did in the 1830s when McCormick revolutionized agriculture when he invented the mechanical reaper. Wade's Mill offers another interesting stop where you can see how flour and corn are still stone-ground as they were circa 1750.

Lexington & the Countryside

To begin the route, from downtown Lexington take US 11 north. Cross I-64 just outside of town and turn left in a quarter mile on 2-lane VA 39, a Virginia Scenic Byway. In a few minutes you pass the **Virginia Horse Center,** one of the country's largest equestrian facilities. Events are held all year, and include competitions as diverse as grand prix jumping and walking horse races to horse-judging shows and auctions, with all of them included in the April horse festival. The center boasts a 4,000-seat coliseum (for people) and more than 700 stables (for horses).

As the winding Maury River Road crosses the **Shenandoah Valley,** you are virtually surrounded by mountains. Behind are the Blue Ridge Mountain peaks; ahead, where you are going, are the rounded slopes of the Allegheny Mountains. The road's namesake—the **Maury River**—flows by on the left.

About 12 miles from Lexington, VA 39 follows the Maury River into the **George Washington National Forest** and the towering cliffs of **Goshen Pass.** For several miles you wind past 1,000-foot-high cliffs of steeply dipping limestone and sandstone that tower over the boulders in the rushing river. Rhododendron, dogwood, and redbud grow to the roadside amid maples, pines, and hemlocks. Several scenic turnouts and roadside parks give picnickers, anglers, canoeists, swimmers, and tube riders access to the water.

After several miles you emerge from the pass into a little valley. As you drive through the small town of **Goshen** you can see the Calf Pasture River on the right where VA 42 merges with VA 39.

Continue on VA 39. A few miles past Goshen the route enters another river pass, narrower and slightly less spectacular than Goshen Pass. This one follows the Cow Pasture River (a little bigger than the Calf Pasture River).

In a few miles you pass VA 629 which leads to **Douthat State Park,** a popular camping and picnicking area. VA 39 leaves the river valley to begin the winding climb over the ridge of **Warm Springs Mountain,** elevation 2,950 feet.

Warm Springs to Hot Springs

The road descends from the ridge to the intersection of US 220 at **Warm Springs,** county seat of Bath County. The town and the county get their name from the numerous hot and warm springs that issue from the fractured limestone of the valley floor.

Jefferson Pools features an octagonal wooden building that was opened in 1761, most likely making it the country's oldest spa. Mineral rich and bubbling up at 98°F, the waters here are mighty inviting for soaking away your aches and pains and, even more important, whatever is stressing your day. The pools are open daily in season, with family and adult-only soaking hours.

With nature as an inspiration, it's understandable that the **Garth Newel Music Center** has been able to create and provide chamber music and other entertainments to discerning guests, particularly those who love listening to exquisite notes in such a gorgeous nature setting.

Among the typical programs executive director Chris Williams might schedule are all Beethoven, Virginia Blues and Jazz Festival, composer competition, Eric Lindell Mardi Gras dance party, Flamenco Aparicio Dance Company, Harvest Moon festival, Independence Day celebration, and a Memorial Day weekend (with student alumni). Pieces may be performed by as few as three musicians or as many as 60 students from the Allegheny Mountain String Project.

Garth Newel, meaning "new home" in Welsh, was a residence created in the 1920s by William Sergeant Kendall and his bride Christine Herter Kendall. For those who are traveling during the summer and plan far enough ahead, you can spend an entire weekend in the 1920s Manor House (complete with continental breakfast each morning) enjoying the fine dinner after the concert prepared by resident chef, Josh Elliott, right in the concert hall kitchen. Yes, you dine with the musicians. If they're filled the weekend you want to attend, there are plenty of bed-and-breakfasts around, and the Homestead Resort is about 5 miles away.

In town is the site of **Terrill Hill,** home of two brothers, both generals, and both killed during the Civil War. They served on opposing sides. Brigadier General William R. Terrill, a graduate of West Point, was on the Union side and was killed in 1862 during a skirmish in Perry, Kentucky. His Confederate brother, Brigadier General James B. Terrill, a graduate of VMI, died during the Battle of the Wilderness in 1864 near Fredericksburg. Legend says that their grieving father erected a monument to his sons saying, "God alone knows which was right."

Turn left on US 220, which follows the valley floor. You will see remains of several bathhouses and resorts, most of which are now closed. One that is still open, and still a major resort, is the huge and imposing **Omni Homestead Resort at Hot Springs.**

The original Homestead opened as an inn in 1766. Today's Omni Homestead Resort sits amid 2,000 acres of lush greenery and features more than 483 distinctive guest rooms and suites. It also has 105-degree mineral baths and spa and offers tennis, three golf courses, a 2-acre year-round outdoor pool and water park, miniature golf, skeet and target shooting, other sports, several restaurants, and even ice-skating and downhill skiing in season. The Omni Homestead recently partnered with the Canyon Ranch Spa Club bringing wellness and healthy lifestyle programs to the popular spa as part of a $26 million renovation. And, as of spring 2013, the property belonged to the Omni Hotels and Resorts. During World War II, Japanese dignitaries were housed at the Homestead.

A quiet stretch of water along VA 39 out of Lexington

Falling Spring Falls to Covington

Continue on US 220, past the Omni Homestead's verdant golf courses. About 8 miles from Hot Springs and about 200 feet past the large rocks at VA 640 are an overlook and small parking area on the right from which to view **Falling Spring Falls.** Use caution because the turnoff is easy to miss. The falls, first described by Thomas Jefferson in 1798, form lacy cascades dropping about 200 feet.

After you view the falls, turn around and drive back 200 feet to VA 640. Turn left on VA 640, a narrow, 2-lane road, toward the town of **Falling Spring.** At Falling Spring turn right on VA 687.

Make an acute left turn on the unnumbered Forest Service road at the sign to Lake Moomaw and Gathright Dam. Cross the Jackson River and make a sharp right turn on VA 600 at another Lake Moomaw sign and continue to follow the signs.

You'll have several views of **Lake Moomaw** and pass the visitor center before reaching **Gathright Dam** itself. The dam, with the road on top of it, is an earth-and-rock structure about 1,310 feet long, rising 250 feet above the Jackson River. On the dam's other side, the road makes a loop several miles long with numerous

lake views with mountains rising from the far shore. You pass several swimming, boating, and fishing areas.

The dam was put into operation in 1979 to help prevent flooding—while still allowing for fishing and water activities—downstream in Covington. The lake has 43 miles of shoreline and covers about 2,500 acres. Today the lake, with its surrounding wildlife management area, is popular with anglers, swimmers, boaters, bird-watchers, and hikers. It is known for its large wild turkey population and has several bald eagle nesting areas. There are half a dozen campsites and campgrounds scattered around the area.

"Moomaw" may sound like an ancient Indian name, but the lake is actually named for Benjamin C. Moomaw Jr., who, as the executive director of the Covington-Allegheny Chamber of Commerce, joined with landowner-sportsman Thomas M. Gathright, in pushing for its construction.

When you leave the dam, retrace your route to the intersection in Natural Well and turn right on VA 687. Stay on VA 687 past Falling Spring (don't turn on VA 640) to the intersection in several miles with US 220. Turn right on US 220 into **Covington** where the route ends. The large plant you see as you approach Covington belongs to the MeadWestvaco (MWV).

Follow signs to I-64 to head east back to Lexington or west to the West Virginia border.

Jefferson Pools

16

Lee's Retreat

Petersburg to Appomattox

General description: Lee's Retreat is a 110-mile, historical route that traces the closing days of the Civil War as Union General Ulysses S. Grant relentlessly pursued Confederate General Robert E. Lee to Lee's surrender at Appomattox. The route crosses much of the rural Piedmont area of central Virginia with numerous stops at historical and military points of interest.

Special attractions: The main attractions are the historical stops which feature short, interpretive radio broadcasts. Sailor's Creek Battlefield Historical State Park is the scene of the last major battle of the war. Appomattox Court House National Historical Park, where Lee surrendered to Grant, has been restored to look as it did in 1865. The route passes through Appomattox-Buckingham State Forest and near two state parks.

Location: Central Virginia, west of Petersburg.

Route numbers: VA 708, 153, 38, 671, 642, 617, 618, 619, 45, 657, 600, 653, 638, 636, and 24; US 360, 460, and Business 460. The route is complicated, but all turns and stops should be well marked by special "Lee's Retreat" signs.

Travel season: All year.

Camping: Camping in season is available at Holliday Lake State Park, a few miles from the main route.

Services: Gasoline, restaurants, motels, and hotels are available in Petersburg and Farmville. Appomattox has restaurants, gasoline, and some motels.

Nearby attractions: Petersburg at the start of the route has numerous historic sites, including Petersburg National Battlefield, the Siege Museum, Blandford Church and Cemetery, and Pamplin Historical Park and the National Museum of the Civil War site.

For more information: Virginia Civil War Trails, (888) 248-4592, civilwartrails.org; Petersburg Area Regional Tourism, (804) 861-1666, petersburgarea.org; Tourism, City of Petersburg, Siege Museum, (804) 733-2403, petersburg-va.org; Pamplin Historical Park and the National Museum of the Civil War Soldier, (804) 861-2408 or (877) PAMPLIN, pamplinpark.org; Sailor's Creek Battlefield Historical State Park, (804) 561-7510, dcr.virginia.gov; Appomattox Court House National Historical Park, (434) 352-8987, nps.gov/apco; The Museum of the Confederacy/Appomattox, (855) 649-1861, moc.org.

The Route

Lee's Retreat traces the ending days of the Civil War in April 1865. It follows Confederate General Robert E. Lee's route as his Army of Northern Virginia was pursued by Union General Ulysses S. Grant's Army of the Potomac from Petersburg to Lee's surrender at Appomattox Court House, effectively ending the Civil War. The route is a winding one, primarily on narrow, 2-lane roads. Lee's Retreat is one of several Civil War motor trails designed and established by the Virginia Civil War Trails. This private organization works with the state and local communities

Lee's Retreat

Appomattox Court House National Historical Park
© BENJAMIN DOYLE /SHUTTERSTOCK.COM

to preserve Civil War sites and make them accessible to the public. Most of the route is also a designated Virginia Scenic Byway.

(Grant and Lee met several times in battle outside Fredericksburg before Lee retreated south to Petersburg. These conflicts are described in Route 11.)

The route lies in the state's Piedmont area between the Coastal Plain to the east and the Blue Ridge to the west. The Piedmont here is characterized by gently rolling hills, thick, fertile soil, farmlands that have been cultivated since colonial days, and extensive second-growth forests. The route gives you a good look from back roads at the rural, mostly unspoiled land of the Piedmont, much of which is little changed since the Civil War. It passes through the Appomattox-Buckingham State Forest and by two state parks.

The route is twisty with numerous road changes because it is laid out from a historical point of view and stops at points of interest. It is easy to follow, however, because the well-marked "Lee's Retreat" signs mark the route. Each stop has an informative display and a short, interpretive AM-radio broadcast that you can listen to on your car radio on 1610.

Because the route is well marked, and to avoid cluttering up the description with numerous road changes, minimal directions are given here. The numbered stops in the text refer to corresponding numbers on the book's map and to the sites designated by the Virginia Civil War Trails. This route covers that portion of Lee's Retreat from Sutherland Station (stop 3) to Appomattox Court House (stop 21).

Before starting you may want to visit some Civil War sites in Petersburg. The visitor center in the Farmers Bank Building on Bollingbrook Street can get you oriented. The Siege Museum and Petersburg National Battlefield preserve the story of Grant's 9.5-month blockade and siege of the city when he slowly surrounded Petersburg and cut off Lee's supply lines from the south. Miles of earthworks, constructed by Union and Confederate troops, are still visible. The role of the US Colored Troops (USCT) is explored at the battlefield. After a final assault on April 2, 1865, at what is now the privately owned Pamplin Historical Park, Union forces broke through Lee's line defending Petersburg. That night Lee abandoned Petersburg and headed west with his bedraggled Confederate forces, some 80,000 hungry and weary soldiers, and a wagon train of supplies and equipment grudgingly pulled by ribs-thin horses.

Sutherland to Farmville

The route begins west of Petersburg at **Sutherland** (stop 3) where VA 708 leads west from US 460. Here Grant cut off the South Side Railroad, Lee's only remaining supply line into Petersburg.

VA 708 traverses gently rolling forest and farmland. At one time thick stands of hardwoods and pines covered the area. Early settlers soon found that the thick, almost rock-free soil grew rich, abundant crops, so that by the time of the Civil War the majority of the land was under cultivation. Tobacco, the main crop, provided the economic backbone and support for Virginia and the Confederate army. Tobacco is still important today, now joined by fields of soybeans, corn, wheat, and other crops.

Traveling mostly at night to avoid Union troops, Lee retreated toward **Amelia Court House** where he had arranged for food and supplies to arrive by railroad. From there, he planned to take his troops from both Richmond and Petersburg to North Carolina to join other Confederate forces.

Union cavalry troops attacked Lee's retreating and lagging rear guard at **Namozine Church** (stop 4), which was used as a hospital after the confrontation. The church, built in 1847, is still standing today.

About 18 miles from Sutherland, turn right on VA 153 (this turn, like the others, is well marked). Turn left in 3 miles on VA 38. Follow the route to Amelia Court House (stop 5) on US 360 where the Richmond & Danville Railroad parallels the highway. When Lee arrived here, he found no train and no supplies, so

he turned south toward North Carolina. On the courthouse lawn (a block off the main route) is an imposing memorial to Confederate soldiers.

At **Jetersville** (stop 6) Lee encountered more Union troops, which forced him to abandon his plans to go to North Carolina. Instead he headed west to Farmville, hoping to find food and supplies for his impoverished army, marching at night to avoid Grant's forces.

The Union forces kept attacking Lee's strung-out rear guard, with minor skirmishes at **Amelia Springs** (stop 7) and **Deatonville** (stop 8). At **Holt's Corner** (stop 9), now the junction of VA 617 and VA 618, the main portion of Lee's army went straight (along VA 618) to cross **Sailor's Creek,** while a wagon train went north (VA 617).

Sailor's Creek was the final major battle of the Civil War. As Lee's army struggled to cross the bogs and muddy creek, Grant's Union forces, nearly 100,000 strong, caught up with them. Overpowered, some 7,000 Confederate soldiers were killed, and about 8,000 surrendered.

This battle scene is preserved in **Sailor's Creek Battlefield Historical State Park** (stop 9—Holt's Corner—and stops 10 and 11). Today the route curves down to a small creek through thick woods, a pleasant change from the nearly flat farmlands that give little hint of its bloody history. Interpretive services are available at the park during the warmer months, but it can be visited all year.

From the creek bottom the route reverses and retraces the route to the intersection with VA 618, passing the **Lockett House** (stop 12), which still has bullet holes from the battle. The Confederate wagon train that went north was attacked as it crossed Sailor's Creek at **Double Bridges** (stop 13). To your left are bridge remains.

At **Rice's Depot** (stop 14) the route heads toward **Farmville** on 4-lane US 460. The Confederates captured several hundred Union troops (stop 15) who attempted to burn the railroad structure over the Appomattox River.

Farmville to Appomattox

Follow the route into **Farmville.** The city today is an agricultural and carpet-manufacturing center, and the site of Longwood College. In 1865 it was a tobacco-growing town of 1,500, and many residents watched fearfully as both armies passed through the area.

Civil War memorial, Petersburg National Battlefield, Petersburg
© RACHEL RAMEY /SHUTTERSTOCK.COMCOM

Civil War Cannon at Petersburg
© RACHEL RAMEY /SHUTTERSTOCK.COM

In the center of town turn right on VA 45 (Main Street). Ahead you will see a few carpet mills in some old brick buildings. Turn left into the parking lot by the Appomattox River (stop 16, Farmville). The supply train Lee was hoping for did not appear. He crossed the Appomattox River and headed north.

Continue north on VA 45. As you cross the river, you will see the current railroad bridge over the river. At **Cumberland Church** (stop 17), Union troops attacked, delaying Lee's march north.

Turn right on VA 657. Confederate troops burned four spans of **High Bridge** (stop 18); only the lower wagon bridge remained, so Grant's troops were able to cross the river and continue their pursuit of Lee. Unfortunately, you can't see the river or the bridge from this spot.

Turn left on VA 600, and left again in about 2 miles on VA 653. The route heads west, crosses VA 45 and becomes VA 636. Lee also turned west, and followed this exact route.

In 7 miles the route crosses US 15. At **Clifton** (stop 19) on April 8, Grant received a letter from Lee suggesting a peace meeting. Grant left the next morning and rode into Appomattox Court House.

For several miles the route passes through the **Appomattox-Buckingham State Forest,** which has extensive stands of second growth of southern pine and hardwoods. Nearby, and within the forest, is **Holliday Lake State Park.** A small lake in the park provides fishing, boating, and swimming. There are 30 campsites. Several archaeological sites within and near the park give evidence that early man lived here some 8,000 years ago.

At **New Store** (stop 20), Lee's army was still being pursued by Grant's troops. Lee turned south toward Appomattox Court House. The route turns left on VA 24, about 5 miles beyond this stop, and heads south toward **Appomattox.**

In 3 miles you pass Confederate General Longstreet's soldiers' hastily built breastworks (chest-high lines of earth—stop 21) to protect Lee's rear troops, although most of his weary army had already reached Appomattox Court House 4 miles south.

Turn right into **Appomattox Court House National Historical Park.** On April 8, 1865, Lee surrendered his men to Grant. The official surrender took place the next day when Robert E. Lee surrendered to Ulysses S. Grant in a ceremony that took place in the home of Wilmer McLean. Among the many paradoxes of the Civil War is that McLean, a civilian, was an unwilling observer at both the war's beginning and end. Originally he lived in Manassas, where he and his family witnessed the First Battle of Manassas. To ensure his family's safety, McLean moved with them to Appomattox Court House where he believed they would be out of danger and far removed from further conflict.

At the surrender ceremony April 9, Grant's soldiers stood at attention, rifles at present arms, honoring and saluting their former Confederate foes as Lee's 28,000 remaining soldiers laid down their rifles. The Confederate soldiers received written paroles enabling them to safely return to their homes.

Four years of Civil War, fought primarily on Virginia soil, resulted in approximately 630,000 deaths and more than one million injured personnel. Some units had been fighting for the full 4 years, and their ranks were nearly eliminated. For example, the 6th Louisiana Volunteers started with almost 1,000 eager recruits in New Orleans in 1861; 55 of them survived to receive their paroles at Appomattox Court House.

The village of Appomattox Court House has been rebuilt to look as it did in 1865, including shops and stores and the **McLean House** where the surrender was signed. Exhibits, guided tours, and reenactments help tell the complex story of this vital part of Virginia and US history.

The route ends here, although Lee's Retreat continues to additional stops. While Appomattox is best known for its role in the Civil War, it is also the birthplace of Joel Walker Sweeney, inventor of the five-string banjo in 1831.

17

The Plantation Road

The Colonial James River

General description: This 55-mile route follows the winding Plantation Road along the James River from Richmond to Williamsburg. In colonial days this was the center of commerce for the state, and the James River was the main means of travel. Well-to-do farmers and statesmen built mansions and plantations along the river. The route follows the inland plantation route, passing by several restored colonial plantations that you can visit. In addition to the plantations, the route passes through wooded groves, rich farmland, and tidewater inlets.

Special attractions: The numerous colonial mansions and plantations along the James River are of primary interest. Most are lovingly restored and furnished, including grounds and gardens, and you can see the buildings and grounds through the eyes of tour guides. Other attractions include Fort Harrison, a part of Richmond National Battlefield Park, which played a crucial role in the Battle of Richmond, and a side trip to a national fish hatchery.

Location: East-central Virginia between Richmond and Williamsburg.

Route numbers: The route follows VA 5 with short side trips or turnoffs on VA 10, 31, 106/156, 608, 615, 619, 633, and 658.

Travel season: All year. Most plantations are open daily except for such major holidays as Christmas. The warmer months attract large crowds.

Camping: The closest campgrounds are at Jamestown, a few miles from the southern end of the route. They are privately operated.

Services: All services are available at Richmond and Williamsburg, and occasionally along the route. Several bed-and-breakfasts and restaurants are scattered throughout the route.

Nearby attractions: The capital city of Richmond and historic Williamsburg offer a variety of attractions. See Route 18, Colonial Parkway, for more details about the Williamsburg-Jamestown-Yorktown area.

For more information: James River Plantations, jamesriverplantations.org; Charles City County, (804) 652-4702, co.charles-city.va.us; Fort Harrison, (804) 226-1981, nps.gov/rich; Harrison Lake National Fish Hatchery, (804) 829-2421, fws.gov/harrisonlake; Berkeley Plantation, (804) 829-6018, berkeleyplantation.com; Evelynton Plantation, (800) 473-5075, jamesriverplantations.org; Sherwood Forest Plantation Foundation, (804) 829-5377, sherwoodforest.org; Shirley Plantation, (804) 829-5121 or (800) 232-1613, shirleyplantation.com; Hopewell Office of Tourism & Visitor Center, (804) 541-2481 or (800) 863-8687, hopewellva.gov; Kittiewan Plantation, (804) 829-2272, kittiewanplantation.org, hopewellva.gov.

The Plantation Road

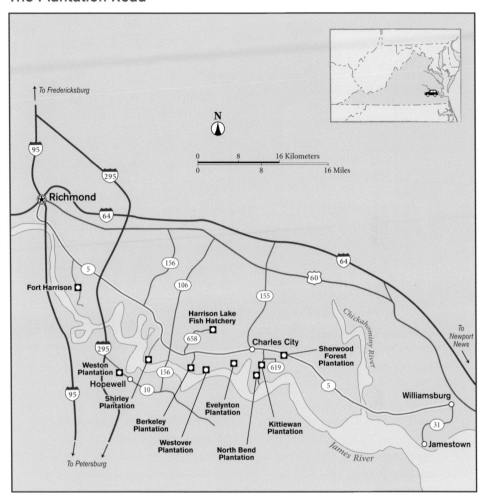

The Route

That part of Virginia along the James River between Richmond and Williamsburg is among the most historical in the country. In the early 1600s Europeans started settling here, and its valuable agricultural products, particularly tobacco, helped make the Virginia colonies a most important economic and political power. Dominating this economy were several large plantations along the James River, each one essentially a self-supporting community and farmland.

There is one working plantations, Shirley Plantation, which is the oldest family-owned business in North America, and many other remaining plantation manor houses, mansions, and outbuildings restored to their colonial splendor are

Historic signs mark the Plantation Road route and relate interesting tidbits about the area.
PHOTO COURTESY GINA PATTERSON

privately owned but open to the public. They are all listed on the National Register of Historic Places; most are also National Historic Landmarks and Virginia Historic Landmarks. They have survived more than 300 years of social, civil, and technological change, including depressions and booms, the Revolutionary War, War of 1812, Civil War, and Reconstruction. Admission fees are charged.

The region has remained rural, with extensive woods and forests, river and tidal lands, and bountiful farmlands, despite its long history of settlement and its proximity to the colonial capitals of Jamestown and Williamsburg, and to Richmond, the Confederate and state capital.

Fort Harrison (Richmond) to Berkeley Plantation

The 55-mile-long route begins near the Fort Harrison section of **Richmond National Battlefield Park.** Fort Harrison, part of a necklace of Confederate forts surrounding Richmond, was captured by General Ulysses S. Grant's troops in September 1864. This crucial battle led to the loss of Richmond, the Confederate capital, several months later. Fourteen black Union soldiers were awarded the Medal of Honor for their bravery during the battle.

To visit **Fort Harrison,** from the intersection at I-295 go north (toward Richmond) on VA 5 about 2 miles to an unnumbered road at the park entrance and turn left. This battlefield park contains miles of Confederate breastworks (trenches) that surrounded and protected Richmond. The visitor center has maps and information.

If you don't want to visit Fort Harrison, from the intersection at I-295 go south (toward Williamsburg) on VA 5. The 2-lane, winding road passes through wooded farmland. Because you are driving down the James River valley, the land is fairly flat. This road has several names that you may notice from signs: Plantation Road, New Market Road, and the John Tyler Memorial Highway. Soon you enter Charles City County.

In a few miles you come to VA 608 and the entrance to **Shirley Plantation** on the right. Like all the plantations, this one was built to front on the main highway of colonial times, the James River. Rivers were the settlers' transportation lifeblood, providing the swiftest and safest means of movement between Richmond, Williamsburg, and the open ocean.

Trees meet in an arch over the entrance roadway. Shirley Plantation has belonged to the Hill-Carter family since 1613 and is still occupied by the 10th and 11th generations of that group. The mansion, completed in 1738, was known for its many modern and innovative features. The most dramatic and best known is the flying, or hanging, staircase in the main hallway, which ascends to the second floor with no support beams. Another modern feature was indoor running water made possible by a cistern in the attic. Although water had to be carried up to the cistern, it cut down on broken dishes because the dishes could be washed in the parlor instead of carrying them outside.

Return to VA 5 and turn right. In less than a mile you come to the intersection with VA 106/156. An optional right turn on VA 106/156 will take you across the James River on the **Benjamin Harrison Memorial Bridge.** This high span will give you a better view of the river, 2 miles wide at this point, than you can get from VA 5 or any other plantations. At the other end of the bridge, go to the stop sign at VA 10, where you can turn around and cross the bridge again to rejoin VA 5, and turn right.

In a few miles VA 658 leads left to the **Harrison Lake National Fish Hatchery.** The hatchery has several ponds where you can see hatchlings, a short nature trail, and an observation platform for spotting egrets and shorebirds. The lake is locally popular for boating and fishing.

Return to VA 5 and turn left. In a few miles you come to VA 633, the turnoff for **Berkeley Plantation,** the most historic of all the plantations.

Its European history began when 38 settlers from England came ashore here on December 4, 1619, and celebrated the first Thanksgiving in America, 2 years

before the Pilgrims arrived at Plymouth Rock, Massachusetts. A reenactment of this event is held the first Sunday of November each year, near a replica of the ship afloat in the James. The early settlers are also credited with distilling the first bourbon. This brew, made from corn liquor, reputedly proved far more popular than their weak English ale.

Berkeley is one of only two houses in the US that is the ancestral home of two presidents plus a Declaration of Independence signer. (The other is the Adams house near Boston, Massachusetts.) The Berkeley property was acquired by the Harrison family in 1691, and the main house was constructed in 1726 by Benjamin Harrison IV. It was his son, Benjamin Harrison V, who signed the Declaration of Independence. His son, William Henry Harrison, born here in 1773, was elected the ninth president in 1840. The president-elect spent many hours at his desk in the mansion composing his inaugural address. Unfortunately, the address took 2 hours to deliver on a raw, rainy day in 1841. Following the speech the new president contracted pneumonia, and he died after just one month in office. He was succeeded by his vice president and neighbor, John Tyler, who lived at nearby Sherwood Forest Plantation, which you will pass later in this route. Benjamin Harrison, William's grandson, who became the 23rd president in 1888, also lived here.

During the Civil War the plantation was the headquarters for Union General George McClellan and his 140,000 troops from the Army of the Potomac who camped here in 1862. President Lincoln conferred here with McClellan several times. And here the poignant bugle notes that sounded "Taps," a memento to those killed in battle, was composed and heard for the first time, echoing over the James, during the encampment.

In addition to the house and authentic furnishings, there are 10 acres of formal, terraced boxwood gardens and lawn extending from the house to the James River. Memorials to "Taps" and the first Thanksgiving are near the ship replica on the river.

Berkeley Plantation to Charles City

Return to VA 5 and turn right. In a few miles you arrive at **Evelynton Plantation,** named for William Byrd's daughter, Evelyn. Since 1847, the Ruffin family has lived here, starting with Edmund Ruffin, credited or blamed with firing the first shot at Fort Sumter in Charleston, South Carolina. Perhaps in some form of retribution, this land was the center of a ferocious skirmish in 1862 as General George McClellan waged his ruinous Peninsula campaign. The buildings were all

Shirley Plantation, Charles City
©CAROLYN M CARPENTER/SHUTTERSTOCK.COM

Charles City County Historic Courthouse (circa 1730) up from Plantation Road
PHOTO COURTESY GINA PATTERSON

burned, and it would take two generations of Ruffin family members before his great grandson, John Augustine Ruffin Jr. and his wife Mary Ball Saunders rebuilt the property.

Today, the 2,500-acre farm is still family owned and operated. The house and grounds are closed at this time.

Farther down VA 5 is **Westover Plantation** and church, built circa 1730, by William Byrd II, the founder of Richmond. The Georgian building is known for its secret passages, magnificent gardens (the tulip poplars are more than 150 years old), and architectural details. The grounds and gardens are open daily, although the house is not open to the public.

Continue on VA 5 to **Charles City, the** county seat where you can see the 280-year-old **Charles City County Courthouse** and visit the county's self-service visitor center, inside the historic 1901 Clerk's Office adjacent to the courthouse. Four outdoor interpretive exhibits provide information about Charles City's courthouse and involvement in the Revolutionary and Civil Wars. The courthouse is on the National Register of Historic Places and is a Civil War Trails Site.

Near here Chief Powhatan ruled an extensive Virginia Indian confederation comprised of more than 30 tribes. You may remember the legend of his daughter,

Pocahontas (whose given name was *Matoaka*), saving the life of Captain John Smith. The Native Americans called the James River the Powhatan, but the early English settlers renamed it after their King, James I.

Less well known is that a free African-American community, one of the first in the Americas, flourished here in the 1600s, and that this is the birthplace of Lott Cary, an African-American Baptist minister who was born into slavery and purchased his freedom along with that of his two children. Cary was the first black American missionary to Africa, became a lay physician practicing in Africa, was instrumental in the founding of the Colony of Liberia, and in August, 1828, became acting governor of Liberia.

Charles City to Williamsburg

Continuing down VA 5 just 3 miles from the courthouse brings you to **Sherwood Forest Plantation,** home of John Tyler, our 10th president. As previously mentioned, Tyler took over the office in 1841 when his neighbor William Henry Harrison died after 30 days as president. Tyler had a long history of political office, serving twice as governor of Virginia and in both the US Senate and US House of Representatives.

Tyler's descendants are still in the area, and a younger Harrison Tyler retains ownership of Sherwood Forest. The evolution of the main mansion spans almost 4 centuries, beginning in 1660. Known as the longest frame dwelling in America, it reached its present length—more than 300 feet—when President Tyler added a 68-foot ballroom for dancing the Virginia Reel.

In addition to the main house and its elegant furnishings, many original outbuildings have been restored, including the tobacco barn, kitchen, laundry, smokehouse, milk house, and law office. A formal garden is included in the 25 acres of terraced gardens, woods, and lawn. While the colonial mansion is not open to the public, the expansive grounds are.

Past Sherwood Forest turn right on VA 619 to visit **North Bend Plantation.** This area was first occupied by the Weanoc Indians. The earliest known owner of the land is recorded as Christina (Shields) Minge. The property passed to her son, John Minge. He and his wife, Sarah Harrison (yes, sister of William Henry) built the first part of North Bend in 1801 in the federal style.

Mr. and Mrs. George Forbes Copland II are the current owners. He is the great nephew of Sarah and William Henry Harrison.

A self-guided tour of the grounds and dependencies of North Bend includes the old well, dairy house, icehouse, cookhouse, smokehouse, and slave quarters.

Farther down VA 619 you find **Kittiewan Plantation,** next the last plantation on this route, and one of the oldest on the river. It overlooks Kittiewan Creek and

Plantation Road, Sherwood Forest Plantation sign
PHOTO COURTESY GINA PATTERSON

the James River, and from the exterior the 18th-century building is a typical colonial-period medium-size framed clapboard plantation house characteristic of the Virginia Tidewater. The interior was done in floor-to-ceiling Georgian paneling.

The 720-acre property, now occupied by the Archeological Society of Virginia, is a working farm and museum. The grounds feature the Rickman family cemetery, earthworks from the Civil War, and a view of Kittiewan Creek. It's open on the second Sat of the month.

Return to VA 5 and turn right and you leave Charles City County and its plantations as you cross the wide **Chickahominy River** with a gorgeous view of the Chickahominy and, to the right, the James River. Follow the VA 5 signs that require a southeastern right turn and soon urban life—subdivisions, signs, condos, and stores—appear.

Turn right at the light at Five Forks taking VA 615 (Ironbound Road) to VA 31/VA 5 (Jamestown Road). A left on to VA 5 will take you into **Williamsburg** and the route's end. And a right on to VA 31 will take you to **Jamestown Settlement** and the entrance to the Colonial Parkway. Williamsburg is at the midpoint of the Colonial Parkway, Route 18, and described in that section.

Or, after you cross the Harrison Bridge on VA 106/156, you can turn right on VA 10. Old City Point, now **Hopewell,** is 4.7 miles down (or up) the road, where General Ulysses S. Grant directed the siege of Petersburg for 9.5 months from the grounds of Appomattox Plantation (c. 1763). President Lincoln also spent 2 of the last 3 weeks of his life, March 24–April 8, at City Point. Although Lincoln stayed on the *River Queen* steamboat docked in the James River, he left the ship to tour battlefields, talk with soldiers, visit the wounded, and see Petersburg and Richmond after they fell.

Weston Plantation (circa 1789) is a 2.1-mile drive from Hopewell. The guided house tour includes 3 floors furnished in period antiques and reproductions. The home is notable for preserving much of its original interior.

18

Colonial Parkway

Jamestown to Williamsburg to Yorktown

General description: Colonial Parkway connects the two sections of Colonial National Historical Park: Jamestown, in 1609 the first English settlement in America, and Yorktown, a colonial town and scene of the last Revolutionary War skirmish. Between the two is Colonial Williamsburg, former colonial capital with more than 500 restored buildings. The parkway itself is a 23-mile, 2-lane highway and can be easily driven in less than an hour. Many historical and other attractions are nearby that may induce you to linger longer. The parkway does not permit trucks or commercial vehicles (tour buses are allowed). Unlike at many other national parks and monuments, there is no fee to use the parkway.

Special attractions: For many visitors, history, theme parks, and shopping malls are bigger draws here than the scenery. You're encouraged to see the shoreline, water, and woods along the parkway. Jamestown, Yorktown, and Colonial Williamsburg each played a unique role in our country's history. Several pull-offs allow a more intimate view of the flora and fauna; the ones at the James and York Rivers are particularly popular because of the panoramic views across each river.

Location: Colonial National Historical Park, off I-64 by Williamsburg in the east-central part of the state.

Route numbers: Colonial Parkway, plus unnumbered loop tours at Yorktown and Jamestown.

Travel season: All year. Summer can be hot and muggy with large crowds.

Camping: None within the federal areas. Nearby are several privately owned campgrounds.

Services: Gas, motels, hotels, and restaurants of every kind and price range are available year-round in the surrounding area.

Nearby attractions: The entire area is a major tourist destination. There is plenty to do for every taste including Carter's Grove, Busch Gardens, Water Country USA, Anheuser-Busch Brewery Tour, and Williamsburg Pottery (outlet center).

For more information: Greater Williamsburg Chamber & Tourism Alliance, (757) 253-2262 or (800) 368-6511, williamsburgcc.com; Colonial Williamsburg, (757) 229-1000, history.org; York County Tourism Development, (757) 890-3500, visityorktown.org; Jamestown Settlement & Yorktown Victory Center, (757) 253-4838 or (888) 593-4682, historyisfun.org.

The Route

This relatively short route—23 miles of scenic parkway, plus 7 or 8 miles of optional loop tours at both ends—spans more than 400 years of American history by joining Jamestown, Yorktown, and Williamsburg. Jamestown, the first permanent, English-speaking settlement in North America in 1607 was the first colonial

Colonial Parkway

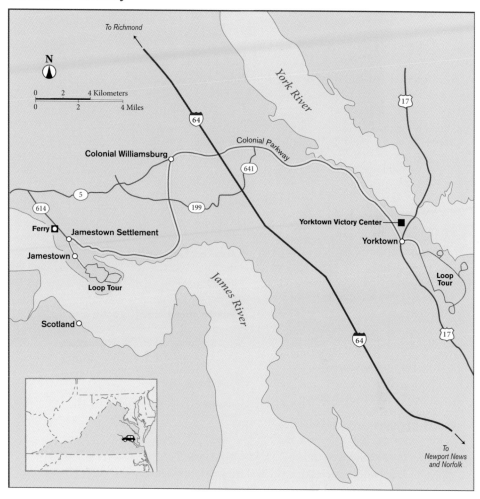

capital. Yorktown was an early colonial port town and site of the Revolutionary War's last battle where the British army surrendered to General George Washington in 1781. Midway between the two is Colonial Williamsburg, the restored second capital of Virginia, with more than 500 buildings restored or renovated to look much as they did in the 1700s.

The three settlements and the parkway make up Colonial National Historical Park. One fee admits you to Jamestown Settlement and the Yorktown Victory Center. Although you can start at either end or at several places in the middle, including Williamsburg, it is chronologically correct to begin where it all began, at Jamestown, southwest of Williamsburg on an island in the James River.

An aerial view of Jamestown

Jamestown

Jamestown was colonized in 1607 by about 100 colonists who made the 4-month trip from England in three small ships. Two years later there were some 500 settlers. It was a difficult and dangerous life in the wilderness; during the winter of 1609–1610, known as the "Starving Time," more than three-fourths of the colonists died.

Despite the many hardships of frontier life, the colonists persevered; the town grew, and became the first colonial capital. Today the town of Jamestown is gone, except for some foundations and ruins adjacent to the river.

An 8-mile loop road through the island's flat marshes gives you an idea of what the original settlers faced, helped by markers and illustrations along the way. Several short trails lead off the loop road so you can see tidal bays and the scenic **James River**. You'll also see numerous wading birds and shorebirds, and possibly distant ships down the river toward Newport News and Norfolk.

The visitor center shares the story of their struggle for survival, with numerous articles of daily colonial life on view. You can walk past excavations and fragile foundations, and may be able to join a tour to see archaeologists continuing their work. One totally unexpected discovery was the foundations of **James Fort,** built in the 1620s and believed to have been eroded away by the James River. Nearby is the reconstructed **Glasshouse,** where craftspeople in period clothing demonstrate 17th-century glassblowing techniques.

Just outside the federal area is the **Jamestown Settlement,** maintained by the state of Virginia. No ghost town here: The three ships, *Susan Constant, God-speed, and Discovery,* have been replicated in full-size. It's amazing that people boarded these small vessels and endured months at sea to get to the unknown shores of this continent. The first fort and an Indian village vividly bring colonial times to life. Costumed guides, with chickens underfoot, lend realism.

And just beyond the Jamestown Settlement are the slips for the **Jamestown-Scotland Ferry.** This free, modern ferry, maintained by the state of Virginia, plies its way between Jamestown and Scotland, Virginia, 24 hours a day. A trip over, even if you turn around and come right back, gives you a waterside perspective of Jamestown that is similar to what the original settlers saw as they made their way up the James.

Colonial Williamsburg

When you're ready to leave Jamestown, head toward Williamsburg and Yorktown on the 2-lane, limited-access parkway. For several miles you pass marshes and inlets along the James. Egrets and shorebirds are common. Frequent turnoffs with roadside markers provide good viewpoints.

The road heads inland through stands of hardwoods, including oak and sycamore. The parkway was built between 1930 and 1957, with a delay in the early 1940s due to World War II. Designed by Calvert Vaux and Frederick Law Olmsted (designers of New York City's Central Park), the route was chosen for its scenic beauty and has no historical significance. The maximum speed limit is 45. Be prepared to share the road with bike riders.

The well-marked exit for **Colonial Williamsburg** is about 9 miles from Jamestown, just before a short tunnel that passes underneath the complex. Williamsburg became the second colonial capital when it was moved from Jamestown in 1699. The restoration of Colonial Williamsburg was created and funded by John D. Rockefeller Jr. A variety of tours, demonstrations of colonial living and activities, and even libations and meals at colonial taverns provide rich insights into 18th-century life.

In addition to the complex of Colonial Williamsburg itself, you may want to visit nearby attractions included in admission, particularly the **Abby Aldrich Rockefeller Folk Art Center** and formal gardens. One walking tour, "The Other Half," focuses on colonial life as experienced by the slaves who made up 50

Battlefield at Yorktown
©N4 PHOTOVIDEO/SHUTTERSTOCK.COM

percent of the population. In addition, there are many private homes and gardens that are open to the public. Adjacent to the historical district is the **College of William and Mary**.

Route 17, The Plantation Road, concludes at Williamsburg.

Yorktown

The parkway continues past Williamsburg. The many bridges and other structures are detailed in brick, laid in English and Flemish bonds, to reflect the region's colonial architecture. As the area grew, new intersections and crossings developed, and each one required a bridge. Modern developments, such as the I-64 underpass completed in 1965, continue to use the traditional brick facing and railing details over concrete arches as designed for the original spans.

The Governor's Palace in Colonial Williamsburg
©STEVE ESTVANIK/SHUTTERSTOCK.COM

You emerge from the woods on the shore of the **York River** at **Felgrass Creek,** a popular local picnic and fishing area. The river is on your left as you drive the last few miles to **Yorktown.** The large structure extending several thousand feet into the river is a US Navy munitions pier where arms are loaded onto naval ships.

The parkway ends at the **Yorktown Victory Center,** which features a full-size mock-up of the gun deck and other sections of a British frigate that was sunk during the Battle of Yorktown. The federal area preserves two distinct sections in addition to the visitor center: the historic town of Yorktown, and the **Battle of Yorktown.** The battle in 1781 followed a 3-week siege by General George Washington that surrounded the British army. The British had been held in place by an offshore French blockade. After a few minor skirmishes, the British, lead by Commander Lord Cornwallis, surrendered to Washington, effectively ending the Revolutionary War; however, a formal peace treaty was not signed for another 2 years.

Two 8-mile loop tours on wooded, winding roads cover the battle area. During the route you can trace the battle and see siege lines (trenches), cannons, and other equipment. Periodically you can see the York River. The route ends at the loop tours.

Unlike at Jamestown, a living town of Yorktown still exists. The park preserves much of the historical area, including some private, historic homes. From the visitor center a guided foot tour of Yorktown passes by the **Yorktown Victory Monument** erected by the US at the centennial in 1881 to commemorate the French alliance during the war.

19

Over & Under Big Walker

Wytheville–Bluefield Loop

General description: This 75-mile loop route through the mountains of southwest Virginia follows the old highway up, down, and around the mountains to West Virginia. From there, you reverse direction and return on a modern interstate, tunneling through the mountains you climbed over earlier. The route is mostly through the Jefferson National Forest and incorporates the Big Walker Mountain Scenic Byway.

Special attractions: Jefferson National Forest, the Big Walker Mountain Scenic Byway and lookout, scenic mountain views, small country towns, and a restored Indian village. The contrast between the winding, hilly old roads and the modern interstate with tunnels adds to the interest.

Location: Southwest Virginia, outside of Wytheville near the intersection of I-77 and I-81.

Route numbers: US 52; VA 717; I-77. FR 206 for the optional trip to the Big Bend Picnic Area and viewpoint.

Travel season: Both spring and fall give the mountain views special hues and colors. Winter travel can be hazardous, but the views of snow-covered mountains from the top of Big Walker are rewarding.

Camping: Camping is available at the Stony Fork campground in Jefferson National Forest near the route's beginning. There are private campgrounds at the Wytheville KOA and at Fort Chiswell and Bluefield, Virginia.

Services: Gasoline, restaurants, motels, and hotels are available in Wytheville and Bluefield, West Virginia. Small towns along the route have gasoline and restaurants.

Nearby attractions: The Shot Tower Historical State Park in Austinville shows how rifle balls were made from chunks of lead. The New River Trail State Park, headquartered in Austinville, provides more than 57 miles of hiking along a former railroad bed stretching from Fries to Pulaski. Bluefield, West Virginia, is the terminal for Coal Heritage Trail, a West Virginia scenic route.

For more information: Blue Ridge Travel Association, (276) 228-7092 or (800) 446-9670, virginiablueridge.org; Wythe County Parks and Recreation, (276) 223-4519, wytheco.org; Wytheville Convention & Visitors Bureau, (276) 223-3355 or (877) 347-8307, visitwytheville.com.

The Route

This 75-mile loop route is a study in contrasts. Beginning near Wytheville, the trip out follows VA 717 and US 52, the old, 2-lane, winding, and hilly road over Big Walker Mountain, past several small towns, and across other ridges to the West Virginia border, mostly within the Jefferson National Forest. From there you reverse direction and take modern I-77 to cruise leisurely through the rugged country on gentle curves, tunneling under Big Walker Mountain to your starting point. The trip out on old roads takes several hours. The return trip on the interstate takes about 25 minutes.

Over and Under Big Walker

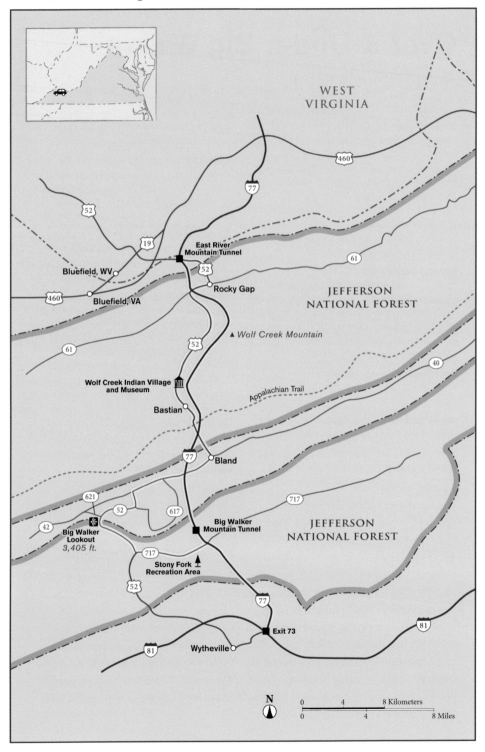

WEST
VIRGINIA

460

77

52

52

19

East River
Mountain Tunnel

Bluefield, WV

52

460

Rocky Gap

61

JEFFERSON
NATIONAL FOREST

Bluefield, VA

61

52

▲ Wolf Creek Mountain

40

Wolf Creek Indian Village
and Museum

Appalachian Trail

Bastian

77

Bland

621

717

52

617

JEFFERSON
NATIONAL FOREST

42

Big Walker
Lookout
3,405 ft.

Big Walker
Mountain Tunnel

717

Stony Fork
Recreation Area

52

77

81

81

Wytheville

Exit 73

81

N

0   4   8 Kilometers

0   4   8 Miles

Big Walker Mountain Tunnel
©THOMASON PHOTOGRAPHY/SHUTTERSTOCK.COM

The area's craggy hills and mountains in southwest Virginia presented a formidable barrier to travel to early settlers. There is little level land; early roads followed old trails across the numerous, unbroken ridges and wound around countless mountains and smaller hills. As automobile travel developed, the highways followed the old trails, and US 52 (formerly known as US 21) between Wytheville and Bluefield, West Virginia, is no exception. Today US 52 still climbs up, over, and down Big Walker Mountain and then follows numerous curves and crosses smaller hills and valleys.

Four-lane I-77 considerably shortened this trip, and made it easier and faster. Cliffs were blasted away to eliminate curves, and cut-and-fill smoothed out many small grades. Two-mile-long tunnels eliminated the long and difficult mountain drives over Big Walker and East River Mountains.

Wytheville, just south of the route, is known for its numerous antiques shops and outlets, many of which reflect its German, Scotch, and Irish heritage. A few more miles south, lead mines near Austinville were important during the Revolutionary and Civil Wars, when the mines became a major source of lead for the Confederacy. The metal was taken to the nearby Shot Tower (now a state historical park) where the lead was heated, then dropped in water to make rifle balls and other shot.

Wytheville to West Virginia

To begin the route, take exit 47 off I-77 at the intersection with VA 717, about 5 miles north of **Wytheville**. This is within the **Jefferson National Forest.** Ahead on I-77 are the long ridge of Big Walker Mountain and the twin portals into the **Big Walker Mountain Tunnel.**

Go west on 2-lane VA 717 which parallels the ridge, following the signs for the **Big Walker Mountain Scenic Byway.** In a few miles you pass the entrance to the **Stony Fork Recreation Area,** which has a campground, hiking trails, and fishing in Stony Fork Creek.

At the intersection with US 52, turn right. The road soon heads uphill for the long climb up **Big Walker Mountain.** At the top, elevation 3,405 feet, is the privately owned **Big Walker Lookout** which features a 100-foot fire tower, gift shop, and restaurant. The most outstanding views are from the tower above the treetops, or you can enjoy excellent views from the gift shop without making that long climb. In one direction lie ridges, valleys, farmlands, and small towns; in the other is an unspoiled sea of mountain peaks and forests.

When Big Walker Lookout opened in 1947, it was advertised as "the highest point on US 21 between the Great Lakes and Florida." US 21 no longer exists, but the lookout is still far higher than anyplace in the Great Lakes or Florida. The facility is open Apr through Oct. A fee is charged to climb the tower.

The lookout also marks the place where Confederate heroine Mary Tynes crossed the mountain in 1863 to warn the residents of Wytheville of a raid by Union Colonel John Toland. Alerted by the alarm, the fighting townspeople turned away the raiders, killing Toland during the skirmish.

A side trip from the lookout on FR 206 leads 4 miles to the **Big Bend Picnic Area.** You can see excellent Valley and Ridge views from this tree-shaded site, at an elevation of 4,000 feet.

After a short ride along the ridge, it's a curvy downhill trip off Big Walker. You emerge in an open valley. At the intersection with VA 42, turn right, continuing on US 52 along a rare level stretch on this section.

In a few minutes you cross I-77, and the Big Walker Mountain Scenic Byway ends. Just beyond is the town of **Bland,** county seat of Bland County, with an imposing courthouse. US 52 turns left in Bland.

It's all uphill and downhill from here. If you look carefully you may spot markers for the **Appalachian Trail** as it crosses the highway a few miles past

Jefferson National Forest
©MATT SMITH PHOTOGRAPHY/SHUTTERSTOCK.COM

Bland. **Wolf Creek Indian Village and Museum,** just at the edge of **Bastian**, is a site carbon dating tells us was occupied as early as AD 1215. Now interpreters wearing native costumes reenact historical times.

For a few miles, US 52 parallels I-77 where it cuts through **Wolf Creek Mountain.** (Before the interstate was built, the old road went up and over this mountain.) Across the interstate, the cliffs and half-mile-long outcrop are composed of Clinch sandstone of Silurian age.

A steep climb after the town of Rocky Gap brings you to the foot of **East River Mountain** to an intersection where US 52 joins I-77. Ahead are the twin mile-long tunnels that bore through the mountain. About halfway through, watch for the boundary marker as you pass into West Virginia several hundred feet underground. Take the first exit after the tunnel (in West Virginia), still following US 52, which turns left at the stop sign.

The "old road–US 52" portion ends here. For a respite, you can follow US 52 a few miles into the town of **Bluefield, West Virginia,** adjacent to its smaller sister city of Bluefield, Virginia. The **Coal Heritage Trail,** a West Virginia scenic route, begins near Bluefield.

And Back Again

If you want to return immediately, turn left (south) on US 52/I-77 and drive through the **East River Mountain Tunnel** again. At the other end, stay on I-77 for sweeping views of the steep hills you recently drove through.

I-77 cuts though the hills with gentle, high-speed curves. It's a fast trip, mostly downhill. In a few minutes you pass the cliff and outcrop where US 52 parallels the highway. The route flattens out for a few miles as you approach the ridge of Big Walker Mountain and the route through the tunnel, several thousand feet below the road you traversed earlier. On the other side is exit 47 for VA 717 where you began the drive at the scenic byway. You can exit here, or stay on I-77 another 7 miles to **Wytheville** and the intersection with I-81.

Shot Tower State Park
©WESLEY DANIEL DAVIS/SHUTTERSTOCK.COM

20

Buchanan to Blacksburg

Mountain Streams & Valley

General description: This 70-mile drive, almost entirely within Jefferson National Forest, follows twisty Craig Creek surrounded by the Allegheny and Blue Ridge Mountains. It then climbs into the mountains and traverses an unspoiled farming valley virtually all the way to Blacksburg.

Special attractions: Unspoiled, clear mountain streams, scenic mountain vistas, curvy roads, and very few towns. This drive appeals to those who want a mountain drive with no tourist distractions or towns. Most of the drive is along a designated Virginia Scenic Byway.

Location: Western Virginia, off I-81 at Buchanan between Lexington and Roanoke.

Route numbers: VA 43, 615, and 42; US 220 and 460.

Travel season: Spring, summer, and fall are the preferred seasons. Heavy mountain snows may temporarily close the road in winter.

Camping: A private campground with about 100 sites is located at Natural Bridge, 10 miles north of Buchanan. There are also two campgrounds in the Buchanan district:

North Creek Campground and Middle Creek Campground.

Services: Gasoline, restaurants, and motels are available in Buchanan at the route's beginning and along US 460 at the conclusion. New Castle, about halfway, has gasoline. Make sure you have sufficient gas.

Nearby attractions: Natural Bridge, a 215-foot limestone arch, is about 10 miles north of Buchanan on I-81, and can easily be combined with this route. Once owned by Thomas Jefferson, it was known as one of the Seven Natural Wonders of the World, and as of this writing, it and the adjacent attractions are for sale. The Peaks of Otter on the northern section of the Blue Ridge Parkway, Route 9, are south of Buchanan. Mountain Lake resort lies north of Newport.

For more information: Botetourt County Office of Tourism, (540) 473-1167, visit botetourt.com; Lexington & the Rockbridge Area Tourism Development, (540) 463-3777 or (877) 453-9822, lexingtonvirginia .com; Roanoke Valley Convention and Visitors Bureau, (540) 342-6025 or (800) 635-5535, visitvablueridge.com; Natural Bridge, (540) 291-2121 or (800) 533-1410, naturalbridgeva.com.

The Route

This 70-mile route leaves from the town of Buchanan. The narrow, 2-lane road follows the Upper James River and one of its twisting tributaries upstream between the Blue Ridge and Allegheny Mountains. Then, in a dramatic change of pace, the route climbs over the ridgeline and passes through a small valley between the ridges. The route concludes in a short stretch of 4-lane highway ending in the city of Blacksburg, home of Virginia Tech (Virginia Polytechnic Institute, or VPI).

Buchanan to Blacksburg

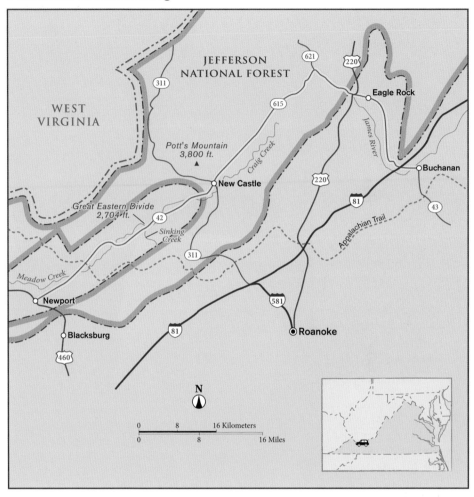

Buchanan is off exit 167 on I-81, about midway between Roanoke and Lexington and about 10 miles south the Natural Bridge exit. You can also reach Buchanan from the northern section of the Blue Ridge Parkway, Route 9, by taking VA 43 north at milepost 90.9, just past the Peaks of Otter.

In the 1850s, the James River and Kanawha Canal western terminus was at Buchanan, making it an important commercial town. Starting at the Fall Line in Richmond, all that's left in this area are some piers and remnants, north of town. Today Buchanan's main industries are beef and dairy cattle, timber, and limestone and crushed stone; tourism is increasing in importance.

Autumn along the James River
©DONNA SMITH PHOTOGRAPHY/SHUTTERSTOCK.COM

Buchanan to New Castle

From downtown **Buchanan,** go north on VA 43, a Virginia Scenic Byway. Note the swinging pedestrian bridge, the only footbridge in Virginia to cross the James River. After you cross I-81, look back at the town and the gap for the James River. The route enters the **Jefferson National Forest.**

The road, known locally as Narrow Passage Road, curves along the James River. This section of the James, many miles upstream from the head of navigation at Richmond, is known to anglers for its sometimes elusive smallmouth bass and muskie.

You drive through a narrow pass at **Eagle Rock** where sandstone outcrops stand almost vertical. Just beyond, the road curves around **Rathole Mountain** on the right to the stop sign at US 220 where VA 43 ends.

Natural Bridge
©IVAN TSVETKOV/SHUTTERSTOCK.COM

The route now follows **Craig Creek,** a much smaller stream than the James. In a few miles, at the intersection with VA 621, go left, still following VA 615. The creek, with its sinuous S-curves, clear water, rocky bottom, and tree-shaded shoreline is popular with trout anglers. Although the stream may (or may not) be shallow enough to wade across at the time of your visit, houses built on stilts attest to frequent floods and high water.

The road follows the creek, although noticeably less curvy. Occasional stretches lead away from the creek to higher ground through thick woods. A few trailheads lead into the adjacent national forest and high country to the right. Gradually you emerge into more open country, viewing the Allegheny Mountains. The prominent peak ahead is **Pott's Mountain,** elevation 3,800 feet.

VA 615 ends at **New Castle,** the county seat of Craig County. Go left 1 block and turn left on Main Street. At the stop sign cross VA 311 and go straight on VA 42.

The route immediately begins a steep and curving climb up from the valley floor. In about a mile is an overlook on the left where you can gaze down on New Castle 1,000 feet below, and at the numerous peaks surrounding the town. After further climbing, the route enters a broad highland valley about a mile wide between mountain ridges.

Great Eastern Divide to Blacksburg

Eight miles from New Castle you cross the almost imperceptible **Great Eastern Divide** at an elevation of 2,704 feet. Behind you, to the east, the waters flow into Craig Creek, then east into the James River, Chesapeake Bay, and the Atlantic Ocean. Ahead, on the other side, to the west, water flows into Sinking Creek, then into the New River, the Kanawha, and Ohio, to join the mighty Mississippi, where it then flows south to the Gulf of Mexico and eventually into the Atlantic. Look for a highway marker delineating the spot. The more famous Continental Divide follows the Rocky Mountain ridges, with the westward flow eventually ending up in the Pacific and the eastern in the Gulf of Mexico, etc.

There is little level ground in this high country. The open fields, too steep in most places for crops, support numerous herds of grazing cattle and sheep. You pass trim and prosperous-looking farmhouses, barns, and silos, many with small gardens wherever a plot of level ground can be found. Many fields also contain grazing teams of Percheron and Clydesdale horses. These big workhorses are used on slopes that are too steep on which to safely use tractors.

The valley flattens out, virtually surrounded by mountain peaks, as the route follows **Sinking Creek.** In a few miles you pass the little town of **Sinking Spring.** As you may guess, the name "Sinking" means that you are in limestone cave

Foggy night in Blacksburg
©MICHAEL METHENY/SHUTTERSTOCK.COM

country where many small streams disappear underground, often emerging several miles farther downstream.

Beyond Sinking Spring, the **Appalachian Trail** crosses the route. A few miles beyond there, VA 42 ends at the intersection with US 460. Off the route and a few miles to the right on US 460 is the road to the resort area at **Mountain Lake.** At 4,000 feet elevation, Mountain Lake is the highest lake in the state.

The route turns left on US 460 for a speedy, downhill trip with several panoramic views ahead to the route's end at Blacksburg.

Blacksburg is home to Virginia Polytechnic Institute and State College, more commonly known as **Virginia Tech.** Also in Blacksburg is **Smithfield Plantation,** an 18th-century mansion restored to its colonial grandeur and open to the public during the warmer months.

21

Burke's Garden

Valley in the Sky

General description: Burke's Garden is a 10-mile-long valley entirely surrounded by mountains. The valley consists of fertile, rolling farmland, pastures, and woods. This unstructured 40-mile route allows you to explore this unique area. You can also visit the Historic Crab Orchard Museum and Pioneer Park which has exhibits ranging from a 500-million-year-old fossil tree to an original 1831 McCormick reaper.

Special attractions: Burke's Garden itself is the main attraction, including the enclosed valley, rich farmlands, woods, and mountains views.

Location: Southwest Virginia, near Tazewell. Tazewell is on VA 16 about 25 miles north of Marion.

Route numbers: VA 61, 623, 666, 625, 667, 627, and 42.

Travel season: In winter, the altitude and bowl-like shape of the valley bring heavy snows which can temporarily close roads. Otherwise the trip can be made at any time. As in most of Virginia, each season has its own special beauty. Autumn is especially beautiful, when the altitude and local climate combine to turn the leaves exquisite shades of yellow, orange, and red. The Burke's Garden Fall Festival, held the last Saturday in Sept, is timed to coincide with the peak leaf season which makes it the year's heaviest travel day.

Camping: Not available.

Services: All services are available in Tazewell. Limited food and gasoline can be obtained in the valley.

Nearby attractions: The Pocahontas Exhibition Mine northeast of Tazewell provides guided tours through an exhibition coal mine.

For more information: Wytheville Convention & Visitors Bureau, (276) 223-3355 or (877) 347-8307, visitwytheville.com; Tazewell Office of Economic Development, (800) 588-9401, visittazewellcounty.org; Lost World Ranch, (276) 472-2347, lostworldranch.com; Burke's Garden General Store, (276) 472-2222.

The Route

Burke's Garden east of Tazewell is an elliptical valley about 10 miles long, totally enclosed by circular Garden Mountain. Inside this sparsely populated valley is some of the richest farmland in the state with views in all directions of rolling country with mountains in the background. This short route, less than 40 miles long and with no specific route to follow within the valley, will allow you to explore the nooks and crannies of this unique area.

Before visiting Burke's Garden you may want to spend some time in the **Historic Crab Orchard Museum and Pioneer Park** west of Tazewell on US 19. Among the historical exhibits (and history as defined by Crab Orchard begins more than half a billion years ago) are mammoth bones and teeth, another

Burke's Garden

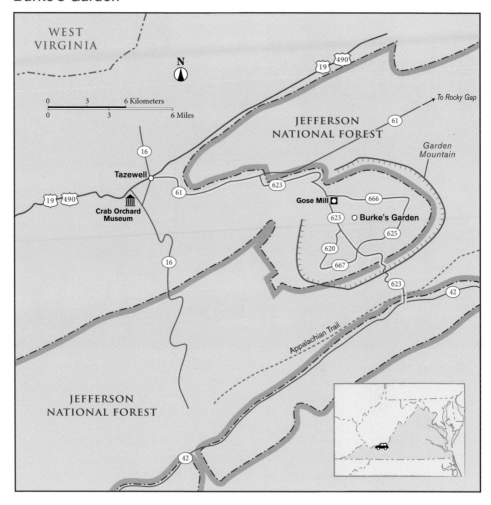

fossil—a Lepidodendron tree that grew during the coal-forming eras—and a replica of a Native American village, surrounded by a wooden stockade.

More recent exhibits include early automobiles and one of Cyrus McCormick's original 1831 reapers. A dozen buildings and associated exhibits depict life in the Virginia mountains in the 1830s. The facility is open all year, with reduced hours in winter.

The valley on this route was discovered in 1748 by James Burke. According to legend, Burke, who was part of a survey crew, buried some potato peelings by a campfire. The peelings took root and provided a welcome crop of potatoes for next year's survey party, who laughingly referred to "Burke's garden." The name for the valley stuck, and the mountain that encircles the valley is now known as

Potatoes are still grown and sold in this fertile farm area.

Garden Mountain. Burke was not able to enjoy his namesake valley. Legend says that he moved to North Carolina and was a neighbor to Daniel Boone.

At an elevation of about 3,100 feet, the valley has the reputation for being the highest, coldest, greenest, and prettiest valley in the state. It is a fact that the rich limestone soils combine with other factors to make this rolling valley floor one of the most fertile farm areas in the state.

Many people think that Burke's Garden is a crater that formed from some ancient, cataclysmic volcanic eruption. Actually the valley and enclosing mountains are the results of erosion of folded sedimentary rocks. In Ordovician time, 500 million years ago, reefs deposited limestone and dolomite in warm ocean waters. These rocks were then covered by sandstone. Later, when the Appalachian Mountains were formed, the rocks that now make up Burke's Garden were uplifted and folded into a dome or plunging anticline.

Millions of years of erosion slowly wore away the uplifted sandstone rocks in the middle of the dome. Today the valley floor is underlain by the dolomite and limestone, and the harder and more resistant sandstone makes up the ring of encircling mountains.

Around "God's Thumbprint"

To begin the route, go east from Tazewell on VA 61. This is a 2-lane road through mostly open farming and cattle country. In a few miles a low range of hills, about 600 feet higher than the valley, appears on the left. This is the southern rim of circular **Garden Mountain;** inside Garden Mountain lies **Burke's Garden.**

Turn right on VA 623, about 8 miles from Tazewell. In a few minutes the narrow road begins the long and curvy climb to the ridgetop. As you ascend, valley views appear through the trees behind, and you see sandstone outcrops as you approach the ridgeline.

As you come over the ridge, the elliptical bowl of Burke's Garden lies before you. A short, downhill run brings you to the valley floor.

For a complete tour of the area sometimes known as "God's Thumbprint" turn left on VA 666 by the bridge at Gose Mill, and follow the complete loop around the valley. The route numbers will change as you drive around, but that will not be a problem. All roads will take you back to VA 623, the main road through the valley.

Along the way you'll pass farms with herds of beef and dairy cattle, fields of corn and other crops, small streams, and groves of hardwoods. Several stands of maple line the road, magnificent in autumn with their orange and red attire. There are several home-based quilt and craft shops, some run by Amish settlers. And visible in all directions is the encircling ridge of **Garden Mountain** rising from the valley floor. What you won't see are many people. About 600 folk—far less than the number of cattle—live within the valley's 20,000 acres.

The "town" of Burke's Garden consists of a general store which has been opened recently by Mattie Schlabach who sells Amish baked goods, crafts, and other products. There's also a post office and the Central Church is the oldest Lutheran place of worship in the state; the adjacent cemetery has hand-carved German headstones dating from the 1700s. The nearby former schoolhouse is now the town meeting hall. (Schoolchildren go by bus over the mountain to Tazewell.)

Lost World Ranch has Appaloosa llamas and two-humped (Bactrian) camels, and with nearly five dozen camels (of which 21 are rare white ones), it's thought to be the largest herd on the continent. Watch them graze in the bucolic pastures, looking perhaps more like a painting than real life. Tours (for a fee) are available on weekdays 10 a.m. to 4 p.m. and on weekends by appointment.

The valley is lovely at any time, with changing leaf colors, highlighted by the brilliant red maples, peaking in late September. The **Burke's Garden Fall Festival** on the last Saturday of September has numerous craft exhibits and sales of local produce. The festival is also a heavy travel day which is about the only time when you will see more than a few cars along the valley roads. Heavy snow

Cows grazing on a hillside field
©JOHN PAGLIUCA/SHUTTERSTOCK.COM

can temporarily close roads in winter; more than 100 inches of snow have been recorded some years.

When you're ready to leave, go north on VA 623 (the way you came in) over Garden Mountain to VA 61 and turn left to return to Tazewell.

An alternative exit is to go south on VA 623 although this is an unpaved, narrow, curvy road with steep grades for 10 miles through a portion of **Jefferson National Forest.** You will see dirt roads, hardwood forests, laurel, dogwood, Virginia creeper, and rhododendron. It is not recommended for trailers or those unsure of their mountain driving skills. It connects with VA 42 between Bland and VA 16.

22

Breaks Interstate Park

Virginia's Grand Canyon

General description: This is a 60-mile, pristine route through woods and mountains with few towns or distractions along the way, giving a taste of rural Virginia as much of the state must have looked years ago. The route ends at Breaks Interstate Park on the rim of the 1,600-foot-deep canyon of the Russell Fork River, the deepest canyon in the eastern US.

Special attractions: The unspoiled nature of the route is perhaps its biggest attraction. At the end of the route on the Virginia-Kentucky border lies the Breaks Interstate Park, known for its canyon of sheer walls and many recreational activities, including whitewater rafting, hiking, fishing, and horseback riding. Nearby is the John Flannagan Dam in Jefferson National Forest.

Location: Southwest Virginia, off I-81 exit 24. This exit is about 7 miles northeast of Abingdon, and about 20 miles southwest of Marion. on I-81.

Route numbers: VA 80.

Travel season: The route can be taken at any time of year, but most facilities at Breaks Interstate Park are closed from late Oct to Apr. Weekends in Oct attract large numbers of whitewater rafters when water

is released from the James Flannagan Reservoir.

Camping: The campground at Breaks Interstate Park has about 120 campsites, most equipped with all facilities. Several camping areas are scattered around the Flannagan Reservoir area in the Jefferson National Forest.

Services: Gasoline and limited services are available in the small towns along the route. The Breaks Interstate Park has gasoline, a restaurant, and a lodge open from Apr to Dec.

Nearby attractions: The John Flannagan Dam and Reservoir in Jefferson National Forest provides numerous recreational activities. Abingdon at the start of the route has many attractions and is described in Route 23.

For more information: Abingdon Convention & Visitors Bureau, (276) 678-2282 or (800) 435-3440, abingdon.com; Russell County Chamber of Commerce, (276) 889-8041, russellcountyva.org; Dickenson County Chamber of Commerce/Visitor's Center, (276) 926-6074, dickensonchamber.net.

The Route

As with most of western Virginia, this is a special route for the scenery. You won't find museums, Civil War or other historical areas, large cities, or tourist attractions. The route follows a 2-lane, paved, sometimes rough, road uphill and down, mostly through the unspoiled beauty of Jefferson National Forest. It ends about 55 miles later at the cliffs and slopes of Breaks Interstate Park, the largest river canyon east of the Mississippi. Along the way you'll pass a few small towns, including Honaker, known as the Redbud Capital of the World. Mostly, the route passes

Breaks Interstate Park

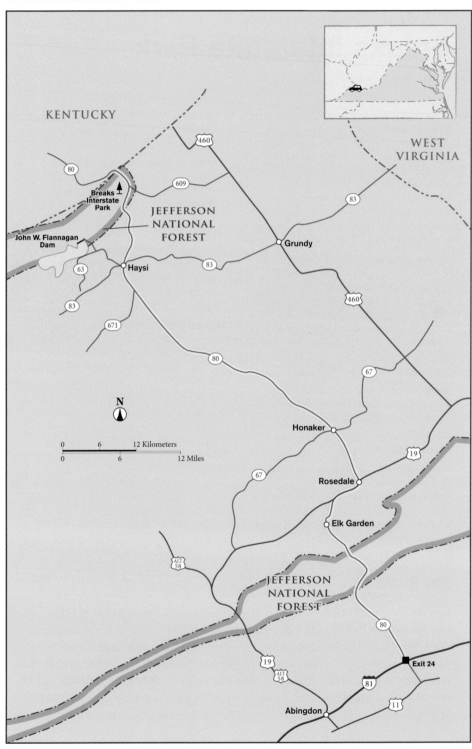

Male northern cardinal (Cardinalis cardinalis) perched in a flowering redbud tree

by woods, streams, and mountains, giving a view of rural Virginia as much of it looked 50 or 75 years ago.

Because of numerous steep grades and sharp curves, you should avoid this route (south of US 19) if you have a trailer more than 30 feet long.

Redbud Highway

The route starts at VA 80 off Exit 24 of I-81. The road is also referred to as **Redbud Highway,** and if you're traveling through here in April, you'll know why. This is about 6 miles northeast of Abingdon via either I-81 or US 11. Abingdon is the starting point for Route 23; its several attractions, including the famous Barter Theatre, are described in that section.

Go north on VA 80, a 2-lane, winding, and hilly road that passes through alternating forests and small farms. This section crosses the Valley and Ridge province of folded rocks made up of sandstone ridges and limestone valleys.

After several miles you cross in short succession the Holston River and the smaller West Fork of the Wolf River. You're now in the **Jefferson National Forest,** and in a series of steep slopes and near hairpin turns, you'll climb and descend several ridges. The forested slopes have restricted views because they are covered with both hardwood and pines, with thick groves of redbud, rhododendron, and other flowering shrubs.

You leave the national forest and descend into a broad, limestone valley. At the stop sign in **Elk Garden** at the intersection with 4-lane US 19, turn right, still following VA 80. In 2 miles at **Rosedale,** turn left, still on VA 80; US 19 continues straight ahead.

Although still 2 lanes, VA 80 is wider here, and with fewer grades. The route crosses the Clinch River and passes through the town of **Honaker,** which holds a **Redbud Festival** in April when the blossoms are at their peak. The Virginia General Assembly gave Honaker the Redbud Capital designation because there are an amazing number of redbud trees here.

Honaker also marks the sometimes indistinct boundary between the Valley and Ridge province of folded sedimentary rocks which you have been crossing and the Appalachian Plateau to the north, of similar, but flat-lying rocks. The Appalachian Plateau in Virginia also includes numerous coal beds; coal mining is a major industry here, although you won't see much evidence of it on this route.

You soon start to follow the **Russell Fork River,** which forms a narrow canyon barely wide enough for the road and the river in most places. Small towns such as **Council** are spread out along the road, 1 block wide and several blocks long. At **Haysi,** the high school is perched on a cliff, and you'll see the stairs and overpass that students must use to cross the road.

In Haysi, VA 63 leads left from VA 80 to the **John Flannagan Dam and Reservoir** in Jefferson National Forest. The rock and earthen dam, 250 feet high and 916 feet long, was completed in 1964 for flood protection. The reservoir is known for its walleye and bass fishing and also provides boating, swimming, hiking, hunting, and picnicking. It is the water supply for several local communities.

Water released from the dam flows down the Russell Fork River and through the canyon in the Breaks Interstate Park just ahead. The river flows north to join the Big Sandy River, which empties into the Ohio River.

Whitewater enthusiasts will instantly recognize the Russell Fork, renowned for its Class VI rapids. The best rafting occurs when water behind the dam is released downstream. Releases from the dam depend on water levels and supply, and major releases are usually scheduled for October weekends, drawing hundreds of rafters.

The Breaks

Stay on VA 80. In a few miles you pass an overlook, giving you the first glimpse of the breaks; just beyond is the entrance to the park, where the route ends. The park's main attraction is the 1,600-foot-deep canyon that curves along the Russell Fork River for 5 miles. A paved road along the canyon's edge leads to several

Whitewater kayaking
©ROBERT PERNELL/SHUTTERSTOCK.COM

overlooks, giving you numerous views of the canyon, river, tiny-looking railroad at the bottom, and distant, rolling mountains.

Reputedly, the breaks were visited by Daniel Boone in 1767. It took until 1951, however, before a paved road was built through the area, linking Virginia and Kentucky; this permitted development of **Breaks Interstate Park** with portions in both states. The only other interstate park is Palisades State Park along the New York–New Jersey border on the Hudson River.

The park is sometimes understandably called the "Grand Canyon of the South" and less reverently as the "Grand Canyon with clothes on," in reference to the thick forest and underbrush that cover all but the steepest slopes. It's called "the breaks" because the Russell Fork gorge breaks up the long ridge of Pine Mountain.

The canyon is formed in limestone capped with red, mottled sandstone. The most impressive overlooks let you see the **Towers,** an almost isolated pyramid of rock surrounded by a 270-degree bend in the Russell Fork River. The gorge also contains an active rail line; you may see long trains loaded with West Virginia coal slowly grind through the canyon and several tunnels on their way to the Newport News seaport. Almost as impressive as the view is the thought of what when into the construction of the railroad through this area.

The region was logged clear in the late 1800s and early 1900s. Today mixed hardwood and pine cover most of the area, with thick growths of rhododendron, dogwood, and other shrubs and wildflowers.

There are several miles of hiking trails, including some leading to the floor of the canyon and to overlooks not accessible by car. The visitor center contains exhibits on the natural history and human history of the area; you can learn the true-life story about the Hatfields (in Virginia) and the McCoys (in Kentucky) whose long-lasting feud resulted in more than 65 murders and numerous fictionalized and dramatized versions in films and on television.

A motor lodge, restaurant, and campground are open April through October. Swimming (in a pool), boating and fishing (in a small lake), and horseback riding are available. Although the Russell Fork has some expert rapids, it also has numerous tamer stretches, and you don't have to be an expert rafter to enjoy the sport. Novices are welcomed by several rafting companies that offer a variety of river trips from gentle to wild during the October rafting season. Check at the visitor center for more information.

When you leave the park, turn right (south) on VA 80 to retrace your route. Turn left (north) on VA 80 to descend to the valley floor and follow the Russell Fork into Kentucky on KY 80 to the intersection with US 460.

23

Abingdon–Big Stone Gap Loop

Coal Country & the Powell Valley

General description: Starting in southwest Virginia in Abingdon, where the famed Barter Theatre presents outstanding theatrical performances, the 75-mile route heads into the Blue Ridge highlands. The route combines visits to Virginia's coal country and Big Stone Gap, including several exhibits and museums, with the outstanding mountain scenery of the Powell Valley and the High Knob Recreation Area in Jefferson National Forest.

Special attractions: Abingdon and the Barter Theatre, coal country, Big Stone Gap, the Coal Museum, the John Fox Jr. Museum, the Powell Valley, Jefferson National Forest, and High Knob Recreation Area and observation tower.

Location: Southwest Virginia. The route begins at Abingdon, off exit 17, I-81.

Route numbers: US 23, Business 23, and Alternate 58; VA 619.

Travel season: Summer is the height of the travel season, when all attractions are open. Except for the side trip to High Knob,

which may be closed because of snow in winter, most of the ride can be taken any time of the year.

Camping: Available in the High Knob Recreation Area near Norton in Jefferson National Forest.

Services: Gasoline, restaurants, and lodging are plentiful in Abingdon, Norton, Big Stone Gap, and nearby Wise, and in most of the towns along the route.

Nearby attractions: The Guest River Gorge, the Virginia Creeper Trail (Route 24), and the town of Bristol (starting point for Route 25).

For more information: Abingdon Convention & Visitors Bureau, (276) 676-2282 or (800) 435-3440, abingdon.com; Henry W. Meador Jr. Coal Museum, (277) 523-9209, bigstonegap.org; Jefferson National Forest, (540) 291-2180, southernregion.fs.fed.us/gwj; Southwest Virginia Museum, (276) 523-1322, dcr.virginia.gov; Wise County Chamber of Commerce, (276) 679-0961, wisecountychamber.org.

The Route

Southwest Virginia is a land of up-and-down with rugged, forested mountains and valleys, open, scenic vistas, and winding roads.

This 75-mile route takes you through the heart of this country, from upbeat Abingdon through Norton and Big Stone Gap. Along the way you'll take a loop through coal mining country, pass through the sweeping grandeur of Powell Valley, and drive to the top of High Knob in Jefferson National Forest for a 360-degree view from the lookout tower. The route ends at Norton.

Although you can complete the route in 1 day, there is so much to see and do that 2 or 3 days are recommended. One almost extinct attraction is the Moonlite Drive In Theater that shows double features on Friday, Saturday, and Sunday

Abingdon–Big Stone Gap Loop

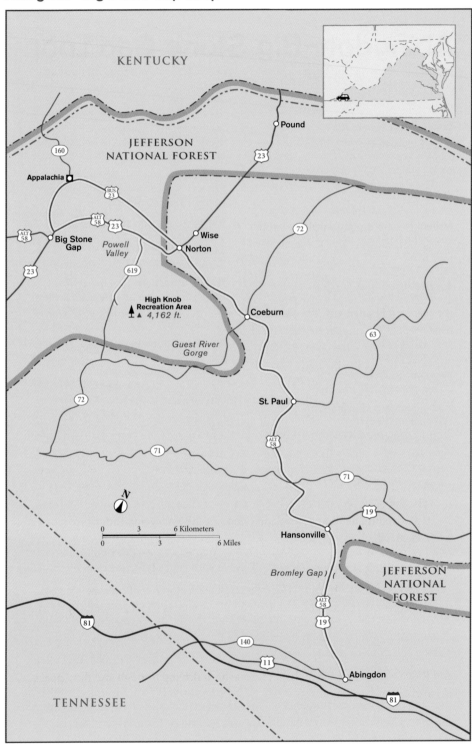

nights during the summer season. Yes, you can catch a first-run family-friendly movie under the stars. This will allow you time to enjoy the many attractions, including a show at the Barter Theatre, a visit to the Coal Museum, an outdoor performance of *The Trail of the Lonesome Pine,* or to just savor the scenery of Powell Valley and the Jefferson National Forest.

Abingdon to Norton

The route begins in **Abingdon** off exit 17 of I-81, the oldest incorporated town west of the Blue Ridge.

The **Barter Theatre** was opened in the Depression year 1933 by Robert Porterfield to help unemployed performers. Cash was scarce, so local residents often bartered for tickets with 40 cents' worth of chickens, eggs, ham, or vegetables. Reputedly, playwright George Bernard Shaw's royalty was paid in spinach; Tennessee Williams received a Virginia ham.

Today the Barter Theatre is the state theater of Virginia, and pigs are no longer accepted in payment. The theater still presents comedy, drama, music, and mystery performances from February through December.

Across Main Street from the Barter Theatre is the venerable **Martha Washington Hotel & Spa.** Built in 1832 as a palatial home for a retired general, this stately institution has also served as a college for young women and a Civil War hospital. The original living room is now the inn's main lobby.

Abingdon is also the northern trailhead for the **Virginia Creeper Trail,** a 34-mile foot, bicycle, and horseback riding trail through the rugged Mount Rogers National Recreation Area to the North Carolina border. The trail follows an old railroad bed and uses several trestles that have been adapted as footpaths; Route 24, Mount Rogers Loop, parallels the Virginia Creeper Trail for several miles.

This route leaves Abingdon heading west and north on 4-lane US Alternate 58/19 past rolling fields and farmland typical of the Valley and Ridge province and the Shenandoah Valley in northern Virginia. After crossing the North Fork of the Holston River, the route passes through **Brumley Gap** in **Clinch Mountain.** The road cuts are mostly in folded sandstone.

As you approach Hansonville, 2,600-foot-high **Hansonville Peak** is visible on your right. At Hansonville, turn left on US Alternate 58; US 19 goes right. The route continues through open valleys, farmland, and rounded hills.

Soon you come down a steep hill and cross the Clinch River at the bypass around St. Paul. This town marks the approximate boundary between the Valley and Ridge geologic province that you have been driving through and the Appalachian Highlands to the west.

The road alternates between tree-covered, steep-sided, narrow valleys and more open farmland, following the bends in the Guest River. Nearby in **Jefferson National Forest** is the **Guest River Gorge Trail.** The trailhead is reached by taking VA 72 south from Coeburn.

In several narrow places it seems there is barely room for the highway and river. You pass some small coal mines; some are still functioning while others are no longer producing. A railroad roughly parallels the road through the nearby hills, and you can occasionally see railroad trestles that span the creek valleys off the main route.

Big Stone Gap Loop

You come over the hill outside Norton for an open view of the small valley and town. The **Big Stone Gap** loop begins here at the four-way intersection with US Alternate 58, US 23, and US Business 23. The outbound section follows an older, narrow 2-lane road along a stream valley through coal country to Big Stone Gap; the return portion is via US 23/Alternate 58, a modern, 4-lane highway through the scenic Powell Valley, with a side trip to High Knob.

On your left at the intersection are small cliffs with the tree-covered hills of **Jefferson National Forest** behind them. Bordering the cliffs and forest you will see a new highway that looks interesting and inviting, and it is: This will be the return route for this loop.

US Business 23 soon leaves Norton on a narrow, winding, 2-lane road through the heart of coal country. You pass several small mines and railroad coal loading sidings. Coal seams are visible in many road cuts, as are the remaining high walls of old strip mines. This stretch gives you a good idea of what much of this area looked like before modern roads.

At **Appalachia** you pass the closed Westmoreland Coal Company Bullit Mine Complex. Bituminous coal from several nearby mines was moved by conveyer belts to the facility where it was temporarily stored in huge silo-like buildings. Coal from more distant mines was transported here by truck and then loaded onto trains of 100 cars or more. More than 90 percent of today's coal production is hauled out by Norfolk Southern Corporation and taken to the port of Hampton Roads, Virginia, where it is shipped to domestic and international destinations. Peak production was in 1990 when the state put out more than 46.5 million tons.

Appalachian Trail marker
CHRISTINA RICHARDS/SHUTTERSTOCK.COM

Virginia creeper
© LIANEM/SHUTTERSTOCK.COM

Almost all of Virginia's coal production comes from Buchanan, Dickenson, and Wise Counties. Virginia coal tends to be in narrow seams, meaning most of the coal is obtained through underground mining which is more expensive than the surface mining of thicker seams in western states. In 1980, there were more than 800 licensed mines, a number that had dropped to 328 by 2001.

From Appalachia to Big Stone Gap is a bucolic, 5-mile route along the **Powell River.** The gap itself, just outside town, is a breach in resistant sandstone where the Powell River has cut through **Big Stone Mountain.**

The town of Big Stone Gap is the setting for local author John Fox Jr.'s best-selling novel, *The Trail of the Lonesome Pine,* published in the late 1890s. The book, which takes place during the coal industry's boom years, describes the love of a local girl for a mining engineer. The novel was the first million-dollar best-seller and has been made into a movie at least three times. A drama created from the book is put on in an outside theater in Big Stone Gap several times a week during the summer months. The author's home is now the **John Fox Jr. Museum** and contains authentic family furnishings and memorabilia. If that isn't enough, there is another museum, the **June Tolliver House,** named after the book's heroine.

The **Southwest Virginia Museum** has numerous exhibits on frontier life of early pioneers in the area. The **Coal Museum,** owned by the Westmoreland Coal Company, has a variety of mining exhibits, artifacts, and photographs, many procured from local mines and miners' homes.

If some places in Big Stone Gap look familiar, it may be because you saw the movie *Coal Miner's Daughter.* Many scenes were filmed here.

When you're ready to leave Big Stone Gap, follow US Business 23 to US 23/Alternate 58. Go north (toward Norton and Wise). In a few moments you will be climbing up the broad, open **Powell Valley.** The 4-lane highway hugs the left side of the valley, at times supported over the valley by cantilevers. An overlook gives sweeping views of farms and houses 1,000 feet below, framed by distant mountains. It is hard to believe that this pastoral scene is only a few miles from the heart of coal country.

As you approach **Norton** again, you can see the town to your left. On the right are alternating cliffs and forest marking the boundary of **Jefferson National Forest.** Take the exit at VA 619 and turn right toward the forest and the **High Knob Recreation Area.**

This 2-lane road twists, turns, and climbs steadily uphill to the observation tower atop **High Knob,** elevation 4,162 feet. The tower is a 30-second walk from the parking area and gives you the best view in the state of Virginia for the least effort. On clear days you can see five states from this 360-degree panorama.

Camping, picnicking, and swimming in a 5-acre lake are other popular activities in the recreation area. On your way down the mountain, look for the turn to **Flag Rock,** which overlooks Norton. The Stars and Stripes were first flown here in the early 1900s by an immigrant who, happy to be in his new country, put up the flagpole; the present flag is maintained by the town.

Return to US 23/Alternate 58 and turn right. In another mile you will have reached the route's end at the four-way intersection of US Alternate 58, US 23, and US Business 23. From here you can return to Abingdon via US Alternate 58, or stop at the nearby towns of Norton and Wise.

24

Mount Rogers Loop

Virginia's Subalpine High Country

General description: This mountain route encircles Mount Rogers (elevation 5,520 feet) and Whitetop Mountain (elevation 5,570 feet), Virginia's highest peaks. It passes from lush, wooded mountain streams along the Virginia Creeper Trail into the subalpine high country in Jefferson National Forest. Most of this 60-mile route is within the Mount Rogers National Recreation Area, known for its hiking, camping, fishing, and scenic beauty. The route encompasses the Mount Rogers Scenic Byway. Several side trips, such as the gravel summit road of Whitetop Mountain, take you into the heart of high country. The route is mostly paved, and very curvy, 2-lane roads with some steep grades. There are numerous campgrounds.

Special attractions: The Virginia Creeper Trail, a loop through the subalpine high country around the two tallest mountains in Virginia, the open meadows of Grayson Highlands State Park, a route to the top of Whitetop Mountain, outstanding views, mountain trout streams, hiking, fishing, camping, biking, and skiing.

Location: Southwest Virginia, south of Marion and east of Abingdon along the North Carolina border.

Route numbers: US 58; VA 16 and 603. Side trips go on VA 600 and 89 for the Whitetop Mountain summit, and on unnumbered roads to Grayson Highlands State Park.

Travel season: All year, but use caution in winter when heavy mountain snow can close roads temporarily. Because there are many sharp curves, the Virginia Department of Transportation does not recommended pulling trailers more than 35 feet long.

Services: Motels, restaurants, and gasoline are accessible in Damascus and nearby Abingdon and Marion. Food and gasoline can be obtained at the intersection of VA 603 and VA 600.

Nearby attractions: Abingdon and the Barter Theatre are about 10 miles west of Damascus. Abingdon is the starting point for Route 23. Hungry Mother State Park is north of Marion, about 15 miles from Troutdale.

For more information: Virginia Creeper Trail, (276) 475-3831, vacreepertrail.com; Smyth County Tourism Association, (276) 646-3305, visitvirginiasmountains.com; Abingdon Convention & Visitors Bureau, (276) 676-2282 or (800) 435-3440, abingdon.com; Grayson Highlands State Park, (276) 579-7092, dcr.virginia.gov; Mount Rogers National Recreation Area Jefferson National Forest, (276) 783-5504, stateparks.com.

The Route

The 115,000-acre Mount Rogers National Recreation Area in Jefferson National Forest surrounds some of Virginia's finest mountain scenery, including Mount Rogers and Whitetop Mountain, the state's two highest peaks. Most of the route is within the Mount Rogers National Recreation Area, which itself is part of Jefferson National Forest.

Mount Rogers Loop

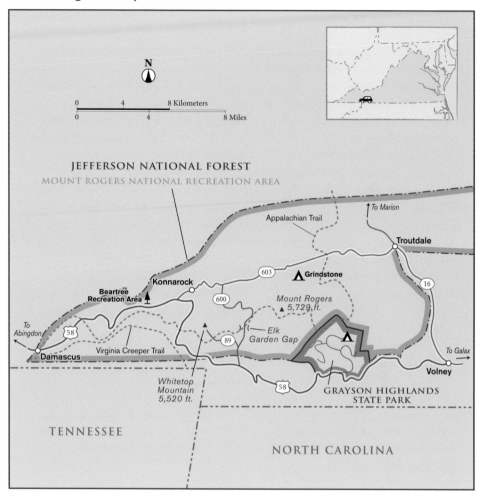

This national recreation area was established in 1966, partly to offset population pressures on Great Smoky Mountain and Shenandoah National Parks. Today
it contains several hundred miles of hiking, skiing, and horse trails, numerous
campgrounds, lush woods, and streams. The route makes a 360-degree circuit
around the high country with several side trips to subalpine areas.

The route begins in Damascus on US 58 about 10 miles east of exit 9 on I-81
at Abingdon; Abingdon is also the starting point for Route 23 to Big Stone Gap.
This route follows US 58 east from Damascus, paralleling the Virginia Creeper
Trail to Volney. From Volney, the route makes a complete circuit around the
two highest peaks in the state: Mount Rogers (elevation 5,729 feet) and Whitetop

Mountain (5,570 feet), following VA 16 and VA 603, and rejoining US 58 past the small town of Konnarock.

Two side trips lead you through the heart high country. The first visits Grayson Highlands State Park, known for its views, hiking, camping, fishing, and other outdoor activities; the second leads you along the uppermost highway in Virginia on a dirt Forest Service road to the summit of Whitetop Mountain.

The route totals about 80 miles, including the side trips, but your total mileage will be higher because you will have to retrace part of the route. You'll want to allow more than a day if you want to do any hiking, biking, horseback riding, or just take a leisurely sightseeing trip.

The route along US 58 from Damascus to Volney, and the portion along VA 603 from Troutdale to Konnarock, comprises the 55-mile Mount Rogers Scenic Byway, a nationally designated scenic route.

A variety of campsites, with facilities that range from the primitive (pit toilets, no drinking water) to upscale (warm showers, hot and cold running water) are available. Reservations are accepted for some campgrounds; others are on a first-come, first-served basis. Check with the Forest Service or Grayson Highlands State Park for current information. Motels are available in nearby Abingdon and Marion.

You can also start at Troutdale at the intersection of VA 16 and VA 603 by joining the route and heading west on VA 603. A complete circuit from here will require retracing part of your route. Troutdale is about 15 miles south of exit 45 on I-81 at Marion via VA 16. This route itself is quite scenic and passes through several miles of Jefferson National Forest. Another possibility is to start at Abingdon and follow US 58 to Damascus to join the route. You can also start at either Abingdon or Marion and end at the other city. This elongated route will be 120 to 130 miles long, depending on which part you retrace.

Damascus to Grayson Highlands State Park

The main route starts in **Damascus.** The **Appalachian Trail** runs down the main street (US 58) of this small mountain town, making it a popular rest stop and resupply area for hikers. Follow US 58 east out of town and into the woods along a narrow, winding stream valley. An understory of rhododendron, spectacular when in spring bloom, covers both sides of the road in many places.

The road parallels the **Virginia Creeper Trail** for several miles, with several points of access to the trail, which runs 34.3 miles from Abingdon to the Virginia–North Carolina border. It follows an old logging railroad bed (as part of the rails-to-trails program), which in turn follows the trace of a Native American footpath. It is known for its 32 converted railroad trestles that cross the numerous gorges

View from Little Pinnacle Overlook, Grayson Highlands State Park
©MARY TERRIBERRY/SHUTTERSTOCK.COM

and gentle railroad-category grades, making it attractive for hiking, biking, horse-back riding, cross-country skiing, and even wheelchair traveling. While the trail is open all year, you're advised to use "extreme caution when using the trail while it is covered with snow. Bridges and trestles can be extremely dangerous. Please walk bikes and horses across." Portions of the trail may be closed due to weather or other conditions, so check the website for current information. The streams, stocked with trout, attract anglers. Look for a view of a trestle near a turnoff with picnic tables.

Some say the trail received its name from the heavily loaded logging trains which crept up the grades, and some say it was named for the Virginia creeper plant, which is commonly found here, along with rhododendron. If you plan to be dropped off for a one-way hiking or biking trip, be forewarned that the trail is constantly downhill from Abingdon to North Carolina, and uphill in the other direction.

In about 4 miles you pass **Beartree Recreation Area,** which features camping, picnicking, a large lake for fishing, and a sandy beach for swimming. At the intersection with VA 603, bear right on US 58. You will end up here at the completion of the main loop.

Summertime view from Horse Trail East, Grayson Highlands State Park
© MARY TERRIBERRY/SHUTTERSTOCK.COM

The route soon begins to climb. The woods thin out as you cross **Whitetop Gap** and come into open fields, leaving the national forest. You may think you are in the land of Christmas trees, which are grown here in profusion. To the left is **Whitetop Mountain;** in the distance to the right, waves of mountains stretch to the horizon in North Carolina.

The route passes the intersection with VA 600, the other end of the side trip to Whitetop Mountain. About 7.5 miles beyond that, at 3,698 feet in elevation, is the entrance to **Grayson Highlands State Park** on the southeast flank of Mount Rogers. The park's roads wind through the alpine high country with its northern hardwood and evergreen forest, open grassy meadows (called "balds"), and outstanding mountain views.

The park's many trailheads provide jumping-off places for numerous hikes, including the summit of **Mount Rogers.** Horseback riding along the **Virginia Highlands Horse Trail** is popular. You can rent horses or bring your own; Grayson Highlands is the only Virginia state park that provides stables. Other activities include camping, picnicking, fishing, and hunting (licenses required), and special cultural events. The park is open all year and, averaging more than 100 inches of snow annually, is popular with winter campers and cross-country skiers.

The visitor center, at almost 5,000 feet, has excellent exhibits of area rocks and mountain crafts, from quilts and musical instruments to children's toys. In the warmer months the **Rooftop of Virginia Crafts Shop** operates a small store in the visitor center.

Volney to Konnarock

When you leave Grayson Highlands State Park, drive down the twisty entrance road back to US 58 and turn left. At **Volney,** about 7.5 miles from the state park at the intersection of US 58 and VA 16, turn left (north) on VA 16. This section of road is outside the national recreation area and national forest and skirts the eastern flank of the loop. You pass many small farms and herds of grazing cattle with occasional views of high country to the left.

VA 16 leads in 7 miles to **Troutdale,** a former logging town, at the intersection of VA 16 and VA 603. When logging was at its peak, around 1900, the town had a population of more than 3,000; today's population is about 200.

Nearby is the former home and burial site of author **Sherwood Anderson,** who lived here from 1925 until his death in 1941. Anderson is known as a founder of the American School of Realism which strongly influenced Ernest Hemingway and William Faulkner. Anderson was also the publisher of two local weekly papers.

Turn left on VA 603 to traverse the northern section of the loop. You soon enter thick woods of the national forest, parallel to **Fox Creek.** In about 2 miles you pass several cascades along Fox Creek, a popular area with trout anglers. Just past this you will see fences along the stream bank that are part of the Fox Creek Riparian Area Recovery Project. The fences are designed to keep livestock away from the stream bank, so as to reestablish vegetation and prevent erosion. Increased vegetation will also provide shade, lowering the temperature of the stream water and benefiting trout (and presumably trout anglers).

You pass by open pastures, often occupied by grazing cattle and horses, and then the route crosses the **Appalachian Trail.** This spot is a well-known drop-off and pickup point for hikers; on summer weekends there may be several cars parked nearby.

Soon you pass the turnoff for the **Grindstone Campground.** Its numerous campsites, hot showers, and 400-seat outdoor amphitheater make it a favorite for family camping and another jumping-off spot for hikers.

Past the campsite on the left are several views of **Mount Rogers** with its bare ridges and spruce- and fir-covered top. Because it is not a prominent peak, it was not recognized as the highest point in the state until accurate surveys in the early 1900s.

Konnarock & Whitetop Mountain

A few stores and gas stations mark most of the town of **Konnarock.** The town is spread out along US 58 between the intersections of VA 603 and VA 600. Like other towns along the route, Konnarock reached its peak population when lumbering was an important industry. When it was a lumber-mill town, around 1900, several thousand people lived here; today there are about 100 residents.

The main loop continues straight ahead on VA 603 through the rest of Konnarock for about a mile to the intersection with US 58 and the end of the route. Many people will turn left on VA 600 for the side trip to the high county and **Whitetop Mountain.**

VA 600 is a paved, 2-lane road that soon begins to zig and zag as it climbs. In about 3.5 miles you come to the broad, open meadows of **Elk Garden Gap.** Several trails lead to the summit of **Mount Rogers,** including the **Appalachian Trail,** which crosses the road, and the **Virginia Highlands Horse Trail,** often used as a winter ski trail. The Appalachian Trail here is the shortest—4.5 miles—and one of the steepest routes to the summit. Mount Rogers itself, Virginia's highest at 5,729 feet, lies to the left as a humpbacked ridge. Although the summit is tree covered, many of the ridges and slopes leading to the top are bare, affording excellent views.

The mountain is named for William B. Rogers, Virginia's first state geologist and a founder of the Massachusetts Institute of Technology.

Continue about a mile on VA 600 to the left turn on VA 89, which leads in several miles to Whitetop Mountain, Virginia's second highest at 5,570 feet. The road is not suitable for recreational vehicles or trailers. Be very careful on this road during cloudy and inclement weather, and remember that the weather can deteriorate in a few minutes in the high country. Fog—low lying clouds here—and thunderstorms are both common year-round.

VA 89 is a narrow, winding gravel road with several steep grades and is the highest automobile road in the state. The last mile consists of switchbacks through open country to a viewpoint just below the summit with good vistas of Mount Rogers. On clear days you see ridge after ridge stretching to the horizon into North Carolina.

The woods behind the parking area are predominantly red spruce; this tree is found in Virginia only near the summits of Whitetop and Mount Rogers. Unfortunately you can't visit Whitetop's actual summit, which is fenced in and covered with a forest of antennas and communication towers.

Turn around and carefully drive back down the switchbacks. Notice the red and white "barber pole" markers that help keep you on the road during foggy weather.

Log cabin in Virginia mountains with fall colors and split rail fence
© JUDY KENNAMER/SHUTTERSTOCK.COM

Retrace VA 89 to the junction with VA 600. What you do next depends in part on where you began the route. Turn right on VA 600 and go 2 miles to the intersection with US 58. At US 58, you can turn right to Damascus or left to Volney and VA 16. Or, you can turn left on VA 600 and retrace the route to VA 603 at Konnarock where you turn left to Damascus (and then to Abingdon) or right to Troutdale (and then to Marion).

25

Cumberland Gap

On the Trail of Daniel Boone

General description: This 100-mile route follows the Wilderness Trail hacked out by Daniel Boone in 1775 through southwest Virginia to the narrow mountain pass at Cumberland Gap where Virginia, Tennessee, and Kentucky converge. Most of the route is through small, mostly unspoiled towns. The route concludes at the 2,440-high Pinnacle Overlook in Cumberland Gap National Historical Park where you can gaze down at the gap and the long range of mountains extending to North Carolina. The route features a stop at Natural Tunnel State Park where you can ride a chairlift down to the huge cave entrance.

Special attractions: Cumberland Gap National Historical Park, Natural Tunnel State Park, Wilderness Road.

Location: Southwest Virginia and adjacent portions of Kentucky and Tennessee.

Route numbers: US 58 and 25E; VA 690 and 871; Pinnacle Road.

Travel season: All year long. Some facilities may be closed during the colder months. Occasional snow may make travel difficult.

Camping: Camping is permitted year-round in Cumberland Gap National Historical Park; the campground in Natural Tunnel State Park closes in winter.

Services: All services are available in Bristol, Virginia; Bristol, Tennessee; Middlesboro, Kentucky; and many of the smaller towns.

Nearby attractions: Jefferson National Forest, Abingdon and the Barter Theatre, and Big Stone Gap. See Route 23 for descriptions of this area.

For more information: Bristol Convention and Visitors Bureau, (423) 989-4850, visit bristoltnva.org; Cumberland Gap National Historical Park, (606) 248-2817, nps.gov/cuga; Natural Tunnel State Park, (276) 940-2674 or (800) 933-PARK, dcr.virginia.gov; Scott County Tourism, (276) 386-6521, explorescottcountyva.com; Big Stone Gap, (276) 523-0115, bigstonegap.org.

The Route

Cumberland Gap is a narrow mountain pass through the Appalachians in southwest Virginia near the Tennessee-Kentucky border. It has been used as a gateway through the mountains to the west, starting with herds of animals that were followed by Native Americans hunting them for food and furs, then pioneers, and now cars and trucks.

Thomas Walker was the European who rediscovered the gap in 1750. The French and Indian Wars prevented additional exploration at that time so it wasn't until 1775 that Daniel Boone, with 30 axmen, marked the Wilderness Trail from eastern cities through Cumberland Gap to the Kentucky frontier. Settlers followed,

Cumberland Gap

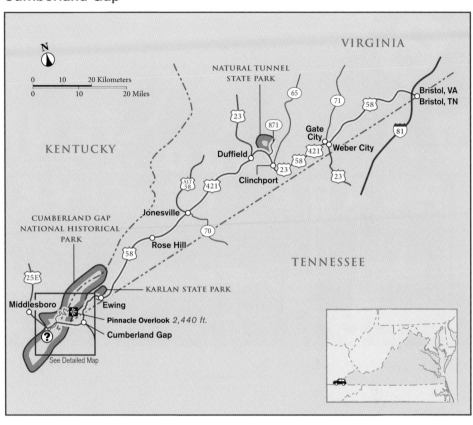

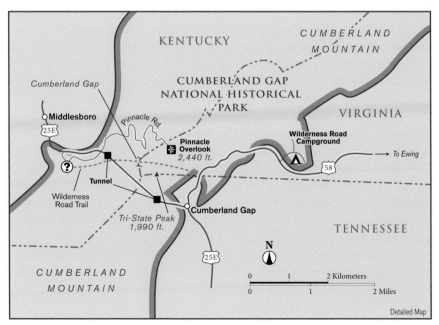

Bristol, a great place to live, straddles State Street and the Virginia and Tennessee state lines.

and by 1792 the population of Kentucky was more than 100,000, and the territory was admitted to the Union.

By 1800 some 300,000 settlers had followed Boone's winding trail through Cumberland Gap on their way to the Kentucky River and the current cities of Lexington and Louisville. It was not a one-way trail: the pioneers were often met by fur traders, hunters, and farmers driving livestock east to the seaboard cities.

Following about 100 miles of US 58, the **Wilderness Trail** used to be 2 lanes along Cumberland Mountain past small towns, fields of corn and tobacco, tobacco barns, and grazing cattle. Woe be anyone caught behind a couple of heavily loaded trucks, for the trip could seem to last for days instead of hours. Today, the 30 miles of winding, mountainous road between Bristol and Gate City (on US 58/421) is still 2-lane, or you can go 28 miles through northern Tennessee on straighter, slightly flatter roads. From Gate City to Duffield is 4-lane, with about 20 miles between Duffield and Jonesville as a 2-lane before it becomes 4-lane again to Cumberland Gap.

The route ends at Cumberland Gap National Historical Park, just over the state line in Middlesboro, Kentucky. The old road that formerly wound through the gap has been replaced by a 4-lane tunnel that bores beneath Cumberland

Mountain. One reason the twin tunnels were constructed was so the original trail through the gap could be restored to as historically correct and natural a state as possible, as it was in 1790. From the park you can drive back into Virginia to 2,440-foot-high Pinnacle Overlook for a magnificent view of the gap and the surrounding states or hike to the gap as it is being restored to look like the wagon trail it once was.

Bristol to Duffield

The route begins on West State Street in downtown **Bristol.** There are two Bristols, and State Street straddles the line between Bristol, Virginia, and Bristol, Tennessee. Yes, if you haven't yet, stop to take a picture of the sign that reads Bristol VA/TN is "A Good Place to Live."

Detour a bit into Tennessee and continue back into Virginia on US 421N. Turn right onto VA 692 for about a minute and then onto VA 689 for another minute or two until you can turn right onto US 421N/58W. Almost immediately you are driving through low, rolling, mostly bare hills past farmhouses and barns. Cattle graze on the slopes, and crops fill the fields.

The route crosses the North Fork of the Holston River and intersects US 23 at **Weber City,** about 26 miles from Bristol. Bear right on US 58/421/23, To the right you look over **Gate City.** There is a distinct, wooded ridge on the left. After you follow the ridge for several miles, the road curves uphill to the right into steep and hilly, wooded country.

You can detour slight to **Duffield** and then to **Natural Tunnel State Park.** The park's stellar attraction is an 850-foot-long cave that is open at both ends. The cave entrance is as high as a 10-story building. A natural stream, Stock Creek, and a man-made railroad, the Southern Railroad, both run through the cave.

Natural Tunnel may have been visited by Daniel Boone during his quest for the Wilderness Road, however, it was Colonel Stephen Long who explored and publicized the tunnel in 1832. It soon became a major tourist attraction and was immensely popular in the late 1800s. William Jennings Bryan called it "The Eighth Wonder of the World."

Like most limestone caves, Natural Tunnel was created from the slow reaction of acidic groundwater with the limestone rock. Stock Creek did not form the cave, but was diverted into it after the cave had begun forming. The creek helped enlarge the cave and shape the spacious walls and roof.

The fastest and easiest way to visit the tunnel entrance is to take the 500-foot-long chairlift to the bottom of the gorge. The chairlift, which is wheelchair accessible, runs daily in summer and on weekends spring and fall. You can also hike to the entrance. Because the tunnel provides an easy grade through the hilly country, railroad tracks were laid through it in 1890. It's still used several times weekly by coal trains; if your timing is fortuitous, you may see one. The tunnel has been a state park since 1967 and offers an amphitheater, bike trails, camping and RV sites (dump facility), fishing, swimming, food, hiking, picnic shelters, restrooms, and a camp store.

The visitor center contains exhibits on the geology and history of the area, including a display of various narrow-gauge railroad tracks. Several hiking trails lead to scenic overlooks or to the tunnel. Moderate fees, which may be seasonal, are charged for the chairlift and for some services.

When you leave the park, follow VA 871 back to US 58/421/23 and turn right. When you reach **Duffield**, head southeast on US 23 toward VA T856 and then back onto US 58W.

Duffield to Cumberland Gap

From here, US 58 heads west, past small towns and farms through a broad, open valley. Parallel to the road on the right is **Powell Mountain** and, farther on, **Cumberland Mountain,** the unbroken ridge that was such a barrier to western exploration. You are following the **Wilderness Road.**

At **Jonesville,** US Alternate 58 heads northeast to Pennington Gap and then to Big Stone Gap. Jonesville is the birthplace of Dr. Alexander T. Still, who headed west to found the first school of osteopathy in 1892 in Kirksville, Missouri.

Cumberland Mountain, actually a long ridge, looms larger and larger on the right with prominent white cliffs of sandstone near the crest. The cliffs were a well-known beacon to the early pioneers, a sign that they were making progress on their western trek, and perhaps giving them the inspiration and hope to continue.

Cumberland Gap National Historical Park straddles Cumberland Mountain north of US 58 from the town of **Ewing** to the gap itself. Several side roads to the right lead to trailheads and are jumping-off places for wilderness camping.

In a few miles, US 58 enters the boundaries of Cumberland Gap National Historical Park. The road begins a gradual climb up the side of **Poor Valley Ridge.** A well-marked road to the right leads to the main campground and some trailheads for the park.

If you have driven through Cumberland Gap prior to 1997, the next stretch of road may confuse you. Before 1997, US 58 led directly through the gap to US 25E and park headquarters in Middlesboro, Kentucky. Today the road through the gap has been closed, and you reach park headquarters in Kentucky, and Pinnacle Gap in Virginia, by passing through a slice of Tennessee and a tunnel under Cumberland Mountain. Follow US 58 to its end outside the town of Cumberland Gap, Tennessee, at the state line at the junction with 4-lane US 25E in Tennessee.

Cumberland Gap National Historic Park
©ZACK FRANK/SHUTTERSTOCK.COM

Go north (to your right) on US 25E, following the signs to the park and Middlesboro, Kentucky. You soon enter one of the twin 4,600-foot tunnels, speeding under Cumberland Gap in a way never dreamed of by Daniel Boone or the settlers who followed. You cross into Kentucky midway through the tunnel. The entrance to Cumberland Gap National Historical Park is about a half-mile past the tunnel portal, before reaching the town of Middlesboro.

Turn into the park. The Pinnacle Road, which leads to the Pinnacle Overlook in Virginia and the end of the route, is the first left-hand turn as you enter the park. Your first stop should be the visitor center for orientation.

Cumberland Gap National Historical Park was established by Congress in 1940 to preserve the history of westward migration, including the Wilderness Road and Cumberland Gap. World War II and a lack of funding delayed the park's opening until 1955. The park today encompasses about 20,000 acres in Kentucky, Virginia, and a small part of Tennessee. Most of the park is a semi-wilderness extending for 20 miles along the ridge of Cumberland Mountain, a portion of the Virginia/Kentucky boundary.

In addition to the gap and the visitor center, the park includes some 50 miles of hiking trails (including the popular **Ridge Trail**), a 160-site campground (electric hookups are available at 41 sites), picnic areas, several wilderness campsites (you must obtain a free permit from the visitor center), and the **Hensley Settlement,** a restored farm community that can be reached by trail or park shuttle. The visitor center has exhibits and a small museum. Guided hikes and other interpretive programs are scheduled during the warmer months.

The **Pinnacle Road** is a narrow, winding, 2-lane road that crosses back into Virginia and climbs to the 2,440-foot-high **Pinnacle Overlook.** The road has

Hiking Cumberland Gap National Historical Park to Pinnacle Peak

several hairpin curves and is closed to trailers and vehicles more than 20 feet long. A short trail leads from the parking area to several scenic vistas.

The view from the overlook shows Cumberland Gap 1,000 feet below, and the otherwise unbroken sweep of the mountain barrier that has had such a profound influence on westward migration in the US. Signs and maps point out other features, including the twin tunnels and **Tri-State Peak** where Virginia, Kentucky, and Tennessee meet. On very clear days it is possible to see the Great Smoky Mountains in North Carolina. However, on days that are not clear, the visibility is understandably miniscule.

The route ends at the Pinnacle Overlook. However, you must turn around and negotiate the hairpin turns back to the visitor center. When you leave the park, turn right (east) on US 25 to return to Virginia and US 58, or turn left (west) on US 25 to go to Middlesboro, Kentucky.

APPENDIX:
FOR MORE INFORMATION

For more information on lands and events, please contact the following agencies and organizations.

Virginia Tourism Corporation
901 East Byrd St.
Richmond, VA 23225
(804) 545-5500
virginia.org

E-ZPass
(877) 762-7824
ezpassva.com

511 Virginia for updates on traffic road conditions highway construction and more

511Virginia.org (sign up for email or mobile alerts)

Route 1: Shenandoah Valley Loop

Belle Grove Plantation
(540) 869-2028
bellgrove.org

Blandy Farm/State Arboretum of Virginia
(540) 837-1758
virginia.edu/blandy

Cedar Creek & Belle Grove National Historic Park
(540) 868-0176
nps.gov/cebe

Endless Caverns
(540) 896-2283
endlesscaverns.com

Kernstown Battlefield
(540) 869-2896
kernstownbattle.org

Luray Caverns
(540) 743-6551
luraycaverns.com

Museum of the Shenandoah Valley
(888) 556-5799 or (540) 662-1473
themsv.org

Old Court House Civil War Museum
(540) 542-1145
civilwarmuseum.org

Rock Harbor Golf Course
(540) 722-7111
rockharborgolf.com

Rocking S Ranch
(540) 678-8501
therockingsranch.com

Shenandoah Caverns
(540) 477-3115 or (888) 422-8376
shenandoahcaverns.com

Shenandoah County Tourism
(540) 459-6227
shenandoahtravel.org

Shenandoah Valley Discovery Museum
(540) 722-2020
discoverymuseum.net

Stonewall Jackson's
Headquarters Museum
(540) 662-6550
winchesterhistory.org

Strasburg Virginia Chamber
of Commerce
(540) 465-3187
viststrasburg.com

Virginia's Heritage Migration Route
or the Wilderness Road
virginia.org/wildernessroad

Winchester–Frederick County
Convention & Visitors Bureau
(540) 542-1326 or (877) 871-1326
visitwinchesterva.com

Route 2: Leesburg Loop

Aldie Mill Historic Park
(703) 327-0777
nvrpa.org/park

Dodona Manor
(703) 777-1880
georgecmarshall.org

Loudoun County Visitors Center
(703) 771-2170 or (800) 752-6118
visitloudoun.org

Loudoun Museum
(703) 777-7427
loudounmuseum.org

Morven Park and the Museum of
Hounds & Hunting
(703) 777-2414
morvenpark.org

Oatlands Plantation
(703) 777-3174
oatlands.org

Town of Leesburg Economic
Development and Tourism
(703) 737-7019
leesburgerva.gov

Visit Loudoun
(703) 771-4964 or (800) 752-6118
visitloudoun.org

Waterford Foundation
(540) 882-3018
waterfordfoundation.org

White's Ferry
(301) 349-5200
visitloudoun.org

Willowcroft Farm Vineyards
(703) 777-8161
willowcroftwine.com

Route 3: George Washington Memorial Parkway

Alexandria Convention &
Visitors Association
(800) 388-9119 or (703) 652-5360
visitalexandriava.com

Arlington Convention &
Visitors Service
(703) 228-0875
stayarlington.com

Dyke Marsh Wildlife Preserve
(703) 289-2500
nps.gov/gwmp or fodm.org

Fort Hunt Park
(703) 289-2500
nps.gov/gwmp

Jones Point Park
(703) 289-2500
nps.gov/gwmp

Lady Bird Johnson Park
(703) 289-2500
nps.gov/gwmp

Mount Vernon
(703) 780-2000
mountvernon.org

Netherlands Carillon
(703) 289-2500
nps.gov/gwmp

Turkey Run Park
(703) 289-2500
nps.gov/ns/gwmp

US Marine Corps War Memorial
(703) 289-2500
nps.gov/gwmp

Women in Military Service For
America Memorial
(703) 533-1155
womensmemorial.org

Route 4: Piedmont–Blue Ridge Vistas

Barboursville Vineyards
(540) 832-3824
barboursvillewine.com

Charlottesville Albemarle Convention
& Visitors Bureau
(434) 970-3635
visitcharlottesville.org

Fauquier County Chamber
(540) 347-4414
fauquierchamber.org

The Inn at Little Washington
(540) 675-3800
theinnatlittlewashington.com

Nelson County Economic
Development and Tourism
(434) 263-7015
nelsoncounty.com

Rappahannock County Office
of Tourism
(540) 675-5330
visitrappahannockva.com

Route 5: Skyline Drive

Blue Ridge Parkway
(828) 670-1924
blueridgeparkway.org

Charlottesville Albemarle Convention
& Visitors Bureau
(434) 970-3635
visitcharlottesville.org

City of Waynesboro
(540) 942-6644
visitwaynesboro.net

Front Royal Department of Tourism
(540) 635-5788
frontroyalva.com

Shenandoah National Park
(540) 999-3500 (particularly for current weather and roadway conditions)
nps.gov/shen
visitskylinedrive.org or nps.gov/shen

Shenandoah National Park concessions
(877) 847-1919
goshenandoah.com

Shenandoah Valley Travel Association
(540) 740-3132
visitshenandoah.org

Virginia Quilt Museum
(540) 433-3818
vaquiltmuseum.org

Route 6: Highland County Barn Quilt Trail

Ginseng Mountain Farm, Store
& Lodging
(540) 474-3663 or (540) 474-5137
ginsengmountain.com

Highland County Museum
(540) 396-4478
highlandcountyhistory.com

Highland County Visitor's Center
(540) 468-2550
highlandcounty.org

The Highland Inn
(540) 468-2143
highland-inn.com

McDowell Battlefield
civilwar.org/battlefields

Shenandoah Valley Battlefields
Foundation
shenandoahatwar.org

Sugar Maple Camp
(540) 458-2550
highlandcounty.org/sugartours

Route 7: Jefferson Heritage Trail

Amherst County Tourism
(434) 946-9400
countyofamherst.com

Bedford City & County Department
of Tourism
(540) 587-5682 or (877) 447-3257
visitbedford.com

Charlottesville Albemarle Convention
& Visitors Bureau
(434) 970-3635
visitcharlottesville.org

Jefferson Heritage Trail
jeffersonheritagetrail.com

Lynchburg Regional Convention &
Visitors Bureau
(434) 845-5966 or (800) 732-5821
discoverlynchburg.org

Nelson County Economic
Development and Tourism
(434) 263-7015
nelsoncounty.com

Snowflex Centre
(434) 582-2308 or (866) 504-7541
liberty.edu/snowflex

Thomas Jefferson's Poplar Forest
(434) 525-1806
poplarforest.org

Route 8: Bedford Wine Trail

Appalachian Trail
(304) 535-6278
nps.gov/appa
Bedford City & County Department
of Tourism
(540) 587-5682 or (877) 447-3257
visitbedford.com

Bedford Museum and Genealogical Library
(540) 586-4520
bedfordvamuseum.org

Bedford Wine Trail
(877) 447-3257
bedfordwinetrail.org

Hickory Hill Vineyards & Winery
(540) 296-1393
smlwine.com

LeoGrande Winery
(540) 586-4066
leograndewinery.com

National D-Day Memorial
(540) 586-DDAY or (800) 351-DDAY
dday.org

Peaks of Otter
(800) 542-5927 or (877) HI-PEAKS
peaksofotter.com

Peaks of Otter Winery
(540) 586-3707
peaksofotterwinery.com

Savoy-Lee Winery
(540) 297-9275
savoy-lee.com

Smith Mountain Lake
(540) 721-1203
visitsmithmountainlake.com

White Rock Vineyards & Winery
(540) 890-3359
whiterockwines.com

Route 9: Blue Ridge Parkway North

Bedford City and County Department of Tourism
(540) 587-5682 or (877) 447-3257
visitbedford.com

Blue Ridge Parkway
(540) 767-2492
nps.gov/blri

Center in the Square
(540) 342-5700
centerinthesquare.org

Charlottesville & Albemarle County
(434) 970-3635
visitcharlottesville.org

City of Waynesboro
(540) 942-6644
visitwaynesboro.net

Lexington & the Rockbridge Area Tourism Development
(540) 463-3777 or (877) 453-9822
lexingtonvirginia.com

Lynchburg Regional Convention & Visitors Bureau
(434) 845-5966 or (800) 732-5821
discoverlynchburg.org

Roanoke Visitor Information
(540) 342-6025
visitroanokeva.com

Staunton Convention and Visitor Bureau
(540) 332-3865
visitstaunton.com

Taubman Museum of Art
(540) 342-6760
taubmanmuseum.org.

Virginia's Blue Ridge
(540) 342-6025
visitvablueridge.com

Route 10: Blue Ridge Parkway South

Blue Ridge Music Center
(276) 236-5309
blueridgemusiccenter.org.

Blue Ridge Parkway
(540) 767-2492
nps.gov/blri

Roanoke Visitor Information
(540) 342-6025
visitroanokeva.com

Virginia's Blue Ridge
(540) 342-6025
visitvablueridge.com

Route 11: Fredericksburg & Spotsylvania Battlefields

Battle of Fredericksburg Visitor Center
(540) 373-6122
nps.gov/frsp

Chancellorsville Battlefield Visitor Center
(540) 786-2880
nps.gov/frsp

Economic Development Spotsylvania County
(540) 507-7210
spotsylvania.org

Fredericksburg Department of Economic Development and Tourism
(540) 372-1216 or (800) 260-2646
visitfred.com

Fredericksburg Welcome Center
(540) 786-8344
virgina.org

History of Wilderness and Spotsylvania
(540) 373-6124
nps.gov/frsp

John J. Wright Educational and Cultural Center
(540) 682-7583
jjwmuseum.org

Route 12: Northern Neck

Caledon, Westmoreland, and Belle Isle State Parks
dcr.virginia.gov

Chesapeake Bay Wine Trail
(804) 435-6092
chesapeakebaywinetrail.com

Coles Point
(804) 472-4011
colespointmarina.com

Colonial Beach
(804) 224-7181
colonialbeachva.net

George Washington Birthplace National Monument
(804) 224-1732
nps.gov/gewa

The Inn at Montross
(804) 493-8624
theinnatmontross.com

James Monroe Birthplace
(804) 214-9145
monroefoundation.org

Menokin
(804) 333-1776
menokin.org

Morattico Waterfront Museum
morattico.org

Northern Neck Tourism Commission
(804) 333-1919
northernneck.org

Reedville Fishermen's Museum
(804) 453-6529
rfmuseum.org

Stratford Hall
(804) 493-8038
stratfordhall.org

Route 13: Eastern Shore

Barrier Islands Center
(757) 678-5550
barrierislandcenter.com

Brownsville Seaside Farm
(757) 442-3049
virginia.org

Chatham Vineyards
(757) 678-5588
chathamvineyards.net

Eastern Shore Railway Museum
(757) 665-7245
parksley.com/seeus.shtml

Eastern Shore of Virginia National
Wildlife Refuge
(757) 331-3425
fws.gov

Eastern Shore of Virginia Tourism
Commission
(757) 787-8268
esvatourism.org

Museum of Chincoteague Island
(757) 336-6117
chincoteaguemuseum.com

Northampton County Chamber
of Commerce
(757) 678-0010
northamptoncountychamber.com

Wallops Flight Facility
(757) 824-2050
nasa.gov/centers

Route 14: Chesapeake Bay Bridge-Tunnel

Chesapeake Bay Bridge-Tunnel
(757) 331-2960
cbbt.com

Virginia Fisherman Identification
Program
(800) 723-2728
mrc.virginia.gov/FIP

Route 15: Goshen Pass & Lake Moomaw

Bath County
(540) 839-7202
discoverbath.com

Garth Newel Music Center
(540) 839-5018
garthnewel.org

Jefferson Pools
(540) 839-7741
discoverbath.com

Lexington & the Rockbridge Area
Tourism Development
(540) 463-3777 or (877) 453-9822
lexingtonvirginia.com

Route 16: Lee's Retreat

Appomattox Court House National
Historical Park
(434) 352-8987
nps.gov/apco

The Museum of the Confederacy/
Appomattox
(855) 649-1861
moc.org

Pamplin Historical Park and the
National Museum of the Civil War
Soldier
(804) 861-2408 or (877) PAMPLIN
pamplinpark.org

Petersburg Area Regional Tourism
(804) 861-1666
petersburgarea.org

Sailor's Creek Battlefield State Park
(804) 561-7510
dcr.virginia.gov

Tourism, City of Petersburg, Siege
Museum
(804) 733-2403
petersburg-va.org

Virginia Civil War Trails
(888) 248-4592
civilwartrails.org

Route 17: The Plantation Road

Berkeley Plantation
(804) 829-6018
berkeleyplantation.com

Charles City County
(804) 652-4702
co.charles-city.va.us

Evelynton Plantation
(800) 473-5075
jamesriverplantations.org

Fort Harrison
(804) 226-1981
nps.gov/rich

Harrison Lake National Fish Hatchery
(804) 829-2421
fws.gov/harrrisonlake

Hopewell Office of Tourism &
Visitor Center
(804) 541-2481 or (800) 863-8687
hopewellva.gov

James River Plantations
jamesriverplantations.org

Kittiewan Plantation
(804) 829-2272
kittiewanplantation.org or hopewellva
.gov

Sherwood Forest Plantation
Foundation
(804) 829-5377
sherwoodforest.org

Shirley Plantation
(804) 829-5121 or (800) 232-1613
shirleyplantation.com

Route 18: Colonial Parkway

Colonial Williamsburg
(757) 229-1000
history.org

Greater Williamsburg Chamber &
Tourism Alliance
(757) 253-2262 or (800) 368-6511
williamsburgcc.com

Jamestown Settlement & Yorktown
Victory Center
(757) 253-4838 or (888) 593-4682
historyisfun.org

York County Tourism Development
(757) 890-3500
visityorktown.org

Route 19: Over & Under Big Walker

Blue Ridge Travel Association
(276) 228-7092 or (800) 446-9670
virginiablueridge.org

Wythe County Parks and Recreation
(276) 223-4519
wytheco.org

Wytheville Convention &
Visitors Bureau
(276) 223-3355 or (877) 347-8307
visitwytheville.com

Route 20: Buchanan to Blacksburg

Botetourt County Office of Tourism
(540) 473-1167
visitbotetourt.com

Lexington & the Rockbridge Area
Tourism Development
(540) 463-3777 or (877) 453-9822
lexingtonvirginia.com

Natural Bridge
(540) 291-2121 or (800) 533-1410
naturalbridgeva.com

Roanoke Valley Convention and
Visitors Bureau
(540) 342-6025 or (800) 635-5535
visitvablueridge.com

Route 21: Burke's Garden

Burke's Garden General Store
(276) 472-2222

Lost World Ranch
(276) 472-2347
lostworldranch.com

Tazewell Office of Economic
Development
(800) 588-9401
visittazewellcounty.org

Wytheville Convention & Visitors
Bureau
(276) 223-3355 or (877) 347-8307
visitwytheville.com

Route 22: Breaks Interstate Park

Abingdon Convention &
Visitors Bureau
(276) 678-2282 or (800) 435-3440
visitabingdon.com

Dickenson County Chamber of Commerce/Visitor's Center
(276) 926-6074
dickensonchamber.net

Russell County Chamber of Commerce
(276) 889-8041
russellcountyva.org

Route 23: Abingdon–Big Stone Gap Loop

Abingdon Convention &
Visitors Bureau
(276) 676-2282 or (800) 435-3440
abingdon.com

Henry W. Meador Jr. Coal Museum
(277) 523-9209
bigstonegap.org

Jefferson National Forest
Clinch Ranger District
(540) 291-2180
southernregion.fs.fed.us/gwj

Southwest Virginia Museum
Big Stone Gap, VA 24219
(276) 523-1322
dcr.virginia.gov

Wise County Chamber of Commerce
(276) 679-0961
wisecountychamber.org

Route 24: Mount Rogers Loop

Abingdon Convention &
Visitors Bureau
(276) 676-2282 or (800) 435-3440
abingdon.com

Grayson Highlands State Park
(276) 579-7092
dcr.virginia.gov/state

Mount Rogers National
Recreation Area
Jefferson National Forest
(276) 783-5504
stateparks.com

Smyth County Tourism Association
(276) 646-3305
visitvirginiasmountains.com

Virginia Creeper Trail
(276) 475-3831
vacreepertrail.com

Route 25: Cumberland Gap

Big Stone Gap
(276) 523-0115
bigstonegap.org

Bristol Convention and Visitors Bureau
(423) 989-4850
visitbristoltnva.org

Cumberland Gap National Historical
Park
(606) 248-2817
nps.gov/cuga

Natural Tunnel State Park
(276) 940-2674 or (800) 933-PARK
dcr.virginia.gov

Scott County Tourism
(276) 386-6521
explorescottcountyva.com

INDEX